KALYĀṆAMITRA
A MODEL FOR BUDDHIST SPIRITUAL CARE

Kalyāṇamitra
A Model for Buddhist Spiritual Care

Volume 1

Rev. Dr. Monica Sanford

Kalyāṇamitra
A Model for Buddhist Spiritual Care
Volume 1

Rev. Dr. Monica Sanford

Text © by Monica Sanford, 2021
All rights reserved

Book design: Karma Yönten Gyatso
Cover photo: Ekachai Prasertkaew, Shutterstock

Published by
The Sumeru Press Inc.
PO Box 75, Manotick Main Post Office
Manotick, ON K4M 1A2

ISBN 978-1-896559-45-2 Volume 1, *print edition*
ISBN 978-1-896559-70-4 Volume 2, *print edition*

LIBRARY AND ARCHIVES CANADA CATALOGUING IN PUBLICATION

Title: Kalyāṇamitra : a model for Buddhist spiritual care / Rev. Dr. Monica Sanford.
Names: Sanford, Monica, 1980- author.
Description: Includes bibliographical references and index.
Identifiers: Canadiana 20200365568 | ISBN 9781896559452 (v. 1 ; softcover) | ISBN 9781896559704 (v. 2 ; softcover)
Subjects: LCSH: Chaplains. | LCSH: Buddhism. | LCSH: Spiritual care (Medical care)
Classification: LCC BQ5305.C4 S26 2020 | DDC 294.3/61—dc23

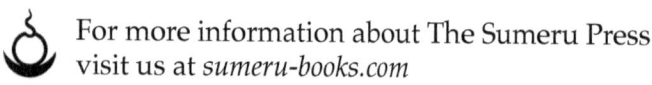

For more information about The Sumeru Press
visit us at *sumeru-books.com*

*This book is dedicated to my parents,
who could not have foreseen this path for my life
and whose support I never doubted.
I would promise no more surprises,
but we all know better, don't we?*

Contents
Volume I

Acknowledgments 9

Introduction: The Four Noble Truths 11

1. What is a Buddhist Chaplain? 15
    Chaplains & Spiritual Care 16
    Three Stories of Buddhist Spiritual Care 23
    Constructing Buddhist Chaplains through
        Education, Reflection, & Practice 30
    Conclusion & Reflection. 35

2. What Do Buddhist Chaplains Do? 39
    The Dharma of Spiritual Care 40
    Sources of Spiritual Care in the Dharma . . 41
    Modern Literature on Buddhist
        Chaplaincy & Spiritual Care 46
    Relationships with Teachers and
        Sanghas. 51
    Integrating through Reflection 53
    The Places of Spiritual Care 59
    Effective Spiritual Care. 68
    Conclusion & Reflection. 73

3. The Three Prajñās Framework 81
    Sutta on Learning & Practicing
        Spiritual Care. 82
    Emergence of the Framework 83
    Literature Review of the Three Prajñās. . . 85
    The Three Prajñās Framework of
        Spiritual Care. 97
    Validating the Framework. 108
    Conclusion & Reflection. 117

4. Kalyāṇamitra, or Spiritual Friendship . 121
    Literature Review of Kalyāṇamitra. 123
    Stage Four: Kalyāṇamitra 135
    Implications, Applications, and
        Limitations 137
    Conclusion & Reflection. 144

Appendix A: Research Methods 147
Appendix B: Sources for Kalyāṇamitra
    within the Pāli Canon. 165
Bibliography 171
Index. 183

Contents: Volume II

Introduction

1. Pragmatic Skills for Every Context
   Presence
   Listening and Responding
   Empathy and Compassion
   Spiritual Assessment
   Personal and Professional Boundaries
   Spiritual Leadership
   Conclusion & Reflection

2. Pragmatic Skills for Particular Contexts
   Ritual and Prayer
   Interreligious Competencies
   Cultural Competencies
   Power, Privilege, and Difference
   Practical Psychology for Chaplains
   Conclusion & Reflection

3. Becoming a Buddhist Chaplain
   Spiritual Formation
   Education and Training
   Professional Formation
   Conclusion & Reflection

4. Developing a Field of Buddhist Chaplaincy
   Buddhist "Practical Theology"
   Buddhist Spiritual Care as an Academic Field
   Buddhist Chaplaincy as a Profession
   Buddhist Diversity Shaping the Field
   Conclusion & Reflection

Appendices
Bibliography
Index

Acknowledgments

My deep and humble thanks to Ken, Vanessa, Victor, Duane, Stephen, and Rochelle for your support throughout this project. Thank you to the thirteen chaplains who generously volunteered to participate in interviews without knowing what might come out of it. Thank you to the members of the Buddhist Ministry Working Group, who expressed excitement and encouragement every time I talked about this project. Thank you to John, my wonderfully patient editor at Sumeru Press, for understanding what I was trying to do with this book. Thank you to Colin, for putting that code lock on the television as I was trying to finish my research, and for tolerating being dragged across the country in pursuit of my career. This was a collective effort of many interconnected people and groups. It wouldn't have come to fruition without you.

Introduction
The Four Noble Truths

This book is intended for those considering a career in Buddhist chaplaincy. It assumes most readers will know little to nothing about chaplaincy. It may still be useful to practicing chaplains, their supervisors, and scholars. As Buddhism is a broad collection of traditions, I also make few assumptions about pre-existing knowledge of the Dharma. Among those interested in chaplaincy, I observe a wide range of Buddhist backgrounds and knowledge, from those who only began studying Buddhism in earnest after they had decided to become a chaplain, to others who have practiced for decades within a particular sangha but may know little about other lineages of Buddhism (or other religions), to those who may have studied the full breadth and depth of Buddhist traditions for many years but not yet applied their knowledge to caring for others. Therefore, I have tried to make this work as accessible as possible to the broadest audience possible at the risk of occasionally telling readers what they already know.

I developed the contents of this book through my own doctoral training in the form of lengthy written essays during my qualifying examinations and, ultimately, a dissertation that was the first of its kind to collect qualitative data – interviews and written reflections – from thirteen practicing Buddhist chaplains in health care, corrections, the military, and higher education. The shape of my studies has followed the shape of the Four Noble Truths, first attempting to describe the situation for Buddhist chaplaincy in North America today, followed by an interpretation of why the situation is that way. From there, I sought to understand how things could or should be in a world that better supports Buddhist chaplains, and then set about outlining a pragmatic response to reach that goal. This process of description, interpretation, normalization, and pragmatic response is both a pattern from the field of practical theology (Osmer, 2008), in which I am trained, and the pattern of the Four Noble Truths themselves (Sanford, 2016).

This correlation between ancient Dharma and modern context is but one of many I shall highlight throughout this book. In fact, very little of what I will say here is new. It is only a recontextualization of ancient wisdom in relation to the emerging profession of Buddhist chaplaincy. While that may make it sound like I have nothing creative to offer, I would not sell myself quite so short. It is precisely this kind of work that I hungered for and did not find in my own training as a Buddhist chaplain, which began in 2010, before a single book on the topic had been published. This book will be the fifth volume intended specifically for Buddhist chaplains and spiritual care givers since then. The other four books are listed on the next page. Hopefully, it shall be followed shortly by many more.

Before going further, I believe it is important to say something about the relevance of the Four Noble Truths to the practice of a Buddhist chaplain.

The Buddha's First Noble Truth is a description of the situation in which living beings, we humans included, find ourselves. It is the called the truth of *dukkha* or suffering. (*Dukkha* has other translations, some more accurate, but I find 'suffering' the most useful because it is the most evocative.) The Buddha describes a world in which all living beings are subject to endless

> The other four books are:
>
> - *The Arts of Contemplative Care: Pioneering Voices in Buddhist Chaplaincy and Pastoral Work* by Cheryl Giles and Willa Miller (Wisdom Publications, 2012);
> - *Benefit Beings! The Buddhist Guide to Professional Chaplaincy* by Danny Fisher (Off the Cushion Books, 2013);
> - *A Thousand Hands: A Guidebook to Caring for Your Buddhist Community* by Nathan Jishin Michon and Daniel Clarkson Fisher (Sumeru Press, 2016);
> - *Awake at the Bedside: Contemplative Teachings on Palliative and End-of-Life Care* by Koshin Paley Ellison and Matt Weingast (Wisdom Publications, 2016).

cycles of birth, old age, illness and death. This world, the world of *samsara* or cyclic existence, is characterized by impermanence, ignorance of the nature of self, and suffering, which is largely caused by clinging. Most religions accept that there is suffering in the world, though many provide alternative explanations and solutions. In fact, I tend to think religions exist because they help us cope with this suffering in meaningful ways. Religions persist inasmuch as this suffering is endemic to the human condition.

Most religions also agree that during times of suffering, we need human companionship. Chaplains exist to help those experiencing acute suffering cope and find meaning in trying times. Chaplains draw on religion to do this, but not exclusively so. Religion (or we may substitute "worldview" when working with secular folk) becomes important in two ways. First, religious systems help the person who is suffering – who I call the 'careseeker' – make sense of their experience and provide resources for coping with their situation, hopefully in ways that minimize their suffering. Second, the deep spiritual formation of the chaplain who is grounded and trained in their own tradition helps the chaplain cope with the empathic suffering they experience as they companion those experiencing acute suffering.

The Buddha's Second Noble Truth is an interpretation of the situation in which living beings find themselves. It is called *samudaya* or the cause of suffering, which the Buddha has identified as clinging or attachment. (In Sanskrit, the word is *taṇhā*, most accurately translated as 'thirst.') We suffer because we are attached to things that are impermanent or to things we mistakenly identify as self, 'me,' or 'I.' Sometimes we suffer more because we are attached to the idea that we *should not be suffering!* Essentially, life will never be what we want it to be. Even happy, content, and joyous experiences fade and we will be full of grief and sorrow. When aging, illness, and death afflict us, we want desperately for our situation to be otherwise. The Second Noble Truth explains why we suffer as we do.

Likewise, in my study, I sought to understand why Buddhist chaplains are as we are and do the work that we do. Chapter 2 includes descriptions of Buddhist chaplains' work in interfaith settings. At the same time that I was attempting to document what chaplains do, as well as who they are and where they work, I was also trying to understand why this was the case. How did they come to the work? How did they understand it? What was their interpretation of the causes of suffering, their own and others, particularly non-Buddhist others? What was distinct about the various sectors – health care, the military, higher education – where Buddhist chaplains find themselves?

During my research, I found a common pattern among the chaplains I interviewed that matched an existing Buddhist idea – the Three *Prajñās* or 'wisdoms.' Some of my fellow chaplains referenced it explicitly, others implicitly. This pattern was fractal, meaning it operated at both large and small scales. It could describe the entire spiritual formation of a chaplain throughout their lifespan and an hour-long encounter between a chaplain and careseeker. As a fractal, it repeats iteratively. One could start or end anywhere within the pattern, though it often followed the standard progression of the Three Prajñās. This book explores and applies this pattern as a comprehensive theory called "The Three Prajñās Framework for Buddhist Spiritual Care." The Framework is an interpretive lens through which we can understand the spiritual formation of chaplains and their work as spiritual caregivers in various contexts. While the Second Noble Truth is universal, applying equally to all living being, The Three Prajñās Framework is situational, applying to Buddhist chaplains in their present contexts (though it may be useful to others).

The Buddha's Third Noble Truth is a normative statement about the highest good that living beings can achieve. It is called *nirodha* or the cessation of suffering. Not only did the Buddha affirm that all beings seek an end to suffering, he also assured us that suffering can, in fact, end. Buddhism has often been called pessimistic or even nihilistic because of the first two Truths, but the Third Noble Truth is fundamentally hopeful. Liberation is achievable. The Third Noble Truth is a normative statement about the way things can and should be – that is, free from suffering. By cultivating wisdom and compassion, we can slowly become aware of our attachments and relinquish them, leading to the cessation of suffering.

Moreover, we can help one another in this process and the Buddhist chaplain has role in this process. To do this role well, the Buddhist chaplain must simultaneously be and do particular things (though 'things' is a rather crude way to describe it). What are these? What kind of person should a Buddhist chaplain be? Can anyone become that kind of person? And what kind of actions should a Buddhist chaplain perform during spiritual care? These are, of course, normative questions and they have normative answers. That is, value judgements are being made here, that one thing is better than another.

Please do not make the easy mistake, as I sometimes do, of assuming this means that a person, virtue, way of being, action, or experience is *intrinsically* better than another. These are not value judgements about personal worth or dignity. These are judgements about skillful and unskillful habits and about cause and effect. The training and education Buddhist chaplains receive is not merely about academic knowledge or professional skills, it also involves the cultivation of personal qualities that will prove essential to the work of the spiritual caregiver. We know that even personal qualities are impermanent, not part of a fixed self, and can be cultivated through certain practices and experiences. We call this process spiritual formation.

In the process of spiritual formation, it is often useful to have a model or ideal to work towards. I have chosen *kalyāṇamitra* as the Buddhist model for chaplaincy and explain in Chapter 4 why I believe this model is suitable for all Buddhist chaplains, Theravada, Mahayana, Vajrayana, and those who prefer not to be categorized. I am saying that kalyāṇamitra should be a model, but I am not saying it need be our only model. Many Buddhist chaplains rely on the model of the *bodhisattva* and that works quite well for them. Though a Mahayana Buddhist myself, I prefer kalyāṇamitra and you might as well, but if you do not, I hope you will add to the literature with models of your own.

The Fourth Noble Truth is a pragmatic formula for how to achieve the cessation of suffering. It is *marga* or the path, in this case, the Noble Eightfold Path of Right View, Intention, Speech, Action, Livelihood, Effort, Mindfulness, and Concentration. This path describes, in very practical terms, what we should understand, say, do, how we should live, and the way we should cultivate our minds. As such, we will already be familiar with many of its aspects as they relate to our own spiritual formation as Buddhist chaplains. Hopefully, we have been following the Noble Eightfold Path in our own lives to the best of our ability.

This book interprets the Buddha's practical advice and applies it to the context of chaplaincy in interfaith settings. It is primarily pragmatic, outlining basic knowledge and skills that a Buddhist chaplain should master to be effective. Many other books about spiritual care and the work of chaplains also outline these skills, though until very recently, few build explicit links between the skills and teachings from the Buddhist tradition. This book does exactly that by drawing on prior literature, both Buddhist and non-Buddhist, the wisdom of the thirteen chaplains interviewed during my research, my own personal experience, and that of trusted colleagues. The normative and pragmatic sections of the book are interwoven in Chapters 3 and 4.

Despite what is provided here, this is only the beginning. Buddhist chaplaincy is a young field that needs further development. This is not to say that spiritual care is new to Buddhists for it certainly is not. We have 2,600 years of Buddhist wisdom on which to rely. However, chaplaincy as a profession is only a few hundred years old in the western world, starting as a Christian profession. As such, we can also rely on the friendly advice of our non-Buddhist colleagues who have been long engaged in this work where we are relative newcomers. We can also draw on examples from the knowledge generated (or confirmed) in the cognate disciplines of social sciences and medicine. This book is a starting place and, I hope, various sections will serve as a template for methods readers can employ to continue this work on their own and contribute to the conversation.

This book is for Buddhist chaplains looking after careseekers of any religious, secular, or spiritual worldview. As such, it is primarily concerned with the contexts in which Buddhist chaplains are trained and work, though it may apply to others. It is also grounded in the experience of Buddhist chaplains working in the United States of America. The rich data that helped develop the theories presented in Chapters 3 and 4 represents the collective wisdom of thirteen Buddhist chaplains working in the U.S., including seven Caucasians (one with Latino heritage) and six Asian or Asian-Americans. The stories they shared about their work often involved working with Christian or secular careseekers and alongside Christian and other monotheistic peers and supervisors. The Framework and kalyāṇamitra model that resulted are deeply grounded in the Dharma and described in Buddhist terms. The Framework and model describe, interpret, normalize, and provide pragmatic guidance for inter-religious spiritual care.

I present this reflection on the Four Noble Truths to start our conversation both as an example of the kind of method I will employ throughout this book and to help readers understand the structure of the work. Chapter 1 contains a description of the situation Buddhist chaplains face. Chapter 2 explores how the Dharma helps us understand and interpret our work as spiritual caregivers. Chapters 3 and 4 present the Framework and kalyāṇamitra model for how we can – perhaps even should – engage with our work as chaplains. In other words, this book contains description, interpretation, normalization, and pragmatic advice. There is more work needed in the final aspect. The pragmatic response, how we get there from here, must be much more communal and detailed. Here it is presented in brief and I hope to address it further in future work.

Kalyāṇamitra, Volume I, presents an overview of Buddhist chaplaincy with a comprehensive theoretical framework and model for Buddhist spiritual care.

Kalyāṇamitra, Volume II, focuses on the development of pragmatic skills throughout the education, training and internship of new Buddhist chaplains, as well as an overview of professional issues facing Buddhist chaplains in North America.

1
WHAT IS A BUDDHIST CHAPLAIN?

Chaplaincy is Right Livelihood for Buddhists who wish to integrate their practice and professional lives. Originally a Christian profession, chaplains today are drawn from all religious traditions and none (e.g., Humanist chaplains), including Buddhism. Chaplains work within large institutions where individuals experience crisis, trauma, and distress, such as hospitals and hospice, prisons and jails, police departments and emergency services, all branches of the military, colleges and schools, some corporations, and elsewhere. Chaplains provide spiritual care and counseling to patients, students, prisoners, members of the military, as well as the staff and leadership of the institutions where they serve. Collectively, I refer to those we serve as 'careseekers.'

Spiritual care theory and practice have evolved throughout the history of chaplaincy, from the Christian paradigm, of the Biblical 'shepherd' who heals, guides and sustains their flock, through various post-modern and inter-religious models. This book presents an original Buddhist framework and model for spiritual care – the Three Prajñās Framework and the model of kalyāṇamitra (or spiritual friendship). Lately, Jewish and Muslim scholar-practitioners have also advanced their own paradigms and theories of spiritual care; Hindu, Humanist, Pagan and other chaplains are not far behind. The activities of spiritual care are not new to any of these traditions and most, including Buddhism, can trace them back to their earliest beginnings and the founders. The Buddha himself provided spiritual care to those suffering from age, injury, illness, and death. Many Buddhist chaplains today provide this care in a religiously plural context where Christians have already developed of body of academic literature and set standards for the profession. This book contributes to this literature from the Buddhist traditions.

This chapter contains definitions and a brief history of several key terms, including chaplain, spiritual care, contemplative care, pastoral care, pastoral theology, practical theology, and careseeker. Following this brief foundation, I have provided three vignettes exploring the work of Buddhist chaplains using a practice known as 'thick description.' Each vignette centers around a chaplain, a careseeker and a context. The stories shared are fictionalized composite accounts drawn from the experiences of multiple Buddhist chaplains.

Following the vignettes, I use my own history to demonstrate the spiritual formation of Buddhist chaplains through a four-stage process. The complete theory behind these four stages is the basis for the Three Prajñās Framework, presented in Chapter 3. For now, it is important for chaplains-to-be who are newly setting out on this path to understand that chaplaincy training is not purely academic. Unlike other college classes, which emphasize what the student can do, what knowledge they recite, or what skills they can demonstrate, chaplaincy also requires personal self-development. In order words, *being* is equally as important as *doing*. This process can be fraught with doubts, anxieties, fears and trauma, based in the student's personal history. Chaplains must work with these experiences during their early training because we inevitably take them with us into the room with careseekers. The process of spiritual formation is an important component of the Three Prajñās Framework, but it is not the sole basis of the Framework, which can also serve as a useful guide to spiritual care practice. As we set out, new chaplains-in-training should know that it may not always be smooth sailing, but your professors and peers are there to support you.

Reflection is a critical skill throughout this process. Reflection is necessary for understanding theory and Dharma, developing and evaluating skills, and personal spiritual formation. Readers who work through this book will be coached in various methods of reflection at the conclusion of each chapter. It may help to read the reflection questions at the end of each chapter first and keep them in mind as you read the chapter. For others, it may be better to leave these questions until the end, lest they draw your attention away from what you might naturally be curious about. Either way, I strongly recommend that you engage deeply with this text as you read. Highlight, underline, annotate, disagree, doodle, and compose notes in the margins. Any text is just a conversation in slow motion, with each author speaking directly to each reader (thus my use of both first person "I" and second person "you" language throughout), and with future authors. When you reach the reflection questions, write out your responses in a page or two. Practice the reflexive skills you will be required to develop, demonstrate and document in your training, employment, and, hopefully, future board certification. Finally, be prepared to share your reflections with your professor and peers and receive feedback. This is critical to refine your own thinking and expressive abilities, grow personally and spiritually, and learn how to accept feedback graciously (whether you agree with it or not!). Reflection is a meta-skill, a skill that refines all other skills, and it can also become a deeply meaningful practice. This very book has grown from my own personal love of written reflection and my deep curiosity about how other Buddhist chaplains reflect on their work. May it be of benefit to future generations of Buddhist chaplains and the careseekers they serve.

Chaplains and Spiritual Care

What is a chaplain? What is a Buddhist chaplain? Why even use this word at all? Given the Christian origin of the term 'chaplain,' this is a pressing question for Buddhists. I personally believe 'chaplain' is a suitable word for Buddhists, particularly those of us working in North America, Europe, and other English-speaking countries. As a vocation, chaplaincy is a path for Buddhists to integrate their practice lives with their professions in the contemporary world. Just as the social structures already existed to support wandering monastics like the Buddha in ancient India, the social structures currently exist to support chaplains in the western world, making this a viable path of practice that enables us to live, work, eat, and practice in alignment with the Dharma. My bias in favor of chaplaincy stated up front, let us explore the meaning of the word 'chaplain.'

The oldest meaning of 'chaplain' describes a Christian clergy member who tends to a chapel (*American Heritage Dictionary*), the word from which the professional term derives. This may not sound significant until one considers that a chapel was historically a small private place of prayer and worship for a particular noble and their family. (Alternatively, a chapel is a small, subordinate space within a larger regular church, though in this case, the chapel would be tended by the clergy assigned to the church as a whole with no special title needed, per *The Chambers Dictionary*.) As the keeper of the chapel, the priest would have unprecedented access to the lord and their family, often acting as far more than the keeper of a shrine, but also as a trusted advisor on religious, spiritual, moral, and political matters and often a tutor to the lord's children. We see this in one of the alternative definitions as "a member of the clergy who is connected with a royal court or an aristocratic household," (*The America Heritage Dictionary of the English Language*). Indeed, such a role is described in the *Kūṭadanta Sutta* (DN

5)[1] of the Pāli Canon for a Buddhist monk. This sutta presents the story of a religious person serving as an advisor in the court of a king and the term 'chaplain' is used for their role when translating the sutta into English. Historically, almost every religion has found it vital to advise the ruling classes (or, at least, gain their favor), even if this means sending their clergy to live with the nobility rather than among their ordained community. In modern times, as the role of nobility has waned, chaplains have become embedded in large institutions. Advising institutional leadership, particularly on religious, spiritual, ethical or moral matters, remains part of their role.

A newer meaning of 'chaplain' describes a member of clergy, still presumably Christian, who holds religious services for an institution whose primary function is not religious, such as a hospital or prison. Lately, this role can also be filled by an educated layperson. The armed forces are one of the oldest institutions to use clergy (in this case, almost exclusively clergy) in this way (*The American Heritage Dictionary of the English Language*). In the history of the United States, chaplains in military service are evidenced by a letter from then Colonel George Washington to Robert Dwinwiddie, then Governor of Virginia, requesting a chaplain to serve his First Virginia Regiment in 1756, twenty years prior to the Declaration of Independence (Abbot, 1984). Since the mid-twentieth century, this role has expanded beyond its Christian origins to include Jews, Muslims, Buddhists, Hindus, Sikhs, and others. Today, several thousand chaplains serve in modern militaries worldwide, while far more serve in non-military settings such as hospitals and hospices, prisons, police departments and emergency services, schools, universities and colleges, nursing homes, and even corporations. While there are no comprehensive statistics on the number of chaplains serving in various settings and geographic areas, I would make a confident estimate that there are at least several hundred Buddhist chaplains serving in these settings worldwide, many in North America. Humanists and other nonreligious folks have recently joined the profession and the breadth of religious representation continues to grow, including Pagans, Confucians, and those representing Native American and other indigenous religions, just to name a few.

The work chaplains do is referred to in this book as 'spiritual care and counseling,' or, more often, just 'spiritual care.' Modern spiritual care according to Carrie Doehring "respects and actively engages religious differences" (2015, p. xxiii). In older and/or predominantly Christian sources, this work is referred to as 'pastoral care.' Pastoral care has pastoral theology as its theoretical counterpart. In the first book on Buddhist chaplaincy (*The Arts of Contemplative Care*, 2012), the editors chose the term 'contemplative care' to describe what Buddhist chaplains do as grounded in a contemplation or meditation practice. I shall explore these terms briefly before explaining why I have settled on 'spiritual care.' No theoretical counterpart has been named for spiritual or contemplative care and the term 'theology' remains hotly contested for its applicability to Buddhism (see Payne, 2011). Rather, most Buddhists simple refer to Dharma as their theoretical grounding. In North America, Buddhist chaplains care predominantly for non-Buddhists, particularly Christians or secular folk, so engaging across religious difference is the norm for the profession, thus my preference for 'spiritual care.'

Pastoral care and counseling was originally understood as "the cure of souls (*cura*

---

[1] For Buddhists unfamiliar with notation related to the Pāli Canon, one can find various scriptures by their reference initials and numbers. AN = *Aṅguttara Nikāya*, DN = *Dīgha Nikāya*, MN = *Majjhima Nikāya*, SN = *Saṃyutta Nikāya*, followed by the chapter and verse or section number. Thus DN 5 is the fifth chapter of the *Dīgha Nikāya* with no verse or section reference. I prefer to use the translations published by Wisdom Publications, mostly by Bhikkhu Bodhi. Most parts of the *Nikāyas* can be found online for free with a simple search of the name or number of the scripture, though the exact translation may differ from what is found here.

animarum)" or the "healing, guiding, and sustaining" of Christians in their spiritual journey (Woodward, Pattison, and Patton, 2000, p. 23). Lartey states the most basic meaning of pastoral care is "pertaining to the ordained Christian," while also suggesting that more "wrestling" with it may be necessary in our "pluralistic, postmodern and postcolonial world context" (Lartey, 2003, p. 13). In the Christian traditions, spiritual care began with the acts of Jesus, as recorded in the Bible. The tradition of looking to Jesus as the ultimate model of spiritual care has not diminished in the two millennia since then and can be found in the work of major scholars in this field such as Howard Clinebell (2011, p. 4-5), Wayne Oates (1982, p. 21), John Patton (1993, p. 23-26), Nancy Ramsay (1998, p. 33-34), Andrew Lester (2003, p. 36-39), and Karen Montagno (2009, p. 6). When relying on Jesus as one's source for pastoral care, his role a shepherd is often cited, and forms the basis of the classical paradigm of pastoral care. Since then, pastoral care can be traced through four paradigms, each building on or critiquing the classical paradigm; these are the clinical, communal contextual, feminist/womanist, and intercultural paradigms. G.R. Evans's edited volume, *A History of Pastoral Care* (2000), provides a detailed overview of how pastoral care evolved from its roots in the Old Testament of the Christian Bible through the end of the twentieth century. E. Brooks Holifield focuses on the national context with his 1984 work *A History of Pastoral Care in America: From Salvation to Self-Realization*. A history of pastoral care that focuses on methods – particularly healing, sustaining, guiding, and reconciling – can be found in Clebsch and Jaekle's 1964 book *Pastoral Care in Historical Perspective*. The *Concise Dictionary of Pastoral Care and Counseling* contains a more abbreviated summary broken down by Christian denomination (Mills, 2010, p. 51-70). Some of these paradigms and definitions for pastoral care resonate more with Buddhist chaplains, while others are relentlessly Christian and inappropriate for those of other religious traditions.

The classical paradigm relied on the model of the biblical shepherd and the acts of healing, sustaining, guiding and reconciling; each act gained different emphasis and interpretations in different eras. Several cultural factors, including the Protestant Reformation, European Enlightenment and rise of Modernism had profound effects on pastoral care. The rise of science and the social sciences and Christian responses to these new sources of wisdom and authority on topics of human suffering, well-being, and morality – previously almost the exclusive domain of religion – ushered in the clinical paradigm in the 1920's. Proponents of the clinical paradigm, such as Seward Hiltner, preserved and promoted the shepherd model within the new clinical training programs for caregivers. The clinical paradigm predominated from the 1940's and into current times, largely through the continuation of formal Clinical Pastoral Education (CPE) programs. In time, Modernism gave way to Post-Modernism and new voices (e.g., women, people of color and LGBTQ+ scholars) joined the field, raising concerns that were not new but previously unaddressed. Starting in the 1990's, three new paradigms emerged: the communal contextual, feminist/womanist, and intercultural paradigms. As with the classical and clinical paradigms, these new models built on what came before. "These paradigm shifts expand and critically adapt more than repudiate previous self-understanding," (p. 13) according to Nancy Ramsay in her 2004 work *Pastoral Care and Counseling: Redefining the Paradigms*. No doubt new paradigms will continue to emerge in the twenty-first century, perhaps beginning with interreligious paradigms for spiritual care and a corresponding body of spiritual care 'theology.' Many of these newer paradigms also made way for the first non-Christian caregivers to enter the field.

Jewish and Muslim theologians have advanced their own definitions of pastoral care. In the book *Jewish Pastoral Care* (2013), Rabbi Dayle Friedman refers to the work of Jewish chaplains as *livui ruchani* or 'spiritual accompaniment' (p. xiii). From the title of the book and the name of Neshama: Association of Jewish Chaplains (which has over 300 professional members), we can see that the terms 'chaplain' and 'pastoral care' are accepted in the Jewish community. Jews also develop their own models and theories, as evidenced by their use of the word Neshama (meaning "soul") and the various theories within the textbook, including *livui ruchani* and *bikur cholim*, the commandment to visit the sick, just for example (Ozarowski in Friedman, et al., 2013, p. 56-57). We do not see the shepherd metaphor in Jewish pastoral care literature. There is a recognition that traditionally educated Jewish rabbis and cantors need additional clinical training to serve effectively as chaplains and that Jewish laypeople can also fill the role of chaplain (Friedman, 2013, p. *vii-xix*). Likewise for Muslims, writing about the British context, Sophie Gilliat-Ray points out that while the role of 'chaplain' and term 'pastoral care' are as new to Muslims as they are to Buddhists, one nevertheless sees learned religious individuals "engaged in the delivery of what one might call 'pastoral care,' beginning with the Prophet Muhammed himself" (in Barker, 2008, p. 145-149). Gilliat-Ray, in *Understanding Muslim Chaplains*, accepts the term Muslim 'chaplain' and distinguishes it from an earlier pre-professional classification of 'visiting minister.' A Muslim chaplain requires training and, in some cases, certification beyond that of a local imam or community elder. Gilliat-Ray and her co-authors state that "Although there is no tradition of institutionalized [sic] chaplaincy in Islam, there is an implicit theology that supports and encourages what might be called 'pastoral care'." While the metaphor of Jesus as shepherd is not used in

---

For more resources on the **communal contextual paradigm**, see: Patton, John. *Pastoral Care in Context: An Introduction to Pastoral Care.* (Louisville, KY: Westminster/John Knox Press, 1993); Ramsay, Nancy. *Pastoral Care and Counseling: Redefining the Paradigms.* (Nashville, TN: Abington Press, 2004); Miller-McLemore, Bonnie J. "The Living Human Web: Pastoral Theology at the Turn of the Century." In *Through the Eyes of Women: Insights for Pastoral Care*, ed. Jeanne Stevenson-Moessner (Minneapolis, MN: Fortress Press, 1996), 9-26; Couture, Pamela. "Weaving the Web: Pastoral Care in an Individualistic Society." In *Through the Eyes of Women: Insights for Pastoral Care*, ed. Jeanne Stevenson-Moessner (Minneapolis, MN: Fortress Press, 1996), 94-106.

For more resources on the **feminist and womanist paradigm**, see: *Feminist and Womanist Pastoral Theology*, eds. Bonnie J. Miller-McLemore and Brita L. Gill-Austern. (Nashville, TN: Abingdon Press, 1999); *Through the Eyes of Women: Insights for Pastoral Care*, ed. Jeanne Stevenson-Moessner (Minneapolis, MN: Fortress Press, 1996); Ramsay, Nancy. *Pastoral Care and Counseling: Redefining the Paradigms.* (Nashville, TN: Abington Press, 2004); Kujawa-Holbrook, Sheryl A., and Karen Brown Montagno. 2009. *Injustice and the Care of Souls: Taking Oppression Seriously in Pastoral Care*. Minneapolis: Fortress Press;

For more resources on the **intercultural paradigm**, see: Ramsay, Nancy. *Pastoral Care and Counseling: Redefining the Paradigms.* (Nashville, TN: Abington Press, 2004); Lartey, Emmanuel Y. *In Living Color: An Intercultural Approach to Pastoral Care and Counseling.* (London: Jessica Kinglsey Publishers, 2003); Lartey, p. 8-9, *Pastoral Theology in an Intercultural World.*

Islamic thought in the same way, "it is possible to identify within Islam significant elements of belief and practice which are perhaps best characterised [sic] as broadly 'pastoral.'" Despite this tentative acceptance of 'pastoral care,' the book also uses 'spiritual care' interchangeably throughout (Gilliat-Ray, Ali, and Pattison, 2013, p. 25). Many Jewish and Muslim practitioners have also advocated for the shift to the more inclusive term 'spiritual care.'

Buddhists, like Christians and other religious traditions, have practiced spiritual care since the beginning of our lineage. Like Christians and Muslims, we can look directly to our founder, the Buddha, as the ultimate model for spiritual care. The Buddha was not referred to as shepherd, but rather as a teacher (meant literally), sometimes a doctor (meant metaphorically), and the Buddha also referred to himself as kalyāṇamitra or a 'good friend,' a concept that serves as an important model throughout this text. Many Buddhist caregivers continue to use the term 'pastoral' to refer to their work. I find this well-intentioned as, after all, pastoral care has been the name of the field in western countries for several hundred years. The word 'spiritual,' an intentionally fuzzy term, is also foreign to Buddhism, (*The Princeton Dictionary of Buddhism* contains no term directly analogous to 'spiritual,' but uses the word as an adjective applied to many other terms to denote religious, soteriological or metaphysical connotations) but at least in its ambiguity remains open to whatever meanings Buddhists care to assign. I posed this conundrum to a panel on Buddhist chaplaincy at the American Academy of Religions National Conference in 2014. Rev. Daijaku Judith Kinst, faculty in the Buddhist Chaplaincy program at the Institute for Buddhist Studies of the Graduate Theological Union, responded that she found the term 'pastoral' easily suited to Buddhists due to its similarity to the *Cowherd Scripture* (MN 34: *Culagopalaka Sutta*) and the Ox Herding Pictures of Zen Buddhism (her own tradition). At the time, this seemed like a reasonable answer from an authority in the field.

Further research into the origin of the term and the meaning of the shepherd model within Christian pastoral care leads me to conclude that we should not rely on the term 'pastoral' merely due to minor similarities between Jesus's biblical shepherd and a small section of the voluminous Buddhist scriptures. This accidental analogy implies greater similarity between the central role of the shepherd model for Christians and the role of the cowherd in Buddhism, which is, in fact, only one somewhat obscure metaphor among many for how Buddhists understand care for others. 'Spiritual care' on the other hand "respects and actively engages religious differences," according to Carrie Doehring (2015) in her discussion of the different between pastoral care and spiritual care, which is used more in the institutional settings where chaplains are employed. Doehring continues:

> Intercultural spiritual care that goes beyond an acknowledgement of religious difference (religious plurality) to creating respectful relationship for working with differences in values, beliefs, and practices (religious particularity) (Greider, 2012). In order for spiritual care to engage religious difference respectfully, caregivers need theological expertise that goes beyond knowledge of their own tradition and includes comparative studies of religion. (p. xxiii)

This is certainly the case for Buddhist chaplains in institutional settings who are mostly working across religious borders with non-Buddhist patients. Doehring even acknowledges that while pastoral care may be suitable for Christians and Jews, spiritual care may be more appropriate for Muslims, Buddhists and others to whom pastoral care is a foreign term. Doehring finds it important for caregivers to examine their "cornerstone religious beliefs and values" in relation to their care practice, particularly how they navigate between exclusive beliefs (i.e., my religion is true) and inclusive beliefs (i.e., many religions contain truths) (Doering, 2015, p. *xxiv*). This focus on belief is itself normatively Christian.

Within Buddhism, Right View and correct understanding about the nature of reality is emphasized, but thus far the literature on Buddhist chaplaincy authored by scholar-practitioners in the field has tended to emphasize practice over belief. "What kind of practice does a Buddhist chaplain need to have to support their work as a caregiver?" seems the more pressing question, though belief is not absent from this conversation. 'Contemplative care,' defined below, may be a suitable alternative to spiritual care; it emphasizes the chaplain's grounding in contemplative practice. However, until more voices have weighed in on the matter, I prefer to rely on spiritual care and counseling to describe the activities of Buddhist chaplains and caregivers. Regardless of what we call our caregiving, the term 'pastoral care' dominates the literature and the clinical paradigm still dominates CPE training programs. The influence of critical theory has made more space for Buddhists (and others) to engage in professional training and join the scholarly conversation, but that space remains marginalized due to many factors, not least of which being that Buddhists still constitute a small minority of chaplains in the workforce.

It is important to acknowledge our viewpoints when making choices over which terms to privilege in our discourse. I am writing from that plural, postmodern and postcolonial context as a white, straight, cisgender, female, American, middle class, educated, able bodied, culturally/post-Christian, *Buddhist* chaplain. In that context, the term 'spiritual' has considerable advantage over the Christian-centric term 'pastoral,' which, even with a broad and generous interpretation of its positive meanings, remains historically rooted in the Christian Gospel. In recent decades, use of the term 'spiritual care' has coincided with a decrease in 'pastoral care,' per Google's NGram viewer.

Despite my preferences, I must also be willing to acknowledge the drawbacks of the recent surging popularity of spiritual care. One problem with spiritual care as a term is that there is

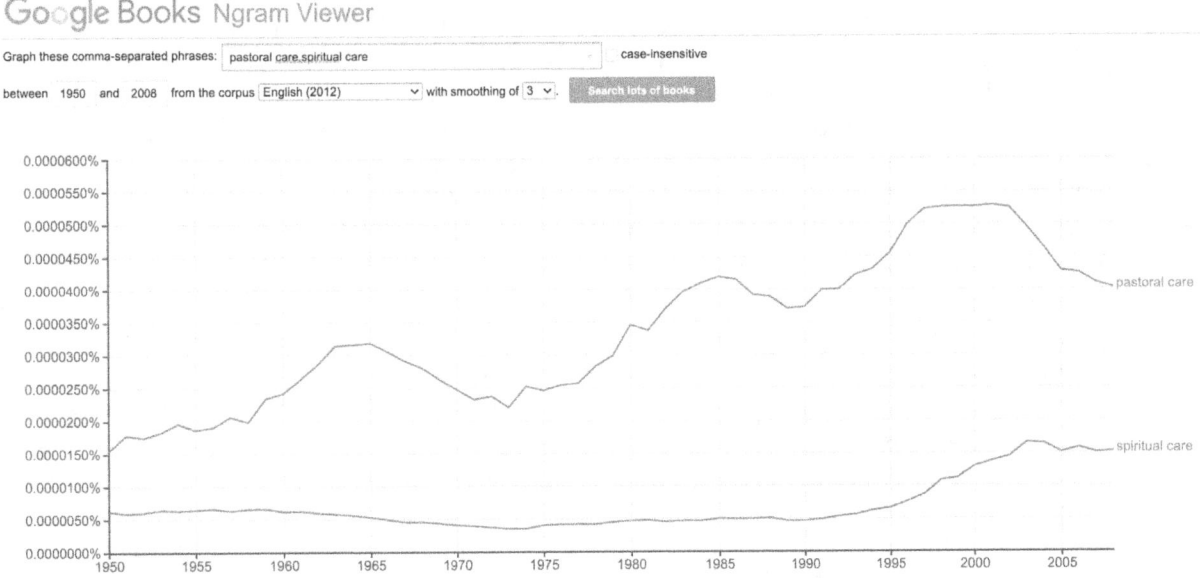

Fig. 1: Screenprint of Google Books Ngram Viewer using the terms 'pastoral care' and 'spiritual care' from 1950 to 2008 (most recent year available), https://books.google.com/ngrams

no corresponding body of 'spiritual theology,' as there is between pastoral care and pastoral theology (which is sometimes a branch of practical theology or vice versa). This is because spiritual care and counseling can be practiced by members of any religious tradition, as well as secular humanists and other 'spiritual but not religious' persons. A person's practice of spiritual care could be rooted in Jewish thought, the Buddhadharma, Hindu wisdom, or shamanic ritual. Meanwhile, Catholics and Anglicans use pastoral theology to cover the theory behind any practical activity, everything from giving sacraments to funeral liturgies. Practical theology, on the other hand, comes from the Protestant traditions, particularly the German theologian Friedrich Schleiermacher, who developed a new subdivision for theological topics and curricula in the 18th Century. For Schleiermacher, pastoral theology was one subject within practical theology, as were other 'applied' subjects such as education, homiletics, and other practical topics. Pattison and Wooward, who summarize these distinctions in *The Blackwell Reader for Pastoral and Practical Theology* (2000, p. 2-3), note that in North America, those primarily concerned with pastoral care of individuals and groups tend to consider themselves as pastoral theologians, whereas practical theologians tend to be more scholarly, and develop theoretical and ethical frameworks for various topics. Buddhist spiritual care as yet has no designated theoretical counterpart aside from the Dharma. I believe that practical theology has useful methods we can learn from as Buddhists, a perspective I outline further in *A Thousand Hands: A Guidebook for Caring for Your Buddhist Community* (Sanford in Michon and Fisher, 2016, p. 55-63).

Another drawback is that definitions of spiritual care as distinct from pastoral care (aside from being inter-religious) are difficult to find. The term 'spiritual care' seems to be more of a legal fiction invented to describe what chaplains do to benefit careseekers in contexts supported by some form of tax funding, which cannot be used to directly support religion (Sullivan, 2014). Perhaps because of this ambiguity, some Buddhist chaplains prefer contemplative care to describe their work.

Contemplative care is "a kind of care that is informed by rigorous training in a meditative or contemplative tradition," according to Cheryl Giles and Willa Miller, the editors of the first book on Buddhist chaplaincy, *The Arts of Contemplative Care*, published in 2012 (p. *xvii*). They describe this form of care as "the art of providing spiritual, emotional, and pastoral support, in a way that is informed by a personal, consistent contemplative or meditation practice" (p. *xvii*). When I first read this definition, I did not believe that it included me. Though I was a Buddhist chaplain-in-training, I had never considered myself a 'contemplative' person. I had certainly never endured "rigorous" or "consistent" meditative practice, regardless of how important my haphazard practice of *śamatha* (calm-abiding) meditation would become to my work. At least one of the chaplains I interviewed evinced similar sentiments.

Indeed, emphasis on meditation is an oft-noted hallmark of western lay Buddhism and, as such, a relative aberration in the long history of Buddhist traditions, where rigorous meditation practice was typically reserved for a select few monastic elites (McMahan, 2008, p. 40-41; he and others characterize "Buddhist Modernism" by its emphasis on meditation as the central feature, in addition to other characteristics, such as democratization and laicization). Nevertheless, this is where Giles, Miller, and their contributors chose to center their dialogue on Buddhist chaplaincy. After six years of campus chaplaincy, my meditation practice has become no more consistent, but I have gained insight into how it contributes to my work as a chaplain and, thus, it is now more central to my understanding of Buddhist chaplaincy. Twelve of the thirteen Buddhist chaplains I interviewed likewise spoke of the deep significance of meditation in relation to their chaplaincy. These practices play important roles in both the formation of Buddhist chaplains and our practice of spiritual care.

For the purposes of this book, I define a chaplain as a professional provider of spiritual care working in a nonreligious institutional context (e.g., a hospital, hospice, prison, military, etc.). Some institutions where chaplains work, particularly hospitals and colleges, are religiously founded and affiliated. I still consider this a nonreligious context because the primary purpose of the institution is not religious, but rather medical or educational, for example, and careseekers and staff are likely to be religiously diverse. The people chaplains care for are called 'careseekers,' whether they are hospital patients or their families, members of the military, prisoners, first responders, students, or staff at the various institutions where chaplains work. Careseeker is a broad term that encompasses all these contexts, but it should not be read to suggest that every careseeker literally actively 'seeks' or even recognizes a need for spiritual care. In many cases, such as in hospitals, chaplains visit careseekers unsolicited on the off-chance they need someone to talk to, even when the careseeker doesn't know what a chaplain is before they knock on the door. I define spiritual care as care for persons with spiritual needs or in spiritual distress; the work done by a chaplain. I refer simple to the Buddha's Dharma or particular aspects and concepts within the Buddhadharma in the role of 'pastoral theology.' (I occasionally use Buddhadharma to emphasize Buddhist teaching from other kinds of Dharma, as the word is common to Hindu, Jain, and other Indian traditions.)

Three Stories of Buddhist Spiritual Care

The following vignettes are fictionalized accounts based on composites of actual spiritual care encounters by Buddhist chaplains in the field. Details about the chaplains, careseekers and situations have been altered and recombined to protect privacy while maintaining verisimilitude. In other words, these vignettes are *like* care encounters that actually happened, though they are themselves fictional. The vignettes present three different Buddhist chaplains working in three different chaplaincy sectors. The chaplains are demographically similar to those working in the field today and all three sectors are known to support Buddhist chaplains.

~

Vignette 1: Higher Education

Chaplain A works at a mid-sized liberal arts college in a suburb of a major metropolitan area, where she is also a full-time faculty member in the social sciences. She is a white, heterosexual, cisgender woman in her late 40's who converted to Mahayana Buddhist as a college student from a non-religious background. While her role as chaplain is voluntary and part-time, she has become well-known among students over the years as someone who cares and who will listen, particularly for those dealing with relationship troubles. Toward the end of the spring term, a student named Alice knocks on her door to ask if they can talk. Alice is a 20-year-old African-American heterosexual cisgender woman from the local area and the first in her family to go to college. Chaplain A has never taught Alice in class, but she has taught several of Alice's close friends and had spiritual care conversations with one of them, who encouraged Alice to come see Chaplain A. It is almost the end of her workday, but Chaplain A beckons Alice to come in, closes the door, and they sit down in the two cozy chairs she keeps in her office for such conversations.

Chaplain A can tell Alice is in emotional distress. She sits carefully, as if trying to make her body small, hunched forward, glancing up occasionally from under dark hair to catch the chaplain's gaze. Her facial expression wavers from flat to very sad as she begins speaking. Alice and her boyfriend, Alex, have been together for two years. They met at the college, where Alex is also a student. He is Alice's first romantic relationship. Alice loves him, but she doesn't like the way he talks to her or treats her sometimes. Recently, he became angry at her and accused her of cheating on him, which she denies. Then he asked her to perform a sexual act and filmed her even though she told him not to. When she became upset with him, he broke up with her and moved out of the room they shared for the last sixth months. He shared the video with his friends and called her insulting names. When Alice told her Aunt about it, her Aunt said it was all Alice's fault because she had agreed to the sexual act, even though Alice insisted she had never agreed to be filmed. Alice told her friend, Abby, what Alex did and Abby told another professor who was legally obligated to report it to the school. Now Alex was being investigated for sexual assault and conduct code violations and he might by expelled. Alice also felt betrayed by her friend Abby and didn't know whom she could trust. Alice cried repeatedly while explaining her story one piece at a time, while Chaplain A reassured Alice that what she shared was confidential[2] and asked gentle probing questions. Here is a sample of their conversation:

> Chaplain A makes an overture, "Alice, earlier you mentioned twice that you felt like you needed to tell someone what happened that night between you and Alex. You told your Aunt and your friend Abby, but you feel like they didn't support you. You don't have to tell me what happened, but you could if you wanted to and I would listen. I promise I won't tell anything to anyone at the school. It's up to you."
>
> Alice sits silently for a minute, then says "It happened last week when I was texting with my sister. She's also in an abusive relationship and I said Alex sometimes does the same things and I didn't want Alex to see that. But he's always reading texts on my phone and I didn't have time to delete these. He came home and he wanted my phone, but I told him no. He was trying to take it from me, but I wouldn't give it to him."
>
> The chaplain notices that Alice said her sister was "also in an abusive relationship," so she may understand that Alex's behavior is abusive. For now, the chaplain just nods and vocalizes acknowledgement.
>
> Alice continues, "So then he started calling me a whore and saying he can't trust me, and he thinks I'm cheating on him. He starts getting his things and says he's breaking up with me."
>
> Chaplain A asks, "Did you want to break up?"
>
> Alice starts crying, "No, I wanted him to stay, so I started begging him to stay." Alice explains how she offered to do sexual things to entice Alex to stay, who then filmed her without her consent, all while calling her names. "So I kept telling him to stop, but he wouldn't. So I went into the bathroom and I was just crying and he just left."
>
> "And you haven't talked to or seen him since then?" the chaplain asks and Alice shakes

---

2   There are limits to chaplain confidentiality. Within most states, chaplains are 'mandated reporters' for a few specific scenarios: 1) neglect or abuse of a child or dependent adult, including an elderly or mentally or physically disabled person, 2) when there is an imminent risk of suicide or homicide. Chaplains-in-training should receive specific guidance on mandated reporting from their educational programs. In some states, risk of suicide and homicide are not covered by mandated reporter laws but may be covered by ethical guidelines within one's profession or institution. A guide and summary of state laws related to child abuse and neglect can be found here: https://www.childwelfare.gov/topics/systemwide/laws-policies/statutes/manda/. Chaplains should advise a careseeker that they may be mandated to report details related to these risks as soon as they suspect a careseeker may share on these topics or at the outset of their conversation.

her head, still crying. "Do you still want him to come back?"

Alice again pauses and takes a few deep breaths, "No, and I feel so ashamed for begging him to stay. I mean, I know it wasn't right. I know he wasn't treating me right. But I just wanted him to understand how he made me feel so horrible. I wanted him to care about how bad I felt, but I don't think he's going to do that. I mean, how could I want him to come back?"

The chaplain responds "I'm so sorry this has happened to you. You don't deserve to be treated that way. What he did, filming you and sharing it, was wrong and it was not your fault." Alice is quiet, so the chaplain checks in, "Do you believe it was not your fault?" Alice nods. "Can you say that it's not your fault?"

Very, very quietly Alice repeats "It's not my fault."

The chaplain continues, very gently, "I know it may not feel that way, but you didn't consent to being filmed or insulted and you didn't deserve to be treated that way."

"But I did offer to do…" Alice trails off, crying again.

"You did," the chaplain acknowledged slowly, carefully, watching Alice's expression, "but earlier you also told me that when you two have fought in the past you would do that and that's what he wanted. So it's possible he knew you would do that and he wanted you to do that this time. Do you think he could have manipulated you?"

Alice is watching Chaplain A very intently, making prolonged eye contact for the first time. She stops crying. Then she says "Now he's going around telling Adam and all his friends that I'm a whore and that I cheated on him, but I didn't. And he's already dating this freshman girl from the dorms and I think he was seeing her before we broke up, but he's telling Adam and the others all these bad things about me."

The chaplain asks "Do you care what Adam and the guys think about you?"

Alice answers with some volume returning to her voice, "No."

Chaplain A responds bluntly, "Then fuck them. Adam's a jerk. Who gives a shit what he thinks?"

Alice smiles and laughs and begins to wipe her eyes and sit up a little straighter.

Chaplain A continues "You've got your parents who love you and friends, and even if they don't always do the things you want them to, they believe you and they support you and want you to be safe. I want you to be safe, too. And I support you in whatever you want to do, even if you don't want to participate in the investigation. I'm just so, so sorry this happened to you."

Alice takes a deep breath and leans back. "Yeah. I just want it to be over now. I don't want him to get in trouble, but I want him to understand how much he hurt me and I want it to be over."

Chaplain A and Alice continue to talk about what she wants to do next, about what resources she has, about how she can talk to her friends and set healthy boundaries. Chaplain A gives Alice information about local domestic abuse counseling services and talks to her a little bit about how to stay safe when breaking up with an abusive partner. Alice doesn't come to see Chaplain A again, but she does email a few days later to say she's gone to one of the support groups and found it helpful. Chaplain A continues to see her around campus until the end of the term. She sees Alex on campus the following day, but not afterward, though she never learns the outcome of the investigation, which is kept private.

Vignette 2: Health Care

Chaplain B works in a major urban hospital in a mid-sized city in the Midwest and works closely with the palliative care team, so he is frequently present for careseeker deaths and accompanies family members at the bedside. He is a Chinese-American heterosexual, cisgender man in his late 20's who was raised in a devout Buddhist family. He is in his fourth unit of Clinical Pastoral Education (CPE) at this particular hospital and has become well-integrated into the multi-disciplinary care team and particularly with the palliative care nurses. He has an affinity for working with those dealing with chronic illness and death due to his own experiences of nursing his father, now deceased, through cancer. Today he is called by the nursing staff to attend a careseeker who had just arrived from a local nursing home following a stroke. The medical staff had determined there was nothing they could do, but was awaiting the arrival of family members from farther away before any decisions were made about life support.

Chaplain B went to visit the careseeker, a white woman in her 70's, who was unresponsive. The chart indicated she was Christian, but no specific denomination was listed. Chaplain B laid his hand on the careseeker's hands and practiced loving-kindness meditation, sending thoughts of wellbeing to the careseeker for several minutes. Then he departed to continue other rounds. When he returned the next day, he found a son (Ben), daughter (Betty), and extended family with the patient. They were glad to see a chaplain and explained they were very devout Evangelical Christians. Their pastor had visited and prayed with them and they asked Chaplain B to pray with them as well, which he did, then stayed to talk.

> "We're just praying for a miracle," Betty says, sitting beside her mother's bed and holding her hand. "She's gonna get through this."
>
> Chaplain B sat next to Betty. Ben sat on their mother's opposite side. Other family members clustered near the window or waited in the hallway. Of the two siblings, Betty seemed more anxious, almost frantic for her mother to make a recovery, while Ben was quieter and calmer. Chaplain B knew the medical staff had already gone over the medical situation with them earlier that day.
>
> "Tell me about your mom," Chaplain B prompts Betty. "Who is she?"
>
> Betty shares stories about her mother from when she was younger. Ben chimes in occasionally and speaks more about their mother in her recent years.
>
> "It sounds like the church was always important to your mother," Chaplain B observes. Betty and Ben nod. "What did she believe would happen after death?"
>
> "Oh, she has a very strong faith," Betty shares. "She was never worried or afraid of death, even after Dad died. She said she missed him, but she wasn't really sad, exactly," Betty sounds a little puzzled as she shares this, and Ben nods again. "She knew she would be reunited with him in Heaven. She has a strong faith in God."
>
> "It sounds like her faith has helped her through a lot of tough situations," Chaplain B ventures.
>
> Betty nods vigorously, "Oh, it has. She believes in the miracles of Jesus and so do we."
>
> "Did your mom ever say anything about situations like this? Maybe when she's known other people who've gone through this?" Chaplain B asks.
>
> Betty blinks and frowns a little. Ben chimes in "Mom was very calm about it all. She had a lot of trust in God. If someone got better, she'd praise Jesus, but if they didn't she'd say it was part of a plan. She'd tell us we had to have faith that they were with God now,"

Ben chuckled, "Mom never thought anyone went to hell."

Betty smiled, "No, she always believes the best of people. She says Jesus loves everyone the way she loves us, but more."

"You Mom sounds like a warm and loving person," Chaplain B replied, following Betty's lead and speaking in the present tense. Both siblings nod again. "Did she ever talk about what she might want for herself in a situation such as this?"

"She'd want us here to pray for her," Betty says immediately and Chaplain B nods.

"Sounds like she'd be happy you're here," Chaplain B pauses, considers, and then presses again. "Do you think she's want to be kept on life support or if she'd want to be allowed to go?"

Betty shakes her head and looks intently at her mother, her eyes tearing up, "No, we're praying for a miracle. The pastors going to come back tomorrow and pray with us. I'm so glad you're here, Chaplain. Can you keep praying for a miracle with us, too?" Ben looks a little more sober, watching his sister.

Chaplain B nods and then speaks very gently, watching Betty carefully, "Well, you know, sometimes the miracles we want – we want Mom to get better – we want her to stay here with us. And, you know, sometimes the miracle is Mom being with God. Maybe that is part of it; it's also like a miracle." Chaplain B could see Betty didn't like this thought, her lips compressed and she looked at her mother rather than the Chaplain. The silence stretches for a while

"Let's pray and then let the Chaplain go. I'm sure he has lots of people to see," Ben suggests.

They pray and then Chaplain B departs.

Chaplain B is not sure what the family will decide or if his words would be welcome. The next day, Betty sees him in the hall and calls his name. Without Ben or other family members present, Chaplain B is prepared for Betty to express her unhappiness with him. He also never mentioned that he's a Buddhist chaplain, not Christian (which he suspected they assume), but he knows they could find out from other staff. That is a constant concern when working with Christian patients, especially when it comes to making suggestions about their own beliefs and doctrines. Instead of being upset, Betty takes a deep breath and says "We have to let Mom go. This miracle is, you know, God. We respect this miracle of her being with God and she's lived a good life and we give her to you. Will you come pray with us again?" Chaplain B is surprised and relieved. He returns to visit the family and prays with them as Mom's life support is withdrawn and she passes peacefully a few hours later.

Vignette 3: Military

Chaplain C serves in the U.S. Navy Reserve and works at a VA center in a mid-sized metropolitan area. She is a half-Korean-American lesbian, cisgender woman in her late 40's who was raised as an Evangelical Christian, but left the church as a young adult and (re)discovered Seon (Zen) Buddhism in her late 20's. After a tour in the Navy as an enlisted sailor, she went to college using veteran's benefits and became a social worker and then a chaplain while serving in the Reserves. An ex-Marine named Charlie made an appointment talk to Chaplain C about his recent breakup with his fiancé. Charlie is a white, heterosexual cisgender male in his late 20's who was enlisted for almost ten years and deployed twice; his is now out of the Marines and trying to go to college for the first time. Chaplain C knows Charlie from a support group for veterans with PTSD and from the local AA meetings hosted at the VA center, but they haven't shared much except casual banter up to this point. Today Charlie shares how he and his fiancé had been getting in more and more fights because they're both really headstrong and want to do things their own way. He says that during their last fight, he got so angry and pushed her and she fell down. That scared her and she told him to leave and then locked him out of the house and now she wouldn't see him or respond to his messages. He knows he "fucked up," but he doesn't know what to do, if he should just accept that it's over or keep trying to fix things. Here is a sample of their conversation:

"I *hate* being single," Charlie states emphatically. "I *hate* coming home alone."

Chaplain C nods. In the groups where Charlie has been present, he usually needs little prompting to continue speaking, so she maintains active listening, focusing on Charlie as she would focus on the object of her meditation.

"I mean, I know Clare and I had problems. And I really fucked that up good," he sighs, "but I miss coming home to her, or to anybody. So I guess I'd rather just go to a bar and drink, but that's all just fucked up, too."

"How long has it been since you did that?" Chaplain C inquires.

Charlie frowns, thinking, "Maybe nine months? The last time Clare and I got into a big fight."

"That's when you got the DUI?" Chaplain C watches carefully, knowing that's another sore point for Charlie that he's talked about in meetings.

"Yeah, so I don't wanna fuck up like that again. And I guess, if I were still in, it would be different. Cause then your guys have your back, through everything, you know? Even the drama with women and life and shit. But now, who am I supposed to talk to? Kevin in my calculus class? Like what the fuck does he even know about what I'm going through? I just feel like there's no one looking out for me. No one has my back. And that was kinda okay when I was with Clare, because we had each other's back. But I fucked that up," he repeats.

Chaplain C refocuses the conversation having already listed through several repetitions of Charlie's failure, "So what do you do instead of going out to a bar?"

"Well, I try to meditate, but that doesn't always work, so I chant instead, or I do PT."

"You meditate? What kind of meditation do you do?" Chaplain C is intrigued; that is not a side of Charlie she expected and she reminds herself not to let her own curiosity dictate the conversation.

"Well, there was a Tibetan Buddhist group that met near base at my last post. So I started going there and learned how to meditate and studied the Dharma a bit. I really felt like the way they understand the world with demons and devas and the visualizations and deity meditation made a lot of sense. And it really fit together with what my martial arts teachers had been talking about since I was a kid. So, yeah…" he shrugs.

"You said meditation doesn't always work when you're upset. Why do you think that is?" Chaplain C asks.

"In the meditation I do, it starts with focusing on the breath, but that's really hard when I'm angry and my mind is full of thoughts. It's easy to get distracted and then pretty soon I'm just so mad I could punch something. So doing the mantras is better, 'cause that's a little more active, ya know, I have to stay focused on what I'm saying, so I can't really think about other stuff at the same time."

Chaplain C thinks of this in light of what Charlie was saying earlier about not being part of the Marines anymore. "So do you have a local sangha or group you meditate with regularly?"

Charlie looks surprised. "No. My group is at my last post, in Virginia."

"That's true. There are some Tibetan groups in the area though. I've visited one of them and they seemed cool. Even had at least one guy who was a veteran, though he was a lot older than you or I."

"Huh, I didn't know that. I mean, I've only been here about a year, and I went to the Zen temple a couple of times, but that wasn't really for me."

"Well, it sounds to me," Chaplain C ventures, "that you're really looking for a new 'home' for yourself. And for a while, you found that in Clare. But since you started dating right after you got here, maybe you missed out on the chance to find other groups that could support you. Like you said, having a bunch of people who have your back is important. You've got me, and the groups here at the VA, and counselors at your college, but where's your sangha? Your teacher? You know, Buddhists say that's important for a reason." This was the most Chaplain C had offered in the conversation so far she watched as Charlie listened intently.

"Yeah, maybe. I have been missing that since I moved here."

"What do your think your teacher or sangha back in Virginia would have said about all this?" Chaplain C asks.

"That I fucked up," Charlie snorts. "That I can't even get the precepts right and they're pretty simple."

"Simple isn't the same as easy," Chaplain C reminds him.

Charlie nods, "That's true."

"You know, in the Order of Interbeing, Thich Naht Hanh's group," Charlie nods to show he recognizes the name, "they call them 'training precepts,' so they remember they're things they use to train behavior, to continuously improve. They don't expect to get them perfect right away. It's like in AA, when they talk about relapse as something most people go through, and how you gotta be prepared for it."

Charlie nods again, a little more firmly, "Yeah, that's true. It's like learning martial arts I guess. First you gotta suck at it, then you practice and practice and practice, and then you get kinda good. But even when you're good you can still miss a block now and then. You can always get better."

Chaplain C and Charlie continue to talk for a little bit. He leaves her office seeming calmer, focused, and more grounded than when he arrived. He takes the contact information for the Tibetan sangha with him and says "See you on Thursday, sis," on the way out.

Chaplain C isn't sure how she feels about being addressed as "sis," but decided to let it pass for now. She realizes that the way they talk to each other does remind her a bit of her brothers, so there may be some transference happening. She'll check in with Charlie at their PTSD group on Thursday. Many of the relationships Chaplain C has formed with soldiers, sailors, marines, and airmen who frequent the VA have lasted for years, so she has patience.

Constructing Buddhist Chaplains through Education, Reflection, and Practice

Buddhist chaplains are made, not born. After reading this chapter, particularly the vignettes, some may be thinking to themselves "That doesn't sound like me *at all*," whereas others might be thinking "I do that already." Both things can be true of any individual at different times of their lives. We all have the capacity to do this work, though it may require careful training and formation to become someone who does it well on a regular basis. Good spiritual care skills can be learned, practiced, and improved. A good chaplain, however, is more than a skilled caregiver. Chaplains also dedicate ongoing effort to cultivating who they are, as well as what they can do. Chaplaincy is about both being and doing. Thankfully, as Buddhists, we believe that character can be cultivated and that we all have the seeds of a fully enlightened Buddha within ourselves. This section uses my own journey to illustrate the formation of a Buddhist chaplain through education, reflection, and a Buddhist practice of spiritual care. It is but one person's story.

When I sold most of my belongings, including my car, to move to Los Angeles and become a Buddhist chaplain I had grave doubts about my ability to do this work. My doubts centered around who I was as a person – deeply introverted, often overwhelmed by too much sensory input, baffled by the behavior of 'normal' people, frequently impatient, frustrated, or derisive of their 'clearly' self-sabotaging behavior, not remotely gregarious, moderately emotionally repressed, and mildly un-social. Many of these traits had already been moderated by several years of Buddhist practice. I developed more patience and compassion towards the people in my life, along with some small understanding of how we are all trapped within maladaptive habitual patterns, myself included. Other traits were modified by eight years of education in a stressful and competitive academic program (architecture). I could pretend to be extroverted during a presentation or committee meeting, but afterward I needed solitude and silence to recover my energy. I was absolutely certain I could learn about Buddhism and that I could even master the skills required for spiritual care, but I was not remotely certain I could *be* the kind of person distressed careseekers needed me to be. Was I really suited for this?

Chaplaincy training programs are not unique in their emphasis on the personal development of the student. Many caregivers, such as therapists and social workers, are likewise asked to examine themselves and given opportunities to grow into both the kind of person and professional they aspire to be. Chaplaincy programs may be unique in the emphasis they place on spiritual and religious growth; they are perhaps unique even from ministry training programs in their insistence on inter-religious growth. Chaplains grow not only within their own religious tradition, but through the careful consideration of their religious experiences, practices, and beliefs in relation to those of other religious traditions. Good Buddhist chaplaincy training programs, of which there are several in the U.S. and Canada today, will facilitate this kind of development, often referred to as 'spiritual formation.'

Despite my misgivings, I chose a Master of Divinity program over a more academic Master of Arts program because I felt strongly that whatever I learned should be pragmatic. It should be able to *help* people directly. While Buddhist studies as a scholarly pursuit helps the world at large progress in knowledge and wisdom, it is often several steps removed from being of direct service to those suffering right now. I see this in much the same way that a person who makes bricks is several steps removed from those who live in the houses made from those bricks. Whereas the mason who assembles those bricks into a structure may know the owners personally. Both are essential, but the brickmaker may never meet the occupants who daily benefit from her handiwork. While I worried about my introversion,

I knew I needed a sense of efficacy in my work that comes from direct engagement. Satisfying my own curiosity was not enough; I needed to help others and see the benefits of my efforts. Despite that motivation, I did not immediately see my path as a direct expression of Right Livelihood the way many of my classmates did. I attribute this mostly to my background as an intellectually curious Buddhist with little direct practice experience and no strong ties to a particular Buddhist teacher or sangha. I would like to say this was unavoidable, given my geographic location, but truth compels me to admit that my disaffiliation was also an expression of my introversion.

I was raised in Nebraska. I studied architecture and community planning at the University of Nebraska, first in Omaha and then in Lincoln. At that time, the university didn't offer a single class that covered Buddhism, not even in a survey of world religions. There are few Buddhists in Nebraska, but enough to form a handful of sanghas. I admit I never visited the Zen temple in Omaha. I read enough on my own to expect that Zen was not going to be my cup of tea, despite an otherwise deep appreciation for Japanese culture. I spent some time with a chapter of the Jewel Heart Sangha in Lincoln, a small offshoot of the main chapter in Ann Arbor, Michigan, which follows the Gelugpa Tibetan lineage of Gelek Rinpoche. That was enough to discover neither was I a Tibetan Buddhist, though I did take refuge from a Tibetan lama who was travelling through town in 2006 and received my first Dharma name, "Tsetan Dolkar" or Long-Lived White Tara. I travelled to Colorado a few times a year to visit Shambhala Mountain Center, where I learned to meditate, completed the first five levels of Shambhala training, and attended talks by Sakyong Mipham Rinpoche (before his fall from grace) and Pema Chödrön. While spending the summer there in 2007, I took bodhisattva vows from Acharya Judith Simmer-Brown and received my second Dharma name. I enjoyed the beauty of the Colorado Rocky Mountains and the camaraderie of fellow Buddhists, but I was never tempted to join Shambhala for both doctrinal and ethical reasons. I read *Tricycle*, the *Shambhala Sun* (now *Lion's Roar*), and *Buddhadharma* magazine when I could find them in the local Barnes & Noble, where I also bought general books about Buddhism by Thich Nhat Hanh, Pema Chödrön, the Dalai Lama and others. I listened to the Buddhist Geeks podcasts and read many blogs, even authoring blogs myself as a way to reflect on my own learning. Reflective writing has long been a major part of my learning and spiritual formation process.

I was still completing a double major in architecture and community planning when the economy crashed in the mortgage bubble of 2008. Architecture graduates failed to find work while doctoral programs in the field filled with newly unemployed professionals. Suddenly, I had not simply the opportunity but the urgent need to sort out what I was going to do with my life when I graduated in 2010. After being rejected from five architecture and planning PhD programs, I asked myself if I was going to work in a shoe store until the economy recovered, like many of my classmates were doing, if I was going to turn fully into planning and work for a municipal government knowing I may never be able to return to architecture, or was I going to do something completely different?

By chance, my family vacationed that year in San Diego. While there, we toured the Midway, a 1950's aircraft carrier now turned into a museum in San Diego harbor. As often happens with my now all-adult family, we went our separate ways, and I found myself wandering through engineering, enlisted barracks, and finally officers' country on my own. I stood in front of a tiny metal cabin, no larger than a walk-in closet, with a bunk against the far wall, a desk to the right, a footlocker to the left, and one long shelf for books. "Chaplain's cabin," the sign read. "I could do this," I thought to myself. I could spend months at sea with a few thousand sailors living in a tiny, windowless cabin and walking along the flight deck to stare at an endless horizon. Maybe others couldn't or wouldn't want to, but I figured I wouldn't mind so much. When I returned to Omaha, I looked up Buddhist chaplain training programs. I was ready to take the step from a solitary practitioner, from what I know recognize as the first stage of a four-stage progression, into the next stage as a formal student.

I arrived at University of the West in August 2010 as a student in the second cohort of Buddhist chaplains admitted to the new Master of Divinity (MDiv) in Buddhist Chaplaincy program. At that time, it was led by Danny Fisher, a bright young product of the more established MDiv program at Naropa University. Danny was completing his doctorate at UWest when he was asked to launch the MDiv program under the supervision of Dr. Kenneth Locke, an Anglican theologian and champion of interfaith collaboration. I entered a program mixing spiritual care coursework with Buddhist studies courses alongside classmates from many different lineages and traditions of Buddhism. The program at UWest meets the learning outcomes for MDiv programs set by the Association of Theological Schools, guaranteeing graduates eligibility for employment and board certification alongside their Christian and Jewish peers. It is a rich three-year, full-time program and I dove in headfirst. I learned I was not the only one with doubts. We all underwent intense spiritual formation during the course of those three years, in addition to studying the history and core texts of the Buddhist traditions, learning rituals and spiritual care skills, studying both Buddhist and western psychology, and expanding our inter-religious knowledge.

Courses in the MDiv often followed a particular pattern, though I didn't notice it at the time. We would be asked to read on a topic before the coming class, complete a written reflection, discuss our reflections with our peers and professors, and then practice the skills covered in the materials, often through role play or contemplative exercises. Practice was also part of our assignments. Homework could involve having a conversation with someone, making notes about it, and reflecting on its various dimensions to reveal insights. In other words, we were asked to develop wisdom through an iterative process of listening/reading, contemplating/reflecting, and practicing. In Buddhism this is known as the Three Prajñās, wisdom by listening, wisdom by contemplating, and wisdom by practicing. The Three Prajñās have been used in many Buddhist traditions as a guide to pedagogy. My research would later reveal their applicability to Buddhist chaplaincy more broadly.

Education for Buddhist chaplains varies considerably based on location and program. In a global survey I conducted with co-author Nathan Jishin Michon, we found Buddhist chaplaincy training programs that ranged from weekend workshops to fully accredited, three-year MDiv programs. Our article on "Buddhist Chaplaincy" for the *Oxford Research Encyclopedia of Religion* includes a summary of the development of the field of Buddhist chaplaincy, an overview of the core competencies, and a helpful survey of Buddhist chaplaincy around the world, including North America, Thailand, Vietnam, South Korea, Japan, Taiwan, the United Kingdom, Australia and New Zealand, and elsewhere (Sanford and Michon, 2019). We listed those programs we could find and the context of Buddhist chaplaincy in those countries. Conditions are changing rapidly, mostly characterized by the growth and professionalization of Buddhist chaplaincy training programs, especially in Asia. Readers outside the North American context should consult this survey for more information on options in your country.

Many Buddhists begin clinical pastoral education (CPE) or internship for chaplains while they are completing their MDiv program, often during the summer following their first or second year. A full-time CPE unit generally lasts three months. A part-time unit can last four to six months with some 'super-extended' units lasting up to nine months. I was employed throughout my MDiv program, often thirty to forty hours a week, and was not able to complete a CPE unit until after my graduation. When I did begin CPE, I realized the wait was a blessing in disguise (for me; others may be ready earlier in their studies). I felt far more prepared to step into my role as a chaplain intern than many of my CPE peers, who were in the first or second year of their training. I also felt more confident in myself after having had three years to learn, reflect, practice, and grow into myself as a Buddhist practitioner. Not being part of a sangha prior to beginning my study made graduate school all the more crucial for my development.

My CPE program was also relatively uncommon. Most CPE takes place in hospitals, where chaplain interns fill out the ranks of the spiritual care department under the oversight of a senior chaplain who is trained in CPE supervision. CPE consists of "clinical rounds" or visiting patients for about 30-35 hours a week, weekly meetings (four to five hours) with one's cohort of peers for ongoing education, sharing, and feedback, and one-on-one meetings with one's CPE supervisor. My CPE experience, by contrast, took place as part of a super-extended out-placement unit offered by the Academy for Jewish Religion. My 'clinical site' was University of the West, from which I had just graduated and where I was not employed full-time as an administrator. My CPE cohort met weekly on Sunday evenings and my supervisor was a Reform Jewish Rabbi with many years of experience. Each unit lasted the length of the academic year, from September to May, and included eight to ten hours of chaplaincy each week, in addition to Sunday meetings. As a result, I may be one of the few campus chaplains to complete all of her CPE training on a college campus. This process took four years, during which I further refined both my own spiritual formation and my spiritual care skills as part of the third stage of the four-stage progression outlined by the Three Prajñās Framework. I moved from the role of student (second stage) into the role of chaplain (third stage).

This was advantageous, as my career aspirations had changed in graduate school. I was unable to attain an endorsement from the Buddhist Churches of America to serve as a Navy Chaplain due to my background, not being associated with the BCA or another Buddhist tradition they found acceptable. The BCA was and still is the only endorsing agency for Buddhist chaplains recognized by the Department of Defense. While they will endorse non-BCA Buddhists for service in the armed forces, my own lack of a long-term affiliation with a recognized sangha gave them pause. Poor communication would not reveal this as the barrier until after my graduation, causing much frustration at the time. Meanwhile, I once again re-evaluated my options and, having demonstrated an interest in and aptitude for research, set my sights on a PhD in spiritual care and work as a campus chaplain, both of which I achieved in 2018.

During my final CPE unit, I often wondered if I had 'arrived.' I knew I would always have more to learn. That is part of the beauty of the work. Yet, I had also achieved my career objective. I was a chaplain. But as I reflected on my work with careseekers, I wondered at a sharp qualitative difference in some encounters over others. While completing my PhD, this also became the unwitting topic of my doctoral dissertation. I interviewed thirteen other practicing Buddhist chaplains and collected hundreds of thousands of words of 'data' in the form of interview transcripts and written reflections.

There was a quality to some of the encounters Buddhist chaplains described that reminded me of Śantideva's descriptions of *bodhicitta*, rare and fleeting, like lightning in a clear sky. When I began my research, I had no expectation that I would find a further stage beyond 'chaplain,' but when it emerged from the research, I felt like it had been right there the entire time. The encounters that stood as exemplifying the best work of Buddhist chaplains are part of the fourth and final stage of development, which I call kalyāṇamitra or spiritual friendship. Some of the chaplains I interviewed named it explicitly in their work, saying that they accompanied careseekers more as friends, rather than as some kind of pastoral authority (a common Christian theme). This clue led me back to the sacred texts and a careful evaluation of kalyāṇamitra, which turned out to be a wonderful model for Buddhist chaplaincy.

In reflecting on the exceptional encounters, I realized three things. First, the chaplain was acting as kalyāṇamitra for the careseeker in distress, exemplifying the qualities and behaviors of the good spiritual friend. These qualities and behaviors are enumerated in detail in the Dharma. Second, this had clear benefits both for the careseeker and for the chaplain. In thinking back to my own spiritual care work, the encounters that went best for careseekers were somehow also 'easiest' on me in terms of vicarious stress and trauma, despite the extreme content of many conversations. Whereas, comparatively less stressful or traumatic situations could often leave me exhausted and the careseeker no better off or, worst case, more frustrated than before. The difference can be characterized by the presence of the chaplain as kalyāṇamitra. This should not be mistaken as an assertion that the chaplain has control over these situations. In fact, most situations are almost always beyond the chaplain's control. The careseeker and the context are major factors. However, even in situations when the chaplain can do little from a practical perspective, embodying kalyāṇamitra seems to prevent emotional distress in the caregiver and, at least, does not add to the careseeker's distress. Third, chaplains who had spiritual friends of their own, who had been accompanied by others exemplifying the role of kalyāṇamitra, were better able to become kalyāṇamitra themselves. Moreover, when these relationships were inter-religious, they were often especially growth-catalyzing and meaningful. Part of the kalyāṇamitra's role includes prompting the careseeker to reflect on their own spiritual worldview in light of their present situation. Working inter-religiously often requires us to pause and really interrogate what we mean and clearly articulate our worldview in a way that benefits both speaker and listener.

I realized that I had been accompanied by many kalyāṇamitra, especially during the eight-year period of my MDiv degree, CPE training, work as a campus chaplain, and completion of my doctorate. Perhaps my first kalyāṇamitra was Dr. Kenneth Locke, the grumpy Anglican theologian who helped start the Buddhist chaplaincy program at UWest. I had the joy of taking two classes from him in 2010 and 2011 and also becoming friends. Then there is Rev. Dr. Victor Gabriel, a Tibetan priest with a multi-religious background and ready laugh, who became an instructor in the MDiv program in 2011, while I was a second-year student. Vanessa Karam, the Dean of Student Affairs, gave me some of my earliest jobs at UWest and welcomed me to experience Ramadan and other Islamic practices alongside her Muslim family. Dr. Duane Bidwell, my doctoral advisor at Claremont School of Theology and self-identified Buddhist-Christian, called personally to tell me that I had been accepted into the doctoral program and then provided wise counsel for the next five years. He also suggested I complete my CPE via the Academy for Jewish Religion, where I met Rabbi Rochelle Robins, who guided me through four units over four years and also helped me work through the habit I have of preemptively sabotaging my student-teacher relationships before my teachers can abandon me, a repetition in my life I was happy to break. Finally, Dr. Stephen Morgan, who was my boss at UWest during the last five years of my work there was the best professional mentor I could have asked for. A devout member of Church of the Brethren and president of the University of La Verne for 25 years, Dr. Morgan came out of retirement to calmly shepherd the little Buddhist university of UWest through a critical five-year reaccreditation process as its president. He was also a wonderful mentor to many of the junior staff, myself included. Without my Buddhist, Christian, Jewish, and Muslim kalyāṇamitra, I would not be the chaplain or scholar I am today. There were others, but these six had an outsized impact.

I find that spiritual formation is an ongoing, lifelong process, and that chaplains are asked to engage with it with greater intensity than most in order to become experts at the process. It is not about reaching some level of spiritual mastery from which you may then calmly teach others. Rather, it is about doing the hard work on yourself that will enable you to be 'in the foxhole' with people who are often going through some of the hardest experiences of their lives. Chaplains go to the places of suffering, to emergency rooms and death row, to oncology wards and on deployment with military units, to hospice and fire station. The people we meet are in crisis, traumatized, or deeply distressed, all of which frequently prompts involuntary reexamination of our spiritual and religious lives. Often, those with a steady religious practice find great comfort in their beliefs and behaviors. At other times, those same people may find themselves cast deeply into doubt and reevaluating everything they thought they knew. Others, with no religious or spiritual identity at all may nonetheless find themselves with deep existential questions and searching for practices to bring them a sense of comfort and support. Our expertise is not in dispensing answers, but rather in the language of the questions. We know how to talk about spiritual, religious, ethical, existential and philosophical questions in the way an architect can describe a building or a conductor can describe a symphony. We know things about what tends to 'work' for those in particular situations, just as a sommelier might suggest a particular wine to go with a meal, in accordance with both the situation and tastes of the diner. But mostly, we are able to tolerate the trauma and stress of the situation, to be in there with the careseeker, to accompany and console, in a way that does not add to that distress and, in many ways, often lessens it. I can't say precisely why or how this happens. Perhaps my more extroverted colleagues will have the words for it. To me, it is merely the mundane magic of our work, and I am quite glad there are those who do it.

Conclusion and Reflection

Readers may have noticed a few patterns in the preceding chapter, some called out explicitly, such as the Three Prajñās Framework with its four-stage progression from self to student to chaplain to kalyāṇamitra. There is one other thread I would like to call the reader's attention to before concluding: the role of reflection. Reflection was implied in the vignettes and described explicitly in the prior section. Reflection is what allows the Buddhist chaplain to become fluent in the language of spiritual care and is essential for the development of other practical skills. Moreover, chaplains are expected to "be self-reflective" (APC standard PIC1) and "Facilitate theological/spiritual reflection for those in one's care practice" (APC standard PPS8). It was the Buddhist chaplains' ability to facilitate reflection for careseekers that I set out to investigate when I embarked on my doctoral research. In the process, I asked chaplains to actively reflect on their work during our interviews and to share written reflections with me. This revealed a great deal of wisdom about the practice of Buddhist spiritual care itself and has culminated in this book. I encourage my readers to read reflexively and each chapter will conclude with reflection questions to help hone a skill many chaplains reported was neglected in their academic coursework but expected during CPE and professional practice.

When I arrived at CPE, I felt that my caregiving skills, such as active listening, responding and reframing, working with a pragmatic psychology, knowing when to refer, holding space for compassion, and setting personal boundaries, were all well formed. However, my ability to describe what I was doing, why I was doing it, and what it all meant was underdeveloped. Christians have the whole genre of pastoral theology literature on this subject. My Jewish peers could similarly cite chapter and verse of Torah, Talmud and academic literature, and relate it to a conversation with a careseeker – who was also likely theocentric – to reflect on the meaning of the encounter in light of both the careseeker's religious/spiritual tradition and their own. My own ability to reflect was not so sophisticated, despite the numerous 'reflection papers' I had submitted throughout graduate school. Fortunately for both my own meaning-making processes and my ability to facilitate such reflection for struggling and confused careseekers at critical periods in their lives, this skill developed rapidly. By the end of my fourth unit, constructing and sharing reflections with others and facilitating reflection among careseekers and peers was one of my strongest aspects of my work as a chaplain.

My preliminary investigation of this topic led me to believe that Buddhist chaplains do, in fact, perform something at least analogous to what Christians call 'theological reflection,' both for themselves and as facilitators for others. A comparison of *The Arts of Contemplative Care* (Giles and Miller, 2012), and *Theological Reflection: Methods* by Elaine Graham, Heather Walton, and Frances Ward (2005) revealed a correlation of methods. Buddhist chaplains do indeed perform and facilitate reflection that is in some ways similar to, yet also distinct from, Christian methods, as several of the authors in Giles' and Miller's anthology demonstrated. However, having been isolated from other Buddhist chaplains during my CPE work, I had few examples to draw on in professional practice. Thus, that seed of curiosity became my dissertation research. How do Buddhists make meaning from/of/about our work as spiritual caregivers?

As we begin, reflect on two parts of this chapter in particular. Start by reading the vignettes again. As you read each, ask yourself the following questions and jot down a few notes.

1. What bodily sensations and emotions arise in me as I read this?
2. What thoughts and memories does this story bring forth in me?
3. What judgements have I formed about the characters in this story?

This process of self-reflection helps us develop a quality known as reflexivity, or the ability to be self-reflective in real-time and adjust our mental states and behaviors accordingly without losing focus on the object of our attention (i.e., the careseeker). Many Buddhist chaplains find reflexivity a natural extension of their meditation practice. Now, you are being asked to go a step further and put what you notice into words. Focus on those sections that surprise you or resonate with you and interrogate those sensations, thoughts and judgements.

When you have finished reading the vignettes, consider the section titled "Constructing Buddhist Chaplains through Education, Reflection, and Practice." This section uses my own spiritual autobiography to outline the progression of a solo Buddhist practitioner to a Buddhist chaplain. Now, consider your own spiritual autobiography using the following questions:

1. Were you raised with a particular religious or spiritual tradition (Buddhism or otherwise) or a certain kind of secular worldview and, if so, how did that manifest in your family and your life?
2. What was your earliest understanding of the Buddhadharma and how did that come about?
3. When did you make the decision to commit yourself to studying the Dharma and why?
4. When and why did you decide to become a Buddhist chaplain?

As you reflect on these questions, it may be helpful to begin outlining your spiritual autobiography as a story. This will not be the last time you are asked to reflect on your path. Throughout your education as a Buddhist chaplain, you will return to this narrative again and again with new eyes. This does not suggest that your first attempts are poor, only that as we learn, we often see our past in different ways.

If you struggle with aspects of your personal history, it may be helpful to pause now and then and engage in compassion and loving-kindness meditation for oneself. Though the Buddhadharma teaches us to be grateful to our parents and ancestors, we must acknowledge that many children and adults experience trauma and abuse. These aspects of your personal history come with you into the caregiving relationship and you will be asked to reckon with them during your training (though perhaps not just yet). Therefore, as you recall your family and your Buddhist path, if this process brings up troubling memories for you, please be gentle with yourself. Direct compassion and loving-kindness towards yourself. If you find yourself struggling, reach out to your professors and the counselors at your school for support. They know that Buddhist chaplaincy students are not immune to such struggles; they will not judge you for them and only seek to support your growth and education. These struggles will not disqualify you from becoming a Buddhist chaplain. In fact, all our past struggles contribute to our ability to empathize and show kindness and compassion to those in our care. At the moment, the person in your care is you, so treat yourself with love.

2
What Do Buddhist Chaplains Do?

How does one actually do the work of a Buddhist chaplain? This chapter attempts to answer this question in two ways. First, it focuses on what makes Buddhist chaplains distinct from other chaplains, that is, we are Buddhist and draw on the Buddhadharma as our spiritual foundation and spiritual care praxis base. Spiritual formation is covered elsewhere, so here I will expand what I mean by 'spiritual care praxis base.' 'Praxis' is a term "used to convey a sense of the constant interaction between *action* and *reflection*," according to Emmanuel Lartey and other pastoral theologians (2003, p. 122). Thomas Groome writes about 'shared praxis' as people's "reflection on life" as part of a commitment to "theory-laden practice" and "practice-laden theory" (Ireland-Verwoerd, 2005). Thus, the term 'praxis' does a few things I find helpful, as a Buddhist. It clearly prioritizes the importance of reflection and theory in our work. Practice may be about doing specific actions, even the Right Actions, but praxis is about knowing *why* we do them through constant reflection – a skill called reflectivity – on our understanding of that *why*. Praxis is a holistic term that integrates multiple aspects of the Noble Eightfold Path into our work, including *prajñā* (wisdom), *śīla* (morality), and *samādhi* (concentration).

The vignettes in the prior chapter demonstrate spiritual care praxis in a few areas. In each case, chaplains are employing a form of reflexivity, drawing on their wisdom (both in the form of theoretical knowledge and prior experience), to inform how they respond to the careseekers. In Vignette 1, Chaplain A waited until after Alice used to term 'abuse' to characterize her own relationship before using the term. This is because domestic abuse victims are often unwilling to acknowledge abuse and will often align with and defend their abusers if they feel the caregiver is against the abusive partner, creating a barrier to a healing relationship with the caregiver and resistance to taking action to keep themselves safe. Chaplain A knows this both from her academic study of relationship theory and her personal experience working with other students in abusive relationships. By being patient and resisting the urge to quickly characterize Alice and Alex's relationship (we can also speculate that Chaplain A drew on her Buddhist training of 'not knowing' and withholding judgement to cultivate this patience during the encounter, though this may have been more subconscious), Chaplain A created the trust needed to be able to give Alice a referral to a domestic abuse support group at a point in their relationship when Alice was receptive, increasing the likelihood that Alice would follow through with the referral, which she did. In Vignette 2, Chaplain B drew directly on her understanding of the Dharma when she practiced loving-kindness meditation for the benefit of the unresponsive patient. In Vignette 3, Chaplain C reflected on her prior experiences with Charlie in group settings and allowed this to guide her interaction with him in a one-on-one setting. Each of these instances illustrate praxis in Buddhist spiritual care.

The two parts of this chapter focus on Buddhist spiritual care praxis in distinct and reciprocal ways. The first section of this chapter provides several reflections on sections of the Dharma that can inform our spiritual care praxis as Buddhists. In that sense, it is the 'theory-laden' section of "theory-laden practice." The second section of this chapter is the inverse, the 'practice-laden' section of "practice-laden theory." It focuses on where Buddhist chaplains provide spiritual care – the military, health care, prisons and schools – and the practical aspects of that care. In other words, how one becomes a Buddhist chaplain in that setting, what a chaplain does on a daily basis, and what common issues they might encounter in different settings. The common issues in each setting should serve as the starting point for further academic study, so that a chaplain-in-training can focus on the theory and praxis of spiritual care in the setting.

In addition to these two sections, the chapter concludes with a summary of outcomes for spiritual care. I should start by saying this is a difficult topic to study. First, chaplains often join careseekers in the middle of their journey and depart before the end. We rarely see the full impact of our work and are often left without a sense of closure. For example, Chaplain A never learned the outcome of Alex's student conduct hearing. She never new if Alice continued going to the domestic abuse support group or if Alice and Alex even stayed separated. Chaplain C may see Charlie again at some of the support groups, or he may simply stop coming and drop off her radar, as so many do. This makes tracking the outcomes of our work difficult and chaplains must cultivate an ability to live with that ambiguity. Second, the outcomes of spiritual care are often reported by the chaplain, not the careseeker. Because of our limited window into the lives of careseekers, these reports will always be partial and biased. Third, while some scholars attempt to do research directly with careseekers about outcomes, this research is often difficult and has not yet been conducted in a way that would distinguish the outcomes of Buddhist spiritual care from any other kind. Careseekers receive spiritual care in some of the most challenging moments of their lives, so any direct research has to be approached very sensitively. There is a great deal of academic research and mounting evidence for the efficacy of mindfulness-based interventions derived from Buddhist teachings and practices, but these interventions are often secularized to remove their explicitly Buddhist content and are delivered by non-Buddhist caregivers. These difficulties stated up front, I will nevertheless attempt to paint a picture of the potential and reported outcomes of spiritual care based on my personal research – interviews with thirteen practicing Buddhist chaplains. While we may rarely receive closure in encounters with individual careseekers, this research does give me hope that, overall, we are of benefit to those who need us. This sense of long-term, collective positive efficacy is important for Buddhist chaplains to cultivate as a strategy for dealing with the ambiguity of our work.

The Dharma of Spiritual Care

What can the Dharma tell us about Buddhist spiritual care? As a Buddhist chaplain, this question is deeply embedded in my particular social and religious location. By Buddhist spiritual care, I do not necessarily mean care for Buddhists, though an important topic, but rather care by Buddhists working in both Buddhist and inter-religious settings. What makes spiritual care 'Buddhist,' rather than Christian or Jewish or secular, aside from the fact that a Buddhist is providing it? This is a question that Buddhists have only recently begun to explore. Some theories and practices for spiritual care can be adopted largely intact from Christian and Jewish sources and secular psychology, though we may value them for different reasons and integrate them with a fundamentally Dharmic view of the world. Other existing theories and practices are of little use to Buddhist caregivers, who must instead develop their own praxis based on our understanding of the Dharma.

Practices of spiritual care easily adopted by Buddhist caregivers include many of the most basic aspects of spiritual care, including listening and responding, empathy and compassion, prayer and ritual, presence, and cultural competency. A survey of the limited literature on Buddhist spiritual care cannot yet fully describe how differences in theoretical understanding have led to differences in practices and outcomes. My preliminary hypothesis is that, in practice, Buddhists, Christians, and Jews are very similar in many aspects of spiritual care, with distinctions in theoretical understanding, practical approaches, areas of focus in the care encounter, and outcomes for careseekers. In other words, we are similar in practice, but distinct in praxis. More research is needed in this area to see if this hypothesis bears out. This chapter, however, is not comparative. Rather, this chapter outlines some of the Dharmic roots of spiritual care. Comparison may be a natural next step in this process but will not be covered in this book.

Sources of Spiritual Care in the Dharma

This section provides only a few examples of spiritual care within the sacred literature of Buddhism. It is broken into two parts. The first part summarizes some sources for spiritual care in the Pāli Canon based on my own surveys and the work of Dr. Pamela Ayo Yetunde. These are important sources for Theravada Buddhists and useful for all Buddhists. The second part summarizes my own reading of the *Bodhicaryāvatāra* or *Way of the Bodhisattva* by Śāntideva from the eighth century CE for its relevance to Buddhist chaplaincy. This is a primary text for both Mahayana and Vajrayana Buddhists. In part, this section serves as a prompt for future chaplains and scholars to explore more of the Buddhist sacred literature for its wisdom on spiritual care. There are two other examples of this kind of constructive exegetical work: in Chapter 3 on the Three Prajñās and Chapter 4 in relation to the kalyāṇamitra model for Buddhist chaplains.

First, let us consider some of the earliest Buddhist literature, the Pāli Canon and, in particular, the *Sutta Pitaka*, or basket of the sayings of the Buddha. The *Mahagopalaka Sutta* (MN33) or *The Greater Discourse on the Cowherd* uses a pastoral analogy to discuss eleven factors that enable a cowherd to keep a herd that will likewise enable a Buddhist to grow, increase, and reach fulfilment in the Dharma. A Buddhist (literally *bhikkhu* or monk)[3] must have knowledge of form as constructed of disparate elements, be skilled in characteristics such as wisdom, remove defilements such as lust and cruelty, must not grasp after sensual objects and restrain desires, teach the Dharma to others, keep company with others for learning and discipline, study and gain inspiration from the Dharma, understand and follow the Noble Eightfold Path, understand and practice the four foundations of mindfulness, accept generosity from others but only for as much as one needs and no more, and revere the elders and leader of the sangha. This sutta describes the relationship between the Dharma teacher (or monastic) and their community. Yetunde describes it as "a powerful message about the pastoral aspect of teaching the dharma – it takes insight, skill, reverence, authenticity and understanding the true nature of being human" (Yetunde, 2011, p. 8-9). Though Buddhist chaplains are not necessarily 'teachers' to those we care for, many of the lessons of this sutta remain applicable. The sutta mentions virtues and characteristics a Buddhist should cultivate, including wisdom and loving-kindness, and appropriate behaviors, such as contemplative practices, studying, and showing respect.

The *Karaniya Metta Sutta* (KN9) or *The Buddha's Words on Loving-Kindness* is a pivotal text

---

3 Every Pāli sutta begins with noting whom the Buddha is addressing, and usually includes a location, some notes about occasion, and sometimes the specific question being answered. The term used in the address of this sutta is "bhikkhu" or "monk" as this lecture was delivered to a group of the Buddha's monastic followers at Savatthi. Some sermons apply to both monastics and laypeople, men and women, even when the audience being addressed consisted only of bhikkhus, while other sermons may only be suitable for monastics. When able, I note which instructions apply only to a particular audience and are not generalizable.

in many south and southeast Asian Buddhist traditions. Not only does it provide guidance on the cultivation of virtue, it is also an important ritual text, composed in verse and often chanted to bring good fortune and instruct Buddhists how to behave towards one another in difficult circumstances. It prescribes characteristics and behaviors for "one skilled in the good," which includes peacefulness, morality (being 'upright'), humility, contentment, judiciousness, and courteousness. These qualities and behaviors appear repeatedly throughout Buddhist teachings and characterize one of the roles of the kalyāṇamitra as moral exemplar. The sutta goes on to describe Right Intention, or the wish we should have for all beings: "May all beings be happy and secure; may they be inwardly happy!" This intention must be equanimous, in that it applies to "Whatever living beings there are...without omission" (*Suttanipata* 1.8.145). The sutta focuses on one of the four "Divine Abodes" or *Brahmavihara*: *mettā* or loving-kindness. However, it hints at the other three: *uppekkhā* (equanimity), *karuna* (compassion), and *muditā* (sympathetic joy). It is worth noting that the *Brahmavihara* must be cultivated collectively for proper balance. *Karuna*, for example, focuses on suffering and without the counterbalance of *muditā*, taking joy in the joy of others, we rapidly find ourselves exhausted. Likewise, *mettā* must be balanced with *uppekkhā*, lest we find ourselves displaying loving-kindness only to our favorites. The four *Brahmavihara* act as the four legs of a stool, providing strength and support equally.

While the practitioner must themselves be good, they may not hold to 'fixed views' that distinguish between 'good' and 'bad' beings in their wish for happiness (they are also included in this wish regardless of their opinions about themselves). In a praxis scenario, this means that Chaplain A would wish for the happiness of Alex (the abusive boyfriend) as well as for Alice. Practitioners extend their wish that others should likewise be skilled in the good, that "no one should wish for suffering for another."

Finally, the sutta circles back around to the virtues of the practitioner, advising them to "cherish" living beings and "radiate kindness" throughout the world, to free themselves from ill-will and hatred, and maintain a state of mindfulness in every action. Yetunde summarizes this teaching:

> The *Mettā Sutta* is clear that loving-kindness is to be bestowed on every being by wishing them well, but the sutta does not stop there. There must be an intense conviction to work toward cultivating loving-kindness. If possible, it should be like the bond and attachment between mother and child. Loving-kindness should be natural, fierce and pervade the universe at all times. It should not be abandoned for a lesser state of being, ever. That is the aspiration. The pastoral care giver in this tradition should transmit and convey to the receiver a loving-kindness that is real. It is embodied. It does not discriminate. It is not limited to the interaction between the caregiver and receiver, but pervades the space in which they meet. (2011, p. 15-16, 22-25)

Here Yetunde describes what I sometimes call the 'circle of care.' Whoever enters our awareness during our work as a chaplain is within this circle of care. This does not necessarily mean we are a chaplain to everyone. Most importantly and as I have heard said many times by many people "You can't 'chaplain' family," though you can continue to cultivate loving-kindness for them. In the hospital, we often speak of the patient as our primary careseeker, yet chaplains also provide spiritual care to family members, as Chaplain B did in Vignette 2. Chaplains also care for friends, other visitors, and even the medical personnel and hospital staff. Chaplains care for the nurses, doctors, orderlies, and administrators jut as much, if not quite as frequently, as the admitted patients. Occasionally, chaplains need to clarify this with administrators, who often view us within the same context as other staff, such as nurses and therapists, all of whom are clearly (even legally) focused on a particular population (e.g., patients in a hospital, students in a school, etc.). Whereas for chaplains, our circle of care includes the entire community, students, families, faculty, staff, alumni, guests, or the random person who has an accident while bicycling across campus and needs someone to hold their hand in the ambulance on the way to the hospital. We are that person. This is an extension of our mission as a religious person. Any chaplain has an expansive circle of care, including Buddhist chaplains who cultivate loving-kindness for all beings without exception as a discipline. This approach distinguishes chaplains in relation to other types of caregivers, though naturally, causes and conditions will bring our focus to those most in need, such as the ill, injured, or distressed.

Several scriptures in the Pāli Canon deal directly with visiting the sick, including the *Girimānanda Sutta* (AN10.60), in which the Buddha encourages his disciple Ananda to visit the sick monk Girimānanda and deliver a teaching on the ten perceptions, which include impermanence, non-self, unattractiveness, danger, abandoning, dispassion, cessation, non-delight in the world, impermanence of all things, and mindfulness of breathing. In short, the ten perceptions remind those who suffer to relinquish their attachments, to accept the present situation rather than compounding it with psychological struggle and self-pity, to cultivate patience and a disciplined mind. In many areas of palliative care, these teachings of the Buddha have been adapted into best practices and mental therapies.[4] Yetunde develops this teaching into contemplations useful for patients in hospitals and those living with chronic illness and presents a ten-step meditation with instructions for how to use it for non-Buddhist careseekers. She carefully explains that "it is important to understand that the affliction to be cured is not physical disease, but mental and emotional dis-ease [sic]. Looking at affliction as mental suffering, let's apply the ten perceptions to one who is physically sick and is also suffering mental dis-ease, or non-contentment, to discover the efficacy of contentment" (Yetunde, 2011, p. 34-41). Thus, while the meditation can benefit those who are physically sick, it does so by primarily addressing the mental and emotional components of their suffering and thus easing the experience of illness. Reductions in mental and emotional stress may also have a general benefit for physical health (such as through the reduction in cortisol, or stress hormone levels, or lowering blood pressure and heartrate). This practice probably will not cure disease or heal injury, despite the sutta's claim that the teachings cured Girimānanda's unspecified affliction. The ability of Buddhist teachings and rituals to cure disease was (and in some places, still is) taken literally for much of Buddhist history. We are left to make of that what we will.

As we can see, the Pāli texts provide a wealth of wisdom for spiritual care. This summary is brief and there is room for much more work in this area. There are many more suttas I could have included, such as the *Gotami Sutta* (SN5.3) with the story of the nun Kisagotami, used by Joan Halifax in her chapter in *The Arts of Contemplative Care* (in Giles and Miller, 2012, p. 219-229), or the first sermon of the Buddha, the *Dhammacakkappavattana Sutta* (SN56.11), where he laid out what would later become the foundations of Buddhist doctrine, including the Four Noble Truths, the Eightfold Path, and

---

4 Resources on the application of Buddhist mindfulness techniques in various contexts including medicine: *Handbook of Mindfulness-Based Programmes: Mindfulness Interventions from Education to Health and Therapy* by Itai Ivtzan, Taylor & Francis Group, 2020; *Mind Cure: How Meditation Became Medicine* by Wakoh Shannon Hickey, Oxford Press, 2019; *Mindfulness-Based Intervention Research: Characteristics, Approaches, and Developments* by Christian U Krägeloh, Routledge, 2019; *Buddhist Thought and Applied Psychological Research: Transcending the Boundaries* by Dinesh Kumar Nauriyal, Routledge, 2010.

the Middle Way. Trudi Jinpu Hirsch references the Four Noble Truths in her chapter in *The Arts of Contemplative Care* (in Giles and Miller, 2012, p. 55-62). There are many other suttas relating to illness and caring for the sick. I encourage all current and future Buddhist chaplains to contribute to this endeavor by composing exegesis and personal reflections and publishing them, whether in journals, books, magazines or blogs. This is something we can all contribute to advance the field and pave the way for future generations of caregivers.

In addition to the Pāli texts, many Mahayana and Vajrayana Buddhists turn to the influential model of the bodhisattva for their inspiration. The *Bodhicaryāvatāra* or *Way of the Bodhisattva* is a foundational text on this topic. I conducted a comprehensive, verse-by-verse review and categorization of the *Bodhicaryāvatāra* for its wisdom on spiritual care, followed by a detailed exegesis of the twelve most common and relevant categories. Many verses applied to more than one category and overlapping meanings demonstrate the interrelatedness of concepts within the text. Approximately 28 percent of the verses referenced care for others in some way; their wisdom is summarized below (a more detailed review can be found in Sanford, 2017). The *Bodhicaryāvatāra* is not primarily concerned with providing detailed instruction for how one should behave in relation to others. Rather, it is interested in the internal formation of the aspiring bodhisattva towards wisdom and compassion and dedicates fully a third of the text to this topic. Nevertheless, it does provide guidance on how the aspirant should regard and treat others, particularly to ensure formation of skillful intentions, management of unwholesome mental states, and so that the aspirant avoids negative merit and accumulates only benefits to aid in her path.

The proper regard for others places their wellbeing on a par or even above that of oneself. To do this, Śāntideva thoroughly explores the negative emotions we tend to harbor towards our fellow human beings and systematically refutes their justification or utility. From these passages (among others), Buddhists today derive the sentiment of treating so-called 'enemies' as our greatest teachers.

> 6.107
> So, like a treasure found at home,
> That I have gained without fatigue,
> My enemies are helpers in my
>   Bodhisattva work
> And therefore they should be a joy
>   to me.

Advice on how best to regard others facilitates the formation of Right Intention and explores the psychology of the defilements or afflictive emotions, such as greed, hatred, and anger, particularly as they are directed outward.

Perhaps most interesting, however, is how regard for others is paired with the exhortation to regard the self as empty of inherent nature, or *anātman*. Indeed, one can (and must) come into the wisdom of the self as empty, as having no real 'I' to cling to, to be fully able to attend to the suffering of the world. Realization of the empty nature of one's own self enables one to regard others in a universally positive, nonjudgmental, and compassionate way.

> 8.120
> Those desiring speedily to be
> A refuge for themselves and others
> Should make the interchange of "I"
>   and "other,"
> And thus embrace a sacred mystery.

The chaplains I interviewed embraced this sacred mystery. Moreover, those whose praxis was infused with a sense of egolessness also reported better outcomes for both careseeker and caregiver. This is a hallmark of stage 4 or kalyāṇamitra caregiving.

Generally, the aspirant should selflessly aid beings wherever they are found. This is often expressed metaphorically (verses 3.18 to 3.22, for example), such as "Let me be a boat/lamp/wishing jewel…", rather than literally, but also includes general exhortations to care for the sick and elderly.

> 1.21
> If with kindly generosity
> One merely has the wish to soothe
> The aching heads of other beings,
> Such merit knows no bounds.

Caregiving is the fruition of Right Intention. The lengthy metaphorical descriptions of the aspiration to do or be the perfect thing or person needed in any given situation are an allegorical expression of skillful means or *upāya kuśala*. Caring actions also correspond with instructions on ethics and the proper regard for others, showing a deep link between inner dispositions and outer actions, working in both the positive and negative directions. This includes a long passage in the fifth chapter exhorting the aspiring bodhisattva not to act on negative impulses, but to remain "like a log" until they have passed.

> 5.48
> When the urge arises in your mind
> To feelings of desire or angry hate,
> Do not act! Be silent, do not speak!
> And like a log of wood be sure to stay.

The treatment of ethical behavior (separate from virtue cultivation) in the *Bodhicaryāvatāra* is brief and mainly concerns passages such as the one above detailing actions from which the aspiring bodhisattva should refrain and the power of vows. One should recall at this point that Śāntideva delivered the *Bodhicaryāvatāra* originally in oral address to an audience of monks, who adhere to a strict ethical and disciplinary code known as the *vinaya*. It was later that the text and its teaching became important to monastics and laypeople of all genders.

> 5.22
> If this is how I act and live,
> Then even in the midst of evil folk,
> Or even with fair women, all is well.
> My steady keeping of the vows will not decline.

There is much here to critique from the feminist perspective, but for now, I simply keep in mind the context in which the text was delivered and attempt a hermeneutic of generosity.

Ethical behavior, or *śila*, is related to soteriology, i.e., descriptions of the path to liberation found in the *Bodhicaryāvatāra*. Thus, one's mental state and the ethical nature of one's behavior connect to the outcomes one will experience in this life and the next.

> 5.47
> And when you feel the wish to move about,
> Or even to express yourself in speech,
> First examine what is in your mind.
> For steadfast ones should act correctly.

As Śāntideva describes at length the torment of mortals still afflicted by their untamed mind, he also describes at length the salvific power of the bodhisattva path and the buddhas who have come before. Those who follow this path to its fruition achieve "supreme joy," reverence from gods and humans, freedom from past negative actions or *karma*, and endless virtue.

> 1.17
> From bodhichitta in intention
> Great results arise for those still turning in the wheel of life;
> Yet merit does not rise from it in ceaseless streams
> As is the case with active bodhichitta.

The author vividly illustrates how unselfishness leads to ultimate bliss for one's 'self' (although by that point all concern with 'I' would be eliminated). In Sanskrit, the word *bodhisattva* means a "being intent on enlightenment" (Buswell and Lopez, 2013, p. 134). The bodhisattva is one who arouses *bodhicitta* or the 'awakened mind.' In both cases, the first part of the word, *bodhi*, comes from the same root as the word *buddha*, the 'awakened' one, so it is the same kind of awakening for both. *Citta* is commonly translated as 'mind,' but also connotes 'thought,' 'attention,' 'desire,' 'intention,' and 'aim,' leading some scholars to describe bodhicitta as the "will of enlightenment" (Brassard, 2000, p. 7).

It may be unclear why a bodhisattva, once enlightened and free from the chains of suffering, would care for the welfare of all beings. For this we must look to the story of the life of the Buddha and the stories of the lives of the great bodhisattvas, who, through countless rebirths, are motivated by *māhakaruṇā* or 'great compassion.' Any motivation aside from compassion simply will not work for the purposes of enlightenment. Only a purely altruistic motivation can abandon the 'I' delusion and realize all phenomena as empty – ultimate wisdom. Suffice to say from this brief review of the *Bodhicaryāvatāra*, we can discern the importance of wisdom and moral behavior (two of the three aspects of the Noble Eightfold Path) in our work as chaplains.

Modern Literature on Buddhist Chaplaincy and Spiritual Care

Literature on Buddhist chaplaincy is limited. The first book on this topic is an anthology, *The Arts of Contemplative Care*, compiled mostly by faculty, students, and alumni of Harvard Divinity School's (HDS) Buddhist Ministry Program and published in 2012. Cheryl Giles, who remain on the faculty at HDS, and Willa Miller, a Harvard University graduate who lectured there from 2013 to 2017, edited this book; they each contributed a chapter to it, as did Daniel Clarkson Fisher (also credited as 'Danny Fisher' in some earlier editions), author and editor of the two later books on Buddhist chaplaincy. Giles' and Miller's anthology begins with a bold statement, situating the profession of Buddhist chaplaincy firmly within 'contemplative care,' rather than the more traditional Christian 'pastoral care' or even the more inclusive 'spiritual care' (p. *xvii*). Contemplative care is defined and critiqued in Chapter 1.

The Arts of Contemplative Care is divided into six sections, each containing several striking essays by its thirty-four impressive authors. The first section outlines the roots of contemplative care, beginning with a definition of Buddhist chaplaincy proposed by Jennifer Block, director of the Zen Hospice Project in San Francisco and a faculty member in various chaplaincy training programs. Block begins with the classic rhetorical move of linking something seemingly new to the oldest traditional precedent: "The Buddha was a chaplain," she writes, because he focused on helping people through the processes of old age, sickness, and death and ultimately on liberating living beings from suffering. Buddhist chaplains today continue this legacy by "accompanying individuals as their awakening and freedom from suffering unfolds." Block succinctly explicates a theoretical underpinning based in non-self, non-clinging, and remaining open to interconnection and change that enable a Buddhist chaplain to perform the basic functions of the profession, including listening, accompanying suffering, and encouraging others to discover their own wisdom (Block in Giles and Miller, 2012, p. 3-7).

Next, there is a chapter by Daijaku Judith Kinst, a professor in the chaplaincy program at the Institute for Buddhist Studies, which explores how Buddhists develop skills for an "appropriate response" to the myriad specific sufferings they will face as chaplains serving multi-religious populations (in Giles and Miller, 2012, p. 9-16). Block plants the roots, and Kinst raises the branches of the tree that is Buddhist practice, academic study, and supervised training in interreligious contexts. Other authors build on these themes, adding flowers and leaves to this growing tree by sharing their own poignant stories of spiritual care, perspectives from their various specific Dharma traditions, concrete methods and tools, and insights into various chaplaincy contexts, which is how the remainder of the book is structured. Section two addresses hospital chaplaincy, section three is on prison work, section four explores both college and military chaplaincy, and section five covers end-of-life care. The book concludes by addressing spiritual care within the context of the sangha itself, with Buddhist chaplains caring for Buddhist communities, and the role of chaplain as Dharma teacher (these roles sometimes, but not always, overlap).

While the anthology presents a balanced representation of male and female authors, a cursory review of the names and biographies indicate that most authors are of non-Asian descent. Thus, the first book on the profession of Buddhist chaplaincy primarily represents the voices of western Buddhist converts. Race, representation, power, and privilege are focal points of recent discussions on American Buddhism. Articles in journals such as *The Eastern Buddhist*[5] and the *Journal of Global Buddhism*[6] have outlined many issues related to race and representation in American Buddhism. Essays by Funie Hsu in *Lion's Roar*[7] and *Buddhist Peace Fellowship*[8] and the late longtime blogger Aaron Lee at *Angry Asian Buddhist*[9] have brought the debate about the public 'face' of Buddhism further into the consciousness of American sanghas. This conversation has been the focus of gatherings such as the "Conference on Buddhism and Race in America" held at Harvard College on March 6, 2015,[10] and again on April 22-23, 2016,[11] at the Sakyadhita USA conference at University of the West in April 2017, whose theme was "Diversity in the Dharma: Buddhist Women Engage Race and Exclusionary Politics in America,"[12] and a dedicated session of the Buddhist Unit at the American Academy of Religion 2019 Annual Meeting focused on "Fostering Diversity in the Study of Asian Religions."[13] I hope future works will include greater Asian and Asian-American representation and cover the concerns of Asian-American communities and *sanghas*, whose needs are often distinct from their non-Asian counterparts.

My own experiences as a campus chaplain and my conversations with fellow chaplains working in other settings, especially hospitals,

---

5 See, for example, Galen Amstutz, "Kiyozawa in Concord: A Historian Looks again at Shin Buddhism in America," *The Eastern Buddhist* 41, no. 1 (2010): 101-150; Judith Snodgrass, "Japan's Contribution to Modern Global Buddhism: The World's Parliament of Religions Revisited," *The Eastern Buddhist* 43, no. 1-2 (2012): 81-102; Julia C. Huang, "Buddhism and Its Trust Networks between Taiwan, Malaysia, and the United States," *The Eastern Buddhist* 44, no. 2 (2013): 59-76.

6 See, for example, Wakoh Shannon Hickey, "Two Buddhisms, Three Buddhisms, and Racism," *Journal of Global Buddhism* 11, no. 1 (2010): 1-25; Scott Mitchell, "'Christianity is for Rubes; Buddhism is for Actors': U.S. Media Representations of Buddhism in the Wake of the Tiger Woods Scandal," *The Journal of Global Buddhism* 13 (2012): 61-79; Ann Gleig, "From Buddhist Hippies to Buddhist Geeks: The Emergence of Buddhist Postmodernism?" *The Journal of Global Buddhism* 15 (2014): 15-33.

7 Fannie Hsu, "We've Been Here All Along," *Lion's Roar*, May 17, 2017, https://www.lionsroar.com/weve-been-here-all-along/.

8 Fannie Hsu, "Lineage of Resistance: When Asian American Buddhists Confronted White Supremacy," *Buddhist Peace Fellowship*, May 8, 2017, http://www.buddhistpeacefellowship.org/lineage-of-resistance/.

9 Lee, *Angry Asian Buddhist* (blog), http://www.angryasianbuddhist.com/.

10 "Conference on Buddhism and Race in America," *Harvard College*, https://college.harvard.edu/college-events/conference-buddhism-and-race-america.

11 "About the HBC Buddhism & Race Conference," *Harvard Buddhist Community*, https://harvardbuddhistcommunity.wordpress.com/.

12 Charlotte Colins, "Report on the Sakyadhita USA One-Day Conference," *Sakyadhita USA*, http://sakyadhitausa.org/conference.html.

13 American Academy of Religion Annual Meeting Program Book 2019, San Diego, CA.

have led me to believe that Asian-American Buddhist careseekers, particularly first- or 1.5-generation immigrants, have different expectations and spiritual requests than their non-Asian Buddhist counterparts. Likewise, Asian-American Buddhist chaplains bring different worldviews to their work as spiritual caregivers. These issues have only begun to surface in the literature, as we shall see in the discussion of *A Thousand Hands*, below. I ensured that six of the thirteen Buddhist chaplains I interviewed during my research were Asian or Asian-American. While this is too few to provide any statistically meaningful significance to differences in the data, it does ensure that broader worldviews are represented in this work than in much of the earliest literature on Buddhist chaplaincy.

The second book on the topic of Buddhist chaplaincy, *Benefit Beings! The Buddhist Guide to Professional Chaplaincy* by Daniel Clarkson Fisher (a white, heterosexual, cisgender American man), was written as a doctoral dissertation at the same time as *The Arts of Contemplative Care* and self-published one year later, in 2013. It follows a similar pattern, first presenting a basic description of the profession, including a brief history of Buddhist chaplaincy, starting with the pioneering work of Rev. Madeline Koi Bastis, the first Buddhist chaplain to gain board certification through the Association of Professional Chaplains, and then offering five chapters describing the common settings for Buddhist chaplains, including healthcare, the military, prisons, law enforcement and emergency services, and higher education (Fisher, 2013). This review is more pragmatic and both less theoretical and personal than the essays in *The Arts of Contemplative Care*. Rather, *Benefit Beings!* covers the factors a chaplain must take into consideration should he or she wish to work in particular sectors, such as board certification standards or Department of Defense regulations. Fisher includes material from interviews with Buddhist chaplains working in these settings (Fisher, 2013, p. 41-42).

The third book on Buddhist chaplaincy is also an anthology: *A Thousand Hands: A Guidebook for Caring for Your Buddhist Community*, edited by Nathan Jishin Michon and Daniel Clarkson Fisher. It echoes similar Christian works, such as *The Church Leader's Counseling Resource Book* (Franklin and Fong, 2011) by providing fifty short chapters summarizing topics such as mental illness, sexuality, organizational management, and addiction. The book is divided into three parts. First, "Working with Ourselves" contains six chapters about presence, listening (by Willa Miller), communication, privilege, finances, and my own chapter on "Buddhist Practical Theology," which provides a method for approaching issues in daily life and relating them to the Dharma (Sanford in Michon and Fisher, 2016, p. 55-65). The second part, "Working with Others," is the largest, with twenty-nine chapters on diverse issues ranging from AIDS to trauma and numerous other sources of suffering. Part three, "Working with Communities," includes thirteen chapters covering topics from group dynamics and community outreach to larger societal issues, such as poverty and race. Each chapter is organized into short sections with breakout boxes and includes an annotated list of resources, such as scriptures, research and scholarship, and books for general audiences. Websites and contact information for organizations related to a given topic are also included.

Unlike *The Arts of Contemplative Care*, which includes no citations, footnotes or endnotes, and only a limited bibliography, most chapters in *A Thousand Hands* are heavily footnoted, guiding readers to more information at every stage. The authors are almost evenly male and female, and at least fifteen Asian and Asian-American Buddhists contributed chapters, including those representing Japanese, Chinese, Thai, and Tibetan traditions (many of the non-Asian authors are also trained in these and other Asian Buddhist traditions as well). I note these statistics – which are admittedly rough, as I cannot definitively verify the gender and ethnicity of all authors – because I believe that representation, inclusiveness, and diversity matter. *A Thousand Hands* also contains chapters explicitly dealing with the issues of power and privilege,[14] acculturation,[15] Asian-American identities,[16] race,[17] and both interfaith[18] and intrafaith considerations,[19] leading me to believe this issue is also alive for other Buddhist authors.

In addition to these books, there are a few chapters in multi-faith anthologies on spiritual care, including Mikel Monnet's chapter in *Injustice and the Care of Souls*, edited by Sheryl Kujawa-Holbrook and Karen Brown Montagno (2009, p. 125-131), and Daniel Clarkson Fisher's chapter in *Multifaith Views of Spiritual Care*, edited by Daniel Schipani (2013, p. 44-64). Both authors also contributed chapters to *The Arts of Contemplative Care*. Monnet is a Board-Certified Chaplain with a background in healthcare chaplaincy and working with veterans and at-risk youth and a member of the Zen Peacemaker Order. His chapter is written explicitly from the Zen Peacemaker viewpoint and connects the practice of interfaith chaplaincy with the path of Mahayana Buddhism. It is one of only three chapters contributed by non-Christians to *Injustice and the Care of Souls* and the only one of a non-Abrahamic religious tradition.

Fisher was the faculty chair of the Buddhist Chaplaincy program at University of the West from 2008 to 2013. His chapter in Schipani's book explores Buddhist spiritual care using the 'three yanas,' a typology that reflects Fisher's own education at Naropa University in Colorado. Fisher points to the internal diversity of Buddhist traditions and then explicates his own approach to care based in mindfulness, the bodhisattva path, bodhichitta, and the *pāramitās*, particularly *prajñāpāramitā*, or the perfection of wisdom (Fisher in Schipani, 2013, p. 44-64). Fisher's chapter is one of six contributed by non-Christian authors and one of four from non-Abrahamic traditions in Schipani's book.

A recent (2019) festschrift in honor of Dr. Kathleen Greider (edited by Jill Snodgrass) from the Claremont School of Theology called *Navigating Religious Difference in Spiritual Care and Counseling* included chapters from Victor Gabriel, faculty (and Tibetan priest) at the University of the West Buddhist Chaplaincy program, Pamela Ayo Yetunde, a black womanist Buddhist on the faculty of United Theological Seminary of the Twin Cities, in Minnesota, and myself. This work also includes chapters from Christian, Jewish, Muslim, Confucian and indigenous religious perspectives, and covers a range of cultural perspectives from the Americas to Africa to Asia and other social locations, including LGBTQ+ considerations (Snodgrass, 2019). Other chapters on Buddhist spiritual care in multi-religious anthologies tend to focus on the needs of Buddhist patients, rather than on the skills and formation of Buddhist chaplains, but new works are published every year.

I note the religious origins of other chapters in these three books, which explicitly seek out

---

14 Mushim Ikeda, "Understanding Our Own Power & Privilege," in *A Thousand Hands: A Guidebook for Caring for Your Buddhist Community*, ed. Nathan Jishin Michon and Daniel Clarkson Fisher (Richmond Hill, ON: Sumeru Press, 2016), 43-48.

15 Hiroshi Sasaki and Kin Cheung (George) Lee, "Acculturation," in *A Thousand Hands: A Guidebook for Caring for Your Buddhist Community*, ed. Nathan Jishin Michon and Daniel Clarkson Fisher (Richmond Hill, ON: Sumeru Press, 2016), 271-276.

16 Chenxing Han, "Young Adult Asian American Identities," in *A Thousand Hands: A Guidebook for Caring for Your Buddhist Community*, ed. Nathan Jishin Michon and Daniel Clarkson Fisher (Richmond Hill, ON: Sumeru Press, 2016), 277-287.

17 Katie Loncke, "Race," in *A Thousand Hands: A Guidebook for Caring for Your Buddhist Community*, ed. Nathan Jishin Michon and Daniel Clarkson Fisher (Richmond Hill, ON: Sumeru Press, 2016), 335-340.

18 Nathan Jishin Michon, "Interfaith Considerations," in *A Thousand Hands: A Guidebook for Caring for Your Buddhist Community*, ed. Nathan Jishin Michon and Daniel Clarkson Fisher (Richmond Hill, ON: Sumeru Press, 2016), 359-362.

19 Bill Aitken, "Intrafaith Considerations," in *A Thousand Hands: A Guidebook for Caring for Your Buddhist Community*, ed. Nathan Jishin Michon and Daniel Clarkson Fisher (Richmond Hill, ON: Sumeru Press, 2016), 363-364.

diversity in their authorship, to demonstrate the pervasive Christian dominance in the field of spiritual care. These first two chapters (Monnet's and Fisher's) are noteworthy both as some of the first published literature on Buddhist chaplaincy and in their clear intention that their primary audience is other professional chaplains; however, the viewpoints they represent are, perhaps unavoidably, personal and limited to only two particular lineages of Buddhism. The chapters in *Navigating Religious Difference* are more constructive, by comparison. Gabriel's chapter presents a teaching on spiritual care from a classic Tibetan scripture on conventional and ultimate truth, much in the way the section above does (Gabriel in Snodgrass, 2019, p. 87-98).

Yetunde's chapter presents a case study of her work as a Black Buddhist woman pastoral counselor with a homicidal white male client and demonstrates the power of interreligious care as she draws on the Biblical story of Jesus's encounter with a woman from Canaan in transforming her own aggression towards this hostile careseeker. Yetunde also describes employing the Four Foundations of Mindfulness and criteria for Right Speech in her chapter (Yetunde in Snodgrass, 2019, p. 235-250). My own chapter, titled "Secret Atheist" focuses on the experiences of Buddhist chaplains within a predominantly theist society and profession and discusses various inner and outer tensions from my own perspective and that of the Buddhist chaplains I interviewed in 2017 (Sanford in Snodgrass, 2019, p. 191-218).

Three further bodies of literature deserve a mention at this stage: the cornucopia of recent books by and for Buddhists on practical topics intended for general audiences, academic books within the intersection of Buddhist and western psychology and philosophy, and works on Buddhist ethics. The first, though not intended to provide guidance specifically for Buddhist chaplains or professional spiritual caregivers, includes Buddhist books on topics ranging from addiction recovery to intimate relationships to death and dying; these can be of great service to the Buddhist chaplain. While writing for general audiences, Buddhist chaplains are contributing to this field, including Joan Halifax, founder and longtime teacher of the Upaya Zen Center chaplaincy training program, and Koshin Paley Ellison, co-founder and teacher at the New York Zen Center for Contemplative Care, which offers the only distinctly Buddhist CPE program. Both Halifax and Ellison focus on care for the dying and bereaved and both are white American teachers in Zen traditions. Both offer a great deal of practical wisdom. Halifax and Ellison are but two examples of this practical genre, which grows daily.

Likewise, the second and third bodies of literature useful for Buddhist chaplains require careful reflection to draw out their full implications for spiritual care. The University of Buffalo (UB) has compiled a helpful list of resources in relation to Buddhist ethics, clinical psychology and psychotherapy, philosophical psychology and philosophy of mind, and the science of mind. Some helpful resources include:

Ethical formation
- *The Six Perfections: Buddhism and the Cultivation of Character* by Dale Wright, Oxford, 2012
- *Know Your Mind: The Psychological Dimension of Ethics in Buddhism* by Bhikshu Sangharakshita, Windhorse, 1998

Ethics in health care
- *Into the Jaws of Yama, Lord of Death: Buddhism, Bioethics, and Death* by Karma Lekshe Tsomo, SUNY Press, 2006
- *Buddhism and Bioethics* by Damien Keown, Palgrave, 2001

Mental health and study of the mind
- *Mindfulness and Mental Health: Therapy, Theory and Science* by Chris Mace, Routledge, 2008
- *The Feeling Buddha: a Buddhist Psychology of Character, Adversity and Passion* by David Brazier, Palgrave, 2005

These and many other resources can be found in UB's research guide on Buddhism, which is so helpful, I highly recommend it for Buddhist chaplains in any stage of training or practice. It provides overviews of Buddhist history, culture, literature, and practice, broken down by topic and tradition, including a section on western Buddhism.

Relationships with Teachers and Sanghas

While scriptures and books teach us a great deal about spiritual care, it will all remain abstract unless we see it practiced and put it into practice ourselves. Spiritual care is fundamentally relational, so our spiritual formation as a chaplain relies on our relationships with others, primarily those within our religious community and our training programs. Sometimes, these may be one and the same, as several Buddhist chaplaincy training programs are based within a particular lineage and draw most of their teachers and students from that tradition. This is not always the case, as many degree programs and most CPE units are now ecumenical or inter-religious. No matter where you find yourself, the importance of your teacher and sangha cannot be overstated.

Nevertheless, I feel I am an odd candidate to write this section, as I myself have never had a traditional teacher-student relationship in the Buddhist sense, nor been a regular member of any sangha. Rather, I have had many teachers and moved between many sanghas throughout my practice. This is the result of numerous causes (my own particular issues) and conditions (my geographic locations), and though it infuses what I write with no little irony, I have been able to observe the effects of a strong student-teacher relationship and a stable sangha on the spiritual formation of my peers and colleagues from various angles. I have also benefited tremendously with my relationships with teachers, peers, and spiritual friends along my journey, even if my refuge in the Buddha, Dharma, and Sangha has not been precisely ideal (whose is, really?).

The *Dhammapada* (v. 188-192) reminds us that the Buddha, Dharma, and Sangha are the highest and most secure refuge from the suffering of cyclic existence. None other can compare (Thanissaro, "Refuge...," 2013). These three are always presented together and sometimes referred to as the Three Jewels or Triple Gem. Thus, a section on the 'Dharma' of spiritual care cannot neglect the Buddha of spiritual care, our teachers, or the Sangha of spiritual care, our community of spiritual friends. Daijaku Judith Kinst refers to these relationships as "The Ground of Practice," saying that "a vital relationship with a Buddhist teacher" undergirds and sustains chaplaincy training. Moreover, she warns, the academic setting is no replacement for the kind of deep personal relationships sustained by refuge in a particular Buddhist teacher and community (Kinst in Giles and Miller, 2012, p. 15-16). So what, precisely, do we mean when we advise chaplains in training to take and sustain refuge in the Buddha, Dharma, and Sangha, through a particular Buddhist teacher and community?

My introduction to Buddhism came through the books of Thich Nhat Hanh, particularly *The Heart of the Buddha's Teaching*, in which he describes refuge as "a fundamental practice in Buddhism," and goes on to present a distinctly modern interpretation of 'Buddha' as "the soil of our understanding." In other words, the Buddha is the innate capacity for wakefulness in each of us. Thich Nhat Hanh composes verses of refuge including "taking refuge in the Buddha in myself...the Dharma in myself...the Sangha in myself," (Hanh, 2015, p. 163). No wonder this book appealed to a lone Midwestern 22-year-old. While Thich Nhat Hanh presented a radically individualized understanding of refuge that did not include the need for a deep student-teacher relationship, he also states unequivocally "we need a Sangha," (Hanh, 2015, p. 164). His community, Plum Village, and the various Order of

Interbeing chapters planted worldwide serve this purpose for many Buddhists. (I briefly sat with two OI groups during my time in Southern California, one led by Larry Ward and his wife, Peggy Rowe, and the other organized by a group of students at University of the West.) Aside from Thich Nhat Hanh himself, the presence of charismatic teachers in the Plum Village lineage appears deemphasized. (This is an outsider view. The actual situation may be somewhat different for those more involved in the Plum Village lineage and the Order of Interbeing.) Thich Nhat Hanh's presentation of the Three Jewels demonstrates what David McMahan refers to as 'democratization' typical of Buddhist Modernism which "discourage[s] the concentration of power and… shift[s] to what [Norman] Fischer calls a 'student centered' rather than 'teacher centered' organization" (McMahan, 2008, p. 242-243). The teacher is not absent in such sanghas, but more traditional hierarchical power structures are diminished.

In his instructions to the layman Sigalaka, the Buddha outlines proper behavior for six traditional relationships: parents and children,; students and teachers; spouses; friends; 'masters' and 'servants;' and between laypeople and religious people such as "ascetics and brahmins." Students should engage in five behaviors towards their teachers: "by rising to greet them; by waiting on them; by being attentive; by serving them; by mastering the skills they teach." Likewise, teachers should engage in five behaviors towards their students: "give thorough instruction; make sure they have grasped what they should have duly grasped, give them a thorough grounding in all skills; recommend them to their friends and colleagues; and provide them with security in all directions" (Bodhi, 2016, p. 172-173). These behaviors are repeated today within the context of Buddhist sanghas and student-teacher relationships. However, most students no longer live together with or in the households of their teachers, as was common in premodern India, and therefore teachers do not provide 'security' in that sense. In the context of western higher education, only some of these behaviors are appropriate and some, such as students 'serving' or 'waiting on' teachers (in this context, this would include doing menial tasks within a teacher's household, including cooking and serving meals), decidedly inappropriate. Nevertheless, it gives us a sense of mutual respect, reciprocal responsibility, and personal intimacy between students and teachers that is fostered within Buddhist sanghas but often absent from formal education, where teachers may not be able to learn all their students' names even if they want to.

If you are new to Buddhism or just starting on your journey to become a chaplain and have not yet affiliated with a particular sangha or teacher, I advise you strongly to seek one. I cannot advise you to seek one particular tradition over another; I have enjoyed my time with diverse sanghas. Through, rhetorically, most lineages will have some claim to superiority, I find that they all have both good and not so good to offer. For example, while the directness of the Pāli Canon is very appealing, Theravada lineages do not ordain or have clear leadership roles for women. (This is changing, with major controversy.) While I appreciate the aesthetics of the Zen tradition, the rigors of form exhaust me. None of us will ever find a "perfect" sangha where we are totally at ease – nor should we! Discomfort is an essential factor in spiritual growth. However, don't be afraid to try different communities and interview different teachers until you find one that is right for you – one where you will be just uncomfortable enough to grow, supported in a way that your discomfort does not become overwhelming and unmanageable, and yet also comfortable and welcome in bringing all of who you are to your relationships within that community.

Teachers should likewise present an appropriate level of challenge, while maintaining clear and transparent ethical boundaries. Teachers should respect your boundaries,

while also asking clarifying questions to help you and other members of the community understand them. I do not believe there is a Dharma teacher alive who is appropriate to every student. That would take an enlightened being, and some teachers will make such claims, but I am a naturally skeptical person. If you should find such a person, stay skeptical for a long time (the Buddha never seemed to mind tough questions), and if they prove to be enlightened, stick with them and don't let go! I advise you to consult these works on your own search for a teacher.
- Pema Chödron on the traditional role of teachers (Chödron, 2007)
- Mark Power on how to consult teachers, including on spiritual care matters (Power in Giles and Miller, 2012, p. 63-72)
- Mikel Monnet on chaplain's responsibilities to their teachers (Monnet in Kujawa-Holbrook and Montagno, 2009, p. 125-131)
- Willa Miller on the difference between teachers and chaplains (Giles and Miller, 2012, p. 25-30)
- Katy Butler on clergy misconduct and abuse within Buddhism (Butler, 1990)

Integrating through Reflection

Dharma and experience have a reciprocal relationship. We study the Dharma and apply those insights to experience. We also learn from our experience and bring those insights to our study of the Dharma. This process of integration results in 'wisdom' (prajñā). Wisdom, in the Buddhist sense, is more than just knowledge or good judgement. Wisdom cannot be gained by reading it in a book or hearing a Dharma talk; it comes through direct experience of spiritual truths. Praxis is action grounded in wisdom.

As mentioned in Chapter 1, pastoral theology is the theoretical counterpart of the practice of spiritual care and counseling. 'Theological' reflection is an important practice in the development of this discipline. The qualifications for professional chaplaincy state that chaplains must be able to "Facilitate theological reflection in the practice of pastoral care" (ACPE Standards). This can be understood in two ways. First, it suggests that chaplains help careseekers perform their own 'theological' reflection. In other words, through skilled conversation and compassionate questioning, they help careseekers: reveal their own understandings of religion, spirituality, God, the universe, or other existential questions; seek out inner strength and direction; and find social supports (both spiritual and mundane) to aid them in their time of need. Chaplains help careseekers make spiritual sense of their past, present and future. Second, it suggests that chaplains perform their own 'theological' reflection, making sense of their lives and work as chaplains. If we are to aid others in making sense of their lives and situations, then we ourselves must be adept at making meaning from our own lives. This section is primarily about this second type of reflection, which begins during a chaplain's earliest education (if not before).

Buddhist chaplains are exposed to reflection as a practice in several ways. They write reflections in graduate school and, more directly, in CPE, where such reflection is an expected part of the verbatim exercise. In addition, they practice such reflections during their training as Dharma teachers and clergy, though it is not called 'theological' reflection in that context. Prior to my work, no scholarly publication has seriously interrogated whether 'theological' reflection is even an appropriate requirement or practice for a Buddhist chaplain. Nevertheless, Buddhist chaplains do engage in reflection, as the essays in *The Arts of Contemplative Care* ably demonstrate, when viewed through the lens of various existing (i.e., Christian) 'theological' reflection methods (Sanford, 2017). Buddhist chaplains report a range of responses and views in relation to these practices, but all reported engaging in reflection to at least some extent, and many reported facilitating reflection for careseekers. I will now attempt to define theological reflection and explore some of its methods. This will be a necessarily Christian exploration, followed by comparisons to Buddhist methods.

James and Evelyn Whitehead's succinct definition states, "Theological reflection in ministry is the process of bringing to bear in the practical decisions of ministry the resources of Christian faith" (Whitehead and Whitehead, 1995, p. *ix*). If we broaden this definition to include the resources of Buddhist traditions, it could quite easily apply to Buddhist chaplains. The Whiteheads' book, *Methods in Ministry*, lays out a three-part model and a three-part method for doing just that. The Whiteheads' model draws on the "religious information" found in religious tradition, personal experience and the "resources of culture," to address practical decisions and problems. Their method involves, first, "attending" to what is occurring and gathering information from each of the three aspects of the model. Much of this information is hidden or subconscious, absorbed uncritically from religious teachings and the dominant culture to color how we interpret our personal experiences. These unconscious assumptions must be brought forward into explicit consciousness to inform the second part of the method. Next, we clarify our insight through dialogue, a stage the Whiteheads call "assertion." The final part of their method is a "pastoral response" in the form of individual or community action. Together, these three stages – attending, assertion, and action – make up the Whiteheads' three-part model (Whitehead and Whitehead, 1995). The Whiteheads revised their method later to rename the three parts "attending, asserting, and pastoral response," but the renaming made little impact on the practical activity involved (Foley, 2015).

We can see each of these stages in action within CPE training, in which chaplain interns are asked to attend to what is happening in a caregiving encounter, assert their understanding of it through a written assignment that is then shared and reflected on within their peer group, and then used to formulate future actions, either in relation to that particular careseeker or future cases. The Whiteheads posit a continuum of theological reflection from the extremely concrete and practical on one end, "in which reflection enjoys almost no role," to a highly academic activity "so abstract that its religious import is all but indiscernible." The Whiteheads situate the kind of reflection conducted in CPE in the former extreme and the work of academics such as Paul Tillich and David Tracy in the latter. (Whitehead and Whitehead, 1995, p. *xi*). The Whiteheads' three-part method is similar to the Three Prajñās of wisdom derived from listening, contemplating, and practicing.

Both Christian and Buddhist chaplains regularly engage in reflection, ranging from the pragmatic to the abstract. Thomas Kilts describes the more abstract extreme as a negative aspect of *vajra*, one of the five Buddha families, calling it "over-reliance on 'heady' or academic theology for reflection" that "leaves us capable of debate, but often lacking in an ability to reflect emotionally about what is happening in the ministry encounter" (Kilts, 2008, p. 279). Harrison Blum's Mindfulness Allies Project provides an example of the concrete extreme, a project designed to test interventions for individuals of low socioeconomic status and people of color to be able to access mindfulness training with allies. It focuses on testing extremely pragmatic interventions, including childcare and dinner, as well as teaching allies how to work with the topic of race and status when raised in discussion by participants. His reflection on this project focuses almost entirely on what worked and what did not, rather than on any theoretical questions (Harrison, 2014, p. 1-18).

These are only two examples of how the abstract and pragmatic both appear in Buddhist reflection. While ultimately practical, directed towards decision-making and action, the Whiteheads' approach is just one among a panoply of Christian methods. Other Christian methods have other types of focus, some directed more towards developing insight or strengthening community bonds. According to J.R. Burck and R.J. Hunter, for Christians, "The exercise of theological reflection is thus one 'in which pastoral experience serves as a context for critical development of basic theological understanding'" (Kilts, 2008, p. 279). In other words, doing and knowing are inextricably intertwined. Reflection enables us to identify and enact what is 'good' in light of our religious traditions.

Another major contribution to the literature on theological reflection is a thorough typology of Christian methods compiled by Elaine Graham, Heather Walton, and Frances Ward. Their book, *Theological Reflection: Methods* (1st Edition, 2010), summarizes seven common methods of theological reflection used by Christians and provides examples of each from early Christian history, through their development in the Modern period, and into their forms today. The authors define theological reflection within the field of pastoral or practical theology as an "inductive" discipline, a "*process* rather than a *product*" (p. 2-6). They provide a typology for theological reflection, devoting one chapter of their book to each of the following seven methods: living human document; constructive narrative theology; canonical narrative theology; corporate theological reflection; correlation; praxis; and local or vernacular theologies. Methods analogous to these, including praxis, correlation, and vernacular theologies, are employed by the Buddhist authors of *The Arts of Contemplative Care*. Applying Graham, Walton, and Ward's seven-part typology to the essays in this book reveals Buddhist chaplains reflecting on their work in ways similar to, but also distinct from, Christians.

The section below analyzes types of reflection within *The Arts of Contemplative Care* using this typology. Unfortunately, I do not have space here to cover all seven methods or analyze each chapter in *The Arts of Contemplative Care*, though this may be a worthy exercise. It is simply not the primary goal of this work to categorize Buddhist reflection according to Christian norms. This analysis is sufficient to demonstrate that both similarities and differences exist and chart their broad outlines. Naturally, some methods seem more suitable than others. For example, I find numerous uses of praxis-based reflection, but few examples of canonical narrative theology. This does not mean Buddhists have no interest in how their identity – both individual and collective – is shaped by their scriptures; quite the contrary. In fact, many sects of the Mahayana form their entire identities around precisely which text they take as most authoritative amongst a broad canon: for example, the *Lotus Sutra* among the Tiantai schools and the *Diamond Sutra* among the Chan schools. Also, the Asian use of *Jataka Tales*, or stories of the Buddha's past lives as ethical and motivational allegories, is similar to canonical narrative theology. These have simply not been emphasized by the western-based, highly educated, culturally pluralistic teachers and chaplains who contributed to Giles and Miller's anthology, possibly due to its relative dearth of Asian and Asian-American authors.

Praxis may be the method of 'theological' reflection most suited to Buddhists, who often use the term 'practice' in the same way Christians refer to their 'faith.' Graham briefly describes praxis as "theology-in-action" and highlights its social justice orientation, "Ushering creation toward an ultimate vision of redemption" (Graham, Walton, and Ward, 2010, p. 14). A contemporary example of praxis is the pastoral cycle of liberation that theologian Juan-Luis Segundo developed from Paul Ricoeur's hermeneutics. The cycle involves experience, social analysis, theological reflection/hermeneutics, and pastoral planning and action, which generates a new immersive experience. The cycle rests on the assumption that each moment calls for reinterpretation of "the word of God" (Graham, Walton, and Ward, 2010, p. 188-189). Likewise, in Jewish theology, Myriam Klotz describes the process of wrestling with blessings "to find redemptive meaning and value in experience" and elucidates the practices of *teshuvah* (repentance), *tefilah* (prayer), and *tzedakah* (good deeds) as orthopraxis in the face of suffering (in Friedman, 2013, p. 4-22). These examples of praxis-based reflection have both similarities and differences to Buddhist praxis.

We find similar, but not identical, methods used by Cheryl Giles, Kristin Deleo, Willa Miller, and Steve Kanji Ruhl, among other authors, in *The Arts of Contemplative Care*. Giles, for example, provides instruction on orthopraxis when she describes the five-fold training of Machig Lapdonma. She cites American Buddhist nun Pema Chödrön, who teaches that compassion is a method for dealing with our own strong emotions and other people's suffering. Giles summarizes Phadampa Sangye's instructions to Machig Lapdronma (through Chödrön's commentary) for cultivating compassion, particularly to overcome racism and other forms of prejudice. This fivefold training involves:

1. REVEALING OUR HIDDEN FAULTS in order to notice when we perceive difference as negative, acknowledge our prejudices, work with uncomfortable feelings, and see how our story about ourselves is constantly changing.
2. APPROACHING WHAT WE FIND REPULSIVE to explore our privilege, how we contribute to systemic injustice, and learn how our prejudices prevent compassion.
3. HELPING THOSE WE THINK WE CANNOT HELP by overcoming our fears of rejection, reaching out with love, caring about others' happiness even when we cannot always make them happy, and giving compassion freely, without judgment. Giles points out that opportunities to help others only arise when we are present with them in their pain.
4. LETTING GO OR GIVING AWAY ANYTHING WE ARE ATTACHED TO, including biased feelings, concepts, and ideas; our own privilege; and our deep subconscious egoic fears of others.
5. GOING TO THE PLACES THAT SCARE US and feeling what we've avoided feeling for years by being willing to cultivate fearlessness to sit with uncertainty, discomfort, and fear (Giles in Giles and Miller, 2012, p. 46-52).

This teaching uses a method common in mind training, or *lojong* practices, reliance on the regular use of slogans during contemplative practice to reshape the mind and/or heart for work in the world. Through this practice, we strengthen our ability "to step into suffering with another [which] is perhaps our greatest act of kindness," according to Carlyle Coash (in Giles and Miller, 2012, p. 263). Giles quotes Pema Chödrön, saying "Through continual practice we find out how to cross over the boundary between stuckness and waking up." Giles applies this teaching to working with racism (in Giles and Miller, 2012, p. 51) within both the Buddhist community and American society in general, thus paralleling the social-justice focus of praxis.

Likewise, Willa Miller's presentation of Patrul Rinpoche's rules for listening assert that these methods of orthopraxis are cultivated over time in real human interactions and linked to meditation practice (in Giles and Millser, 2012, p. 284-290). Miller, an American Buddhist lama in the Tibetan traditions, draws on the teachings of Patrul Rinpoche (1808-1887) to describe three ways *not* to listen and three ways one *should* listen. First, do not listen like an upside-down pot into which nothing new can be placed. That is, listen attentively without being distracted by judgments, feelings, obsessions, other sounds, or physical sensations. Value the speaker's words, cultivate curiosity, and let go of one's own need to be heard. Second, do not listen like a pot with holes that only catches some things, but not others. Listen to remember and understand, imagine what that situation must have been like, and empathize with the speaker. Miller describes this as "an *energy* of receptivity paired with willingness to feel with" the other and "come alongside" them. Finally, do not listen like a pot containing poison that contaminates anything put into it. Miller asserts that good listening comes from having the right motivation to listen, which, according to Patrul Rinpoche, means not wanting to "glorify oneself and vilify others." Become a selfless and nondual listener, totally absorbed in listening beyond self-consciousness of subject and object. This does not mean we forget ourselves, as we listen both to the careseeker and to how we are receiving their words to monitor for our own poisons, but that we do so with equanimous awareness (Miller in Giles and Miller, 2012, p. 284-290).

Miller's description, based on this Nyingma master's teaching, shows striking resemblance to Howard Clinebell and Bridget Clare McKeever's description of active, empathic listening used to understand and overcome one's own blind spots and obsessions (Clinebell and McKeever, 2011, p. 70-74). It also follows Robert Kidd's instruction to stay attuned to the present (in Roberts, 2012, p. 93-94) and Barbara Breitman's concern that the caregiver should receive the careseeker's message accurately and take it into their heart (in Friedman, 2013, p. 98-101). Christian, Jewish, and Buddhist caregivers all agree on the importance of listening as a primary skill for chaplains. Miller's chapter aligns with Graham, Walton, and Ward's description of praxis inasmuch as she emphasizes the Patrul Rinpoche's teaching as one of "performative knowledge" – there is no true knowing apart from doing (Graham, Walton, and Ward, 2010, p. 175). It fully expresses the Buddhist understanding of prajñā as being akin to gnosis, an embodied wisdom that "cannot be perceived by the intellect," (Dalai Lama, 1992, p. 118-119) but only performed by the one who possesses it, in the manner of orthopraxis.

From these few examples, we can already see the shape of the praxis method emerging from Buddhist reflection, with its emphasis on action, assumption that insight is gained from direct experience in addition to scripture, descriptions of orthopraxis leading to liberation, and "solidarity with the suffering of the world" (Graham, Walton, and Ward, 2010, p. 14). It diverges from Christian methods inasmuch as it does not seek a final redemptive end for the world (in the Christian sense), nor does it rely on divine revelation or seek to enact God's will in the world.

Jensen, for her contribution to Giles and Miller's anthology, uses a method similar to Graham, Walton, and Ward's "theology by heart," which relies on Anton Boisen's "living human document" model. This model "speak[s] through the interiority of human experience" for "theological reflection and construction." Jensen documents various encounters with careseekers and family members to explore the theme of Right Speech, drawing more insights from her life than from Buddhist scripture and even managing to quote George Orwell in an example of the correlation method (drawing wisdom from multiple sources). Jensen explores Right Speech in relation to religious prayers and rituals when the caregiver does not hold the same beliefs as the careseeker. She equates speaking in contradiction of what one personally believes with 'lying.' However, it appears that Jensen is conflating her own personal belief with verifiable truth. Therefore, praying for someone to go to heaven is a 'lie' because she does not believe in heaven, not because she can prove heaven does not exist. Jensen concludes it is acceptable to lie – contradicting the Buddha's own teaching on the topic, which she references – when it benefits the careseeker and when one's heart "consents" (Jensen in Giles and Miller, 2012, p. 291-299). She neglects the Buddha's own practice of teaching according to the needs of the audience, including some instances where he taught about the self in seeming contradiction to the doctrine of nonself.[20] Jensen relies on herself as a living human document and interprets the lives and needs of her careseekers as living

---

20 For some examples of how the Buddha tailored his message to his audience, see, "Befriending the Suttas: Tips on Reading the Pāli Discourses," *Access to Insight (BCBS Edition)*, last modified November 30, 2013," http://www.accesstoinsight.org/befriending.html.

human documents, a skill that, as a Buddhist chaplain in a medical setting, she may very well have learned from a predominantly Christian CPE program. (Anton Boisen is known as the 'father of CPE.') Thus, we can also see overtones of the vernacular method (context-based reflection using a shared language) coming to influence the ways Buddhist reflection has developed in the U.S.

In contrast to Jensen, I conclude that Right Speech includes statements such as, "May you find peace in Christ," because it is an honest wish. I do not believe it is *likely* that the historical man called Jesus Christ was the son of God, but in that moment, I can hope for the careseeker's sake that he is God incarnate and capable of granting lasting peace. I can live in this as-if hope for a moment by practicing another Zen skill: not-knowing.[21] Other Zen writers from *The Arts of Contemplative Care*, including Mikel Monnet and Steve Kanji Ruhl, describe the function of "not-knowing" in their caregiving practice, but Jensen does not, though also a Zen practitioner. I do not *believe* in Christ, but I do not *know* for certain, either. I hold what I think I know lightly and remember all that I do not know and all that is beyond conventional knowing. In my own Buddhist worldview, certain knowledge is unattainable apart from total, complete enlightenment, which, among other things, is understood as the complete apprehension of reality and occasionally characterized by omniscience, depending on the tradition. My criteria for Right Speech in these situations are very simple: 1) it is possibly true; and 2) it reduces suffering or increases comfort and joy. In this sense, I also practice 'theology' of the heart, as described by Graham, Walton, and Ward, and treat my own life and experiences of prayer as a living human document. This is an area where Buddhists could do some deeper 'theological' digging, as the Buddhist chaplains I interviewed often grappled with the interfaith nature of prayer in healthcare settings.

I share this personal reflection to highlight another area of alignment between Buddhist and Christian 'theological' reflection: Buddhist not-knowing, or beginner's mind, and Christian *docta ignorantia*, or "knowing unknowing." Duane Bidwell describes the latter as a situation wherein spiritual caregivers "have knowledge of God and the spiritual journey but cannot guess how to create spiritual growth or healing or even know for certain what parishioners experience in a particular situation" (Bidwell, 2001, p. 127). As Clarke, Monnet and Ruhl note, it is not-knowing that enables Buddhist chaplains not merely to practice reflection and make sense from their own experiences, but, more critically, to maintain the basic openness necessary to facilitate theological reflection for careseekers as the chaplaincy standards for professional practice require. Bidwell brings this to bear in a Christian context, encouraging the 'not knowing' attitude as one that allows the Holy Spirit to serve as the true caregiver. His strategies do not rely on a theistic worldview or on a precise correspondence between the worldview of the caregiver and careseeker. They remain accessible to Buddhist caregivers because careseekers "are experts about their own lives," and through not-knowing, we enable an attitude of respectful curiosity that emphasizes the careseeker's own worldview, strengths, resources, and goals (Bidwell, 2001, p. 126-127).

Madeline Koi Bastis's various books, articles and chapters provide an interesting glimpse of many methods for reflection. Her first short article on "Thom's Garden" is a lovely example of "theology by heart" or Boisen's "living human document." Although it lacks an "intimate relation with God" (Graham, Walton, and Ward, 2010, p. 18) or any explicit mention of the Dharma, it clearly describes a close relationship between a careseeker and caregiver, and for a Buddhist reader, it points

---

21 For a brief description of "not-knowing," see Gil Fronsdale, "Not-Knowing," *Insight Meditation Center*, accessed February 10, 2004, http://www.insightmeditationcenter.org/books-articles/articles/not-knowing/.

directly to impermanence (Bastis in Dossey and VandeCreek, 1998), one of the three hallmarks of existence. Bastis's chapter on prayer is an example of reflection through correlation; Bastis correlated Buddhist devotional practices both with science and with theistic devotional practices, particularly Larry Dossey's definition of prayer as "communication with the Absolute" (Bastis in Dossey and VandeCreek, 1998, p. 87-92). While Buddhists and Christians may have very different ideas of the 'Absolute' and its soteriological significance, the practice of mental devotion is an effective coping mechanism employed by both traditions.

From this brief and very unsystematic review, we can see that reflection is an essential skill for Buddhist spiritual caregivers, who use methods similar to Christian and Jewish caregivers. One major difference lies in attribution. Whereas a theist may construct theology from human experience on the basis of God's immanence, a Buddhist may do likewise on the basis of the buddha-nature within all people. Whereas a Christian may see praxis as the conversation between secular culture and divine revelation, a Buddhist may see it as the dialogical relationship between culture and the universal Dharma. Due to these differences in theoretical understanding, Buddhist reflection will continue to develop and explicate its own unique methods. This book provides a structure – the Three Prajñās Framework for Buddhist Spiritual Care – within which to continue to develop and employ such methods. The Framework itself can even be viewed as a method for reflection, similar to the Whiteheads' model.

The Places of Spiritual Care

Military

The military has the longest documented history of chaplaincy in the United States, stretching back to colonial times, when then Colonel George Washington wrote to the then Governor of the colony of Virginia, requesting a chaplain to serve his First Virginia Regiment in 1756 to improve both the morale and morals of his troops (Abbot, 1984, p. 414-418). Chaplains now serve in every branch of the U.S. military and many other militaries worldwide. Buddhist chaplains, as of this writing, can be found in the U.S. Army and Navy, the latter also supplying chaplains to the Marines and Coast Guard. Buddhist chaplains also serve in the National Guard and Reserve, including U.S. Air Force Reserve (though there are none in the active duty Air Force, yet). Chaplains are also employed by the Veterans Administration, serving both VA hospitals and outpatient programs. Chaplains continue to care for both the morale and morals of military members and their families. Chaplains are military officers, but they are also non-combatants, per the Geneva Convention (Article 43), and shall not, if captured, be considered a 'prisoner of war' (while they may be detained, they must be allowed to continue their ministry to other prisoners of war and deal with prison authorities on their behalf, per Article 33). In fact, in the U.S. military, chaplains are actively prohibited from using firearms and are assigned an enlisted chaplain assistant who, in part, has the job of protecting the chaplain in combat zones. This status as non-combatant officers can often help Buddhist military chaplains reconcile Buddhist teachings (and vows) of nonviolence with military service.

The process of becoming a military chaplain is not simple and contains many stages. If one is interested in becoming a military chaplain, one should first reach out to a chaplain recruiter for the branch in which one is interested. Chaplain recruiters are distinct from other kinds of recruiters, so be aware that you will need to talk to this specialist. Each branch will also have a slightly different process, which the chaplain recruiter will be familiar with. Working with your chaplain recruiter, one must submit an application to the selection board including a medical exam (to be conducted at a military recruiting center) and an ecclesiastical endorsement from an endorsement body recognized by the Department of Defense. The only DOD approved endorser for Buddhist chaplains is currently the Buddhist Churches of America, a Jodo Shinshu organization headquartered in San Francisco, CA. Regardless of their Jodo Shinshu roots, the BCA has endorsed a number of Buddhist chaplains of various backgrounds including those of Thai, Japanese Shingon, Korean, and Chinese lineages. In order to provide this endorsement, the prospective chaplain's home tradition will need to work with the BCA to provide evidence of a steady, long-standing practice and appropriate training, education, and ongoing oversight. In addition to the endorsement letter, recruits must meet basic age and fitness requirement, possess a graduate degree in theological or religious studies equivalent to at least 72 credit-hours (3-years) of work, be a U.S. citizen, and able to obtain a security clearance through a rigorous background check. Some chaplains may be able to commission directly, especially if they already have a few years of ministry experience, but most enter via the chaplain candidate program during graduate school. As a chaplain candidate, they receive supplementary training as commissioned officers in the Reserve or National Guard. Chaplains also attend a chaplain basic officer course before being assigned to their first unit. The military does not generally require CPE, though it is often encouraged, if and when it can fit into a military chaplain's busy schedule. Some VA hospitals host CPE programs that may be a good fit for military-bound chaplains.

Before signing on the dotted line, it is also a good idea to talk to chaplains who are currently or have recently served. A handful of Buddhist chaplains have served in the U.S. Army, Army Reserve, and Army National Guard to date, including Captain Thomas Dyer, who became the Army's first active duty Buddhist chaplain in 2008 (after serving in National Guard since 2004), Captain Somya Malasari, a former Thai monk (who started a small trend among his Dharma brothers), Captain Christopher Mohr, and Captain Niphon Sukuan, also a former Thai monk. A number of other Buddhist chaplains have since served in the Army Reserves and National Guard, including several more former Thai monks. Two Buddhist chaplains have served in the U.S. Navy; Lieutenant Jeanette Shin joined in 2004 (also the first and still only active duty woman Buddhist chaplain in the U.S. military) and Lieutenant Aroon Seeda (another former Thai monk) is currently the only Buddhist chaplain serving the Navy branch, which also supplies chaplains to the Marines and Coast Guard. First Lieutenant Brett Campbell became the first and, thus far, only Buddhist chaplain serving in the Air Force branch (Reserve) in 2012. Buddhist chaplains in the military tend to generate press in both military news outlets and mainstream media, so a simple internet search should provide the names of Buddhist chaplains serving as you read this.

Each sector in which Buddhist chaplains serve will have particular areas of focus and common problems and stressors chaplains are called upon to handle. In the military, these include PTSD, moral injury, addiction, relationship stress, domestic abuse, and other family issues, including death notifications, grief, and bereavement of family members when a service member is injured, missing, or killed. The chaplain cares for the entire military unit to which they are assigned, as well as the military families attached to the servicemember in that unit. Over half of military servicemembers are married and just under half have children; single parentage is relatively rare, especially among active duty personnel (5.4%). Military chaplains also serve as advisors to the commanders 'above' and 'beside' them as well as seeing to the needs of the soldiers 'below' them in their units. As such, confidentiality and equanimity (i.e., fairness) are important values in a chaplain's work. Military chaplains also work with other support members, including military psychologists and health care staff, though chaplains tend to be more 'embedded' within their units. This includes accompanying units on deployments overseas, including in active combat zones. Buddhist chaplains serve the militaries of other nations, particularly Southeast Asian countries such as Myanmar, Thailand, and Vietnam, sometimes as civilian specialists and sometimes as uniformed members.

Buddhist resources helpful to military chaplains include:
- "Buddhist Pastoral Ministry in the Military" by Thomas Dyer in *The Arts of Contemplative Care*
- "Grief and Bereavement" by Tenzin Kacho Kiyosaki and "Suicide Intervention" by Duane Bidwell in *A Thousand Hands*
- "Family Systems" by Jesse Howard Lash Masterson, "Military Families" by Raymond M. McDonald, and "Domestic Abuse" by Ouyporn Khuankaew in *A Thousand Hands*
- "Trauma and PTSD" by Daniella Dahmen Wagner and "Addictions and Substance Abuse" by Tom Moritz in *A Thousand Hands*

Non-Buddhist resources helpful to military chaplains:
- *Miracles and Moments of Grace: Inspiring Stories from Military Chaplains* edited by Nancy B. Kennedy (2011)
- *Trauma and Recovery: The Aftermath of Violence – from Domestic Abuse to Political Terror* by J.L. Herman (2007)
- *The Spiritual Side of Traumatic Stress Normalization: Christian Spirituality and Social Neuroscience Consideration for Clinicians and Military Chaplains* by J. Michael Hakanson (2008)
- *Care for the Sorrowing Soul: Healing Moral Injuries from Military Service and Implications for the Rest of Us* by Duane H. Larson and Jeffrey L. Zust (2017)
- *Moral Injury Reconciliation: A Practitioner's Guide for Treating Moral Injury, PTSD, Grief, and Military Sexual Trauma through Spiritual Formation Strategies* by Lewis Jeff Lee (2018)

HOSPITALS, HOSPICE, AND HEALTH CARE

Many hospitals and hospices were founded by religious orders, so health care and spiritual care are deeply intertwined. Chaplains continue to be most numerous in the health care sector. Hospitals and hospice are the largest employers of chaplains, though they can also be found in nursing and elder care facilities, psychiatric centers, and various outpatient care settings such as oncology and dialysis clinics, home hospice and palliative care services, and addiction recovery organizations. The first Board Certified Buddhist Chaplain, Rev. Madeline Koi Bastis, worked in health care settings. Almost all CPE units and residencies are carried out in health care settings, usually hospitals, where chaplain interns add to the spiritual care staff. Trudi Jinpu Hirsh believes Buddhist chaplains are a "perfect match" for health care work, as it involves stepping directly into the suffering of old age, sickness and death with patients and families. Buddhism's emphasis on the impermanence and interconnectedness of all things supports both the chaplain and those they serve (Hirsh in Giles and Miller, 2012, p. 56).

Most chaplaincy students complete a unit of Clinical Pastoral Education (CPE) after their first or second year of training, usually as a full-time unit at an in-patient hospital setting under the direction of a supervisor and program accredited through the Association of Clinical Pastoral Education (ACPE). This is both the most common way to complete a CPE unit and most chaplains' introduction to spiritual care in any setting. Many congregational ministers are also required to complete a CPE unit as part of their journey into the pulpit. A full-time hospital CPE unit involves 40 hours of work per week, including some on-call weekends and evenings, over 10 weeks. Within those 40 hours, chaplain interns will spend three quarters of their time seeing patients and the remainder receiving further education and feedback on their work. One can apply to CPE without any formal chaplaincy training and even work in a hospital or hospice as a volunteer without CPE, but such situations depend very much on the background of the individual and the structure of the health care institution. Generally, one's first unit of CPE is unpaid and requires a fee paid to the hospital. Thereafter, one becomes eligible for paid residencies, which are generally 9-month full-time positions that include a stipend and provide three more units of CPE. Lists of CPE units and residencies can be found on the ACPE website (www.acpe.edu) or by contacting the spiritual care department of the hospital in question. Four units of CPE are required to qualify for board certification (along with other requirements) with the Association of Professional Chaplains (APC). Many hospitals require chaplains to be board certified or on a track to becoming board certified within a few years of being hired. Chaplains in health care work on a full-time, part-time, or *per diem* (per day) basis. Many also volunteer if they do not wish to work so many hours, such as local clergy only called as needed, or if their credentials do not quite meet employment standards (even when their skills may).

In the hospital, a chaplain can expect their day to include patient rounds, visiting rooms either based on referral from the medical staff or doing 'cold calls' to patients on an assigned unit. Families are frequently present with patients, or chaplains may be asked to visit with families in the waiting room, especially during emergency visits, surgeries, scans or intensive care, which may limit presence of family members with the patient. In most hospitals in the United States, chaplains will provide interfaith care; that is, they will visit patients of various religious, spiritual or secular identities. For Buddhist chaplains, this means that they tend to serve very few Buddhist patients and families; instead, they see predominantly Christian or unaffiliated careseekers. Some hospitals prefer to provide co-religionist care; that is, chaplains will be matched to the religious identity of the patients. For Buddhist chaplains, this means serving Buddhist patients and families as well as those who do not identify with the predominant theistic religions, such as the spiritual-but-not-religious, agnostic, atheist, secular humanist, or no-particular-religion careseekers. Even in hospitals where interfaith care is the norm, staff will typically try to match chaplains to patient and family religious identities whenever requested. Religious identity, if known, is often recorded in the patient's chart. It is also part of the chaplain's role to discern if a specific religious representative, such as a Catholic priest or Orthodox rabbi, is needed and facilitate a visit of that party, who may be another chaplain on staff or, more frequently, a member of the local clergy on a list of commonly called-upon volunteers.

Chaplains do many things during these visits under the heading of spiritual care. Patient and family visits commonly include presence and listening, conversation and counsel, and prayer or ritual. Chaplains are also occasionally asked to help diffuse or mediate conflicts between family members, the patient, and/or medical staff. In some hospitals, chaplains may be tasked with working with patients and families on advanced directives, organ donation, or dispensation of the body. Medical staff occasionally use chaplains to help elicit medically relevant information patients and families were otherwise reluctant to disclose or encourage patient compliance with medical directives. In these instances, chaplains carefully navigate the boundaries between doing their job as a spiritual caregiver and being instrumentalized by the medical staff. Likewise, chaplains discern when the patient has needs beyond their scope of practice and make the necessary referrals to therapists, psychologists, psychiatrists, social workers, and other staff. Chaplains both maintain patient and family confidentiality and make chart notes to share relevant information with the medical staff. This skill takes practice as charting is necessarily brief, whereas other forms of writing in spiritual care rely on thick description. Chaplains also spend time checking in with staff at the nursing station, break rooms, and staff meetings. Buddhist chaplains, in particular, are frequently asked to host mindfulness programs for staff due to the effectiveness of mindfulness practices in stress coping and mental/emotional health. Chaplains are often members of hospital ethics committees and participate in case review with other staff. Chaplains may also be asked to host holiday services and rituals or perform rituals around critical life events, even in some instances, for religious traditions not their own. For example, the Buddhist chaplains I interviewed were occasionally asked to baptize at-risk babies born at times when no other chaplain was available. They each found different ways to maintain personal integrity while also providing (if not always performing) the needed ritual for the careseekers.

Hospice chaplains have a special role to play in spiritual care for patients, families and staff, as issues of life and death tend to elicit deep religious, spiritual, and existential questions. What happens afte death? How does one have a 'good' death? How does one respond to the death of a loved one? These are all pressing questions that chaplains help hospice careseekers navigate. Chaplains who work in hospice, nursing and elder care, and treatment centers may develop longer-term and ongoing relationships with patients and families over weeks, months, or even years, which calls for skilled navigation of personal and professional boundaries. The loss of a patient is always difficult, but especially so for a patient one may have grown close to over an extended period. Likewise, bereavement of medical staff depends very much on the circumstances of both the loss and the life of the patient. Chaplains in health care settings need a strong personal practice and support structure to assist them in coping with the vicarious trauma and ongoing grief of their work.

Buddhist resources helpful for chaplains in health care settings include:

- Part II: Serving the Sick: The Arts of Hospital Chaplaincy and Part V: Living with Dying: The Arts of End-Of-Life Care in *The Arts of Contemplative Care*
- Chapters 7 through 13 in *A Thousand Hands*
- *Awake at the Bedside: Contemplative Teaching on Palliative and End-of-Life Care* by Koshin Paley Ellison and Matt Weingast (2016)
- *Being with Dying: Cultivating Compassion and Fearlessness in the Presence of Death* by Joan Halifax (2009)

Non-Buddhist resources for chaplains in health care settings:
- *Pastoral Care in Hospitals* by Neville Kirkwood (2005)
- *Spiritual Care in Practice* edited by George Fitchett (2015)
- *Professional Spiritual & Pastoral Care: A Practical Clergy and Chaplain's Handbook* edited by Stephen B. Roberts (2011)
- *Chaplaincy and the Soul of Health and Social Care: Fostering Spiritual Wellbeing in Emerging Paradigms of Care* edited by Ewan Kelly and John Swinton (2019)
- *Spiritual Care in Common Terms: How Chaplains Can Effectively Describe the Spiritual Needs of Patients in Medical Records* by Gordon J. Hilsman (2016)

Prisons

Prison ministry has a long history among various religious traditions. In the modern day, prison chaplaincy is conducted both by employed staff and trained volunteers, with Buddhist chaplains more commonly falling into the latter category. Prisons includes both state and federal penitentiaries with convicted criminals and city and county jails where the accused await bail or trial. Some Buddhist prison chaplains may also be employed by non-profit organizations dedicated to prison outreach and reintegration of previously incarcerated individuals, rather than direct employees of the correctional institutions. Fleet Maul, one of the most famous Buddhists involved in prison chaplaincy, has stated he believes it is more ethical for a chaplain to work from outside the system than from within. Being employed by a prison makes one beholden to the interests of one's employers in what Maul perceives as an unethical system. (Per remarks he made at the Awakened Leadership Conference I attended in Los Angeles in 2016.) Richard Torres, the only full-time employed Buddhist prison chaplain to contribute a chapter to *The Arts of Contemplative Care,* acknowledges the conflict of interest it creates, while also describing the benefits of greater access to prisoners this provides (Torres in Giles and Miller, 2012, p. 141-148). In some states, such as California, Buddhists are not eligible for direct employment in state prisons, but may be employed by federal prisons. Some prison systems limit volunteer chaplains to contact with prisoners who officially identify as Buddhist, while others are more open and allow prisoners of any religion to attend meditation sessions and Dharma talks.

Prisons are the most tightly controlled environment in which chaplains regularly work. Access to prisoners is controlled by numerous rules and authorities, all of which a prison chaplain must satisfy to provide spiritual care. Applications to become a volunteer and mandatory training sessions can take months or even a year or more to complete. Rules cover what to wear, what can be brought into the prison or not, where and when to meet with prisoners, gifts, and physical contact and distance. Buddhist chaplains often work under the supervision of a Christian chaplain employed by the institution and so must make inter-religious allies to gain access to prisoners. This has not always been easy, but a pivotal court case in 1972, Cruz vs. Beto, upheld the right of a Texas prisoner to correspond with a minister of the Buddhist Churches of America over the objection of prison staff (including the Christian prison chaplain) and helped ensure the religious rights of prisoners in the U.S. gained better protections (Fisher in Michon and Fisher, 2016, p. 235).

The contributors to the prisons section in *The Arts of Contemplative Care* still warn of discrimination and disapproval they face from prison officials, including chaplains, while also affirming that many are very open and welcoming. They warn of mail that never arrives and books that go missing. Margot Neuman and Gary Allen advise that patience is one of the most important virtues for this work, for both chaplains and prisoners (Neuman and Allen in Giles and Miller, 2012, p. 121-132).

Prison chaplains can form long-standing relationships with prisoners through in-person visits and/or correspondence. In-person visits often take the form of weekly meditation training, Dharma talks and rituals, or other group activities within prison chapels or classrooms. Before and after group sessions, chaplains may spend time talking with individual prisoners, but private pastoral care and counseling is often not possible. Chaplains may provide books and reading materials, which they often source from donations. They may also assist prisoners in acquiring ritual objects, such as images, beads, or prayer/meditation mats, subject to approval of prison authorities. Many chaplains continue to work with prisoners after release through formal reintroduction and anti-recidivism programs. For example, the Greyston Bakery founded by Roshi Bernie Glassman of the Zen Peacemakers Order in 1982 regularly hires former convicts and helped them reintegrate to life after prison (www.greyston.org). However, in some cases, contact between paroled or released prisoners and prison volunteers is strictly prohibited.

Terry Conrad provides a vivid and succinct summary of what the prison environment is like in his chapter in Giles and Miller's anthology, describing it as "an environment that appears to contradict anything we might imagine as conducive to contemplation and meditation," being loud, crowded, full of human smells, and subject to frequent interruption and disruption, full of anger and the fear of imminent violence (Conrad in Giles and Miller, 2012, p. 165-166).

Many chaplains described the source of the fear and anger among a population that is both forgotten by the outside world, isolated and alone, while simultaneously being constantly monitored and controlled, and dehumanized to little more than their prisoner number and punished for the smallest infraction of prison rules. They all describe their role as chaplains as being someone who treats prisoners as fully worthy human beings, equally capable of enlightenment through their own efforts. And they report the amazing changes that can occur in prisoners through dedicated practice and study.

Violence, abuse, trauma, addiction and mental health issues are common in the background of many prisoners. This leads to a prevalence of post-traumatic stress disorder symptoms among prison populations, affecting around six percent of men and 27 percent of women, both of whom are often victims of domestic violence and/or sexual abuse (Baranyi et al., 2018, p. 134). Many prisoners were under the influence of drugs at their time of arrest, somewhere between 63-83 percent depending on city. Marijuana and cocaine were the most common but the effects of opiates are on the rise (prisonerhealth.org). As of 2010, two-thirds of prisoners met the diagnostic criteria for substance abuse, but only one in ten received treatment (The National Center of Addiction and Substance Abuse at Columbia University, 2010). A report from the Urban Institute (urban.org) estimated around half of state and federal prisoners and closer to two-thirds of jail inmates have a mental health problem. Depressive disorders are most common, followed symptoms of bipolar disorder (also known as manic-depression), anxiety disorders, PTSD, personality disorders, and schizophrenia and other psychotic disorders. The CDC estimates that a large number of prisoners suffer from traumatic brain injuries (TBIs), which can result in mental health symptoms, such as those above, as well as disordered thinking that makes it difficult for prisoners and parolees to comply with even simple instructions such as making a court appointment, resulting in re-incarceration. Different research studies estimate the percentage of prisoners with TBIs between 25-87 percent. A history of domestic and other forms of violence is associated with TBIs (cdc.gov/traumaticbraininjury). It will help the prospective prison chaplain to familiarize themselves with the ways these issues affect prisoner behavior.

Racism and inequality in policing and criminal justice means that prison populations do not reflect broader American demographics. According to the Sentencing Project (sentencingproject.org), a black man born in 2001 has a one-in-three chance of being imprisoned during his lifetime, and an Latino man a one-in-six chance, compared to a one-in-seventeen chance of a white man. Men are also imprisoned at far higher rates than women. While there has been a 716 percent increase in the number of incarcerated women in the U.S. since 1980, they still only make up around five percent of the overall prison population. Overall, the U.S. incarcerates more of its citizens than any other nation on earth, both in terms of total population and as a percentage of the population (sentencingproject.org); this phenomenon is referred to as mass incarceration.

Buddhist resources helpful for prison chaplains:
- Daniel Clarkson Fisher's chapter in *A Thousand Hands*
- Part III: Dharma Behind Bars: The Arts of Prison Ministry in *The Arts of Contemplative Care*
- *Dharma in Hell: The Prison Writings of Fleet Maul* by Fleet Maul (2017)
- Part IV: Bearing Witness to the System in *Bearing Witness: A Zen Master's Lessons in Making Peace* by Bernie Glassman (1998)
- *Be Free Where You Are* by Thich Nhat Hanh (2002)

Non-Buddhist resources for prison chaplains:
- *A Ministry of Presence: Chaplaincy, Spiritual Care, and the Law* by Winnifred Fallers Sullivan

- *Spiritual and Religious Diversity in Prisons: Focusing on How Chaplaincy Assists in Prison Management* by Josiah Opata (2001)
- *Counseling Criminal Justice Offenders* by Ruth Masters (2003)
- "Religion in Prisons: A 50-State Survey of Prison Chaplains" by the Pew Research Center, https://www.pewforum.org/2012/03/22/prison-chaplains-exec/
- *The New Jim Crow: Mass Incarceration in the Age of Colorblindness* by Michelle Alexander (2020)
- *Waiting for an Echo: The Madness of American Incarceration* by Christine Montross (2020)

Colleges & Universities

As with many hospitals, college and universities in the west were originally founded by and for religious orders. The office of the chaplain has a centuries-long history and has endured even as institutions moved away from their religious roots and opened their doors to students of all religions and no religion. 'Religious life' staff on campuses today serve the needs of all students, regardless of religious affiliation. In some cases, they do so while remaining true to the founding order of their particular school. In other cases, they do so on public campuses where explicit support for religion is legally prohibited while freedom of religion is legally mandated, creating a hybrid of institutional partnerships between schools and the religious institutions that serve the needs of their students. Buddhist chaplains enter into this context mostly as volunteers, either members of a local sangha with an outreach effort at the institution or as paid faculty or staff serving in another role and volunteering as the Buddhist chaplain 'on the side.' While there are paid Buddhist chaplains directly employed by institutions, their numbers are few, and they tend to be limited to the largest and best-funded private universities.

There is no particular career path for becoming a Buddhist college chaplain as there is in other sectors. Buddhist chaplains employed by institutions tend to be hired as either the overall administrator of a multi-faith religious life program, a position I have held since 2018, or as faculty or staff in some other role. For example, the Zen Buddhist Chaplain at Rochester Institute of Technology, where I work, is also the faculty chair of the philosophy department. His role in religious life is entirely voluntary and uncompensated. I am presently aware of less than a dozen schools that directly employ a Buddhist chaplain as such, including Yale, Harvard, and the University at Southern California. Due to the limited availability of such posts (and the limited capacity of institutions to find or judge the quality of the Buddhist 'chaplains' available to them), Buddhist chaplaincy on college campuses tends to be the least professionalized of all sectors. Most serving in the capacity of 'chaplain' lack the rigorous training in spiritual care we expect of Buddhist chaplains in health care or the military. Instead, most have been trained by their sanghas in the particular traditions of that lineage and some may also be religious studies scholars with a deep understanding of the history of Buddhism, but no clinical training or formal education in pastoral skills. Nevertheless, their deep care for students leads them to the path of chaplaincy and many become very successful and important resources for students.

Buddhist chaplains, whether employed or voluntary, work with college-aged young adults who need spiritual support and religious services. Going to college is often the first time that young adults are dislocated from their families and religious communities. At this age, students begin a process of spiritual questing to develop a 'self-authored worldview' that is either a renewed commitment to their religious upbringing (integrating their family traditions with new ideas they encounter in college), an exploration of alternative spiritual/religious (or non-spiritual/religious) paths, or both. Chaplains are integral to this process while also providing general support to student undergoing other common college stressors, particularly in relation to young adult relationships, career and vocational discernment, risky behaviors, mental health, and basic academic and life skills. Finally, chaplains provide crucial religious services to students who are unable to attend their home temples or sanghas and may find it difficult to leave campus due to lack of transportation. Attending regular religious services on campus is a crucial support during their education. Students are very judicious about how they use their time (though it may not always seem so) and reducing 'barriers to entry' to healthy activities and support services is one of the most effective strategies for student engagement and success. On campus groups become surrogate communities for young adults during their college years. Campus chaplains often have the joy of working with the same students over many years, including cultivating student leaders within their young adult communities. Much of a campus chaplain's day is involved in organizing 'programs' (i.e., services and activities) for students to participate in. Through these programs, students get to know one another, their religious tradition, and the chaplain, which may later result in one-on-one spiritual care.

Buddhist chaplains face their own structural barriers that currently prevent them from operating on college campuses at a level similar to Christian and Jewish counterparts. Structural barriers are related both to the institutions of higher education and the Buddhist communities. Institutions place requirements on campus chaplains that are tailored towards Christian and Jewish chaplains, but difficult to meet for Buddhists, Hindus, Muslims, Pagans and other religious minority groups. However, even when Buddhist chaplains can meet these requirements, there is often a lack of support for their work on college campuses from within the Buddhist communities. Part of the structure for religious life in higher education in western countries is a reliance on the religious communities themselves to fund the work of their representatives on college campuses.

Christian and Jewish institutions have developed funding structures to support this work. Buddhist and other minority religions have not, resulting in an underrepresentation of services on college campuses at precisely the time when student enrollment from their religious traditions is increasing.

Buddhist resources for campus chaplains:
- "May You Always be a Student" by Danny Fisher and "Changing Our Mind, Transforming Our World" by Ji Hyang Padma in *The Arts of Contemplative Care*
- "Young Adult Asian American Identities" by Chenxing Han and Part III: Working with Communities (chapters 37-50) in *A Thousand Hands*
- *Blue Jean Buddha: Voices of Young Buddhists* by Sumi Loundon (2001) and *The Buddha's Apprentices: More Voices of Young Buddhists* by Sumi Loundon Kim (2005)

Non-Buddhist resources for campus chaplains:
- *Cultivating the Spirit: How College can Enhance Students' Inner Lives* by Alexander W. Astin, Helen S. Astin, and Jennifer A. Lindholm (2010)
- *Big Questions, Worthy Dreams: Mentoring Emerging Adults in Their Search for Meaning, Purpose, and Faith,* 10th Edition, by Sharon Daloz Parks (2011)
- *Encouraging Authenticity and Spirituality in Higher Education* by Arthur W. Chickering, Jon C. Dalton, and Liesa Stamm (2005)
- *College & University Chaplaincy in the 21st Century: A Multifaith Look at the Practice of Ministry on Campuses across America,* edited by Lucy A. Forster-Smith (2013)
- *No Longer Invisible: Religion in University Education* by Rhonda Hustedt Jacobsen and Douglas Jacobsen (2012)

OTHER SECTORS

Chaplains in the U.S. can be found in small numbers in several other sectors, including first responders and emergency services, corporations, various charitable and activism-focused non-profits, and within Buddhist communities, temples and sanghas. Many Buddhist caregivers also receive cross-training in order to be formally employed as mental health therapists and counselors, social workers, and psychologists. Given that training for mental health professions and chaplaincy requires a similar level of rigor and time commitment, this can be a long path, but also a rewarding one for Buddhists who are able and inclined for such work. However, this area is not the focus of this book and has been ably covered elsewhere. Resources related to Buddhism and mental health have been listed earlier in this work.

Effective Spiritual Care

This section connects the insight gained from interviewing Buddhist chaplains working in interfaith settings with the sources of Dharma and modern literature on spiritual care in order to define some of the factors that contribute to effective spiritual care in any context. Several important concepts appeared throughout my interviews, including presence, connection, emotional intelligence and authenticity. I have also observed the importance of these factors in my own work and attempted to illustrate them in the vignettes.

The chaplains that I interviewed universally reported 'being present' as an important aspect – if not the most important aspect – of spiritual care, and many explained the importance of 'connecting' with careseekers. Some chaplains used the professional (Christian) term 'ministry of presence,' but most did not. The praxis of presence was a common subject for the chaplain's reflexivity, in that 'being present' entails being aware of what was going on as it occurs and enables memory of the event for later reflection. One chaplain said, "I mean, certainly I reflect a lot on my own presence. Like how much am I paying attention? How much anxiety am I bringing to the room, or distraction, or whatever? I really try kind of before I go into the room to kind of center myself and take some breaths." A chaplain's meditation practice was integral to developing the skills of mindfulness, awareness, and concentration necessary to ensure presence in several different ways. Meditation builds mental 'strength' and 'endurance' in much the same way as physical exercise, which can then be employed 'off the cushion' as part of what we call 'presence' in spiritual care.

Being present can be understood in three respects: the intention behind it, what one actually does to be present, and the outcomes of being present with and for careseekers (and oneself). Chaplains described the intention as one of: goodwill, love or loving-kindness, compassion, equanimity, respect, being open hearted, not preoccupied with doing or saying the 'right thing,' comfortable with silence, nonjudgmental, non-anxious, and having unconditional positive regard – the final trait is a professional term popularized in spiritual care by pastoral care scholar Howard Clinebell and based on the work of psychologist Carl Rogers (Clinebell and McKeever, 2011, p. 466). Chaplain B's short loving-kindness meditation with the unresponsive patient in Vignette 2 is one example of presence, as was the listening he employed in his conversation with the patient's children regarding their mother's faith. In an interview, one chaplain also described the quality of being non-attached, or being compassionate and "fully there, but I don't bring it home with me." Other chaplains called this having no agenda, not trying to fix things, and having good boundaries. Likewise, Chaplain A in Vignette 1 offered some resources to Alice without fixating on whether Alice followed through on them or not. This enabled Chaplain A to make the recommendations in a open way that was not perceived as 'pushy' (which is often more effective) and to avoid later anxiety for herself over Alice's choices, which were beyond the chaplain's control.

When they are being present with careseekers, words rarely described what chaplains were actually doing. Many chaplains said they were "just being present," "just be[ing] there," or "showing up," but when those statements are further questioned, chaplains tended to describe practices of attention, focus, flexibility, active listening, eye contact, body language, skillful response, gentle questioning, praying, and noticing and remembering details, even small ones, about the careseeker. For example, Chaplain A noticed when Alice used the word 'abuse' to characterize her own relationship. Chaplain C watched Charlie carefully when bringing up what she knows for him is a sore topic, watching facial expression and body language to gauge his reaction.

When chaplains can be present successfully, the fruition (to use a Buddhist term) can be positive in almost counterintuitive ways. It doesn't seem like they're doing much of anything, yet careseekers express profound gratitude and undergo amazing transformations. Careseekers reported feeling more peaceful, respected, better connected to their emotions, and better able to make sense of things. They appreciated "someone being there" and experienced moments of levity or joy in otherwise difficult situations. Chaplains also talked about the negative consequences of not being present, of not being mindful, or of being self-conscious and anxious. Sometimes, not even the best ministry of presence could help a careseeker, but by continuing to be present in such situations, chaplains seemed better able to cope with the suffering they themselves experienced. (As a side-note, the analytical paradigm of intention-task-fruition revealed through the investigation of being present and connecting became an important way of organizing theoretical categories within the Framework described in Chapter 3.)

Being present helped chaplains connect with careseekers, because, "If I'm not totally present, I'm gonna lose that connection." Evidence relating to the concept of connecting quickly grew as the interviews progressed and conversations began to focus on particular topics revealing several different aspects of connecting. First, in relation to being present, connecting refers to the connection between two people, specifically the chaplain and careseeker(s). Building connection could be as simple as being present and having a conversation that both parties are interested in having. One chaplain described how connecting with careseekers "felt like magic and I didn't have [to] work so hard [scoffs], which is odd." Many chaplains associated a sense of joy with connection, even in traumatic circumstances, and even on days when they would drive home crying. Sometimes connecting involved a sense of identification with or transference (or counter-transference) based on the careseeker's situation. Transference is illustrated at the end of Vignette 3 when Charlie refers to Chaplain C as "sis," and Chaplain C reflexively ponders how she feels about that. She may decide to continue to embody the 'older sister' paradigm as part of her therapeutic relationship with Charlie (counter-transference) if she feels it facilitates a trusting and growth-inducing process. In any case, connecting often involved empathy and almost always involved compassion. For example, Chaplain B could empathize with the family's desire for a miracle that would save their mother's life based on the losses he had experienced in his own life. This longing created a connection between chaplain and careseekers' that facilitated their conversation. When chaplains could remain present and be mindful of these psychological processes, they did not appear to interfere with care. However, when chaplains were not aware of them and became overwhelmed, they reported needing to step back, calm down, and/or seek support before being able to continue offering spiritual care.

Second, chaplains also understood that connection could have a more spiritual dimension as people sought to connect with themselves or things greater than themselves, such as God, the divine, or the big existential questions of the universe. The big questions that all people ask "break down all labels and barriers." Chaplains empathized with careseekers' desire to or sense of connection with God based on the chaplain's own sense of connection with something larger than themselves, even though they did not call that thing 'God.' In these instances, being open to a sense of mystery or not-knowing helped chaplains empathize with careseekers who felt connected to things the chaplains did not personally feel connected to, but could imagine based on their own sense of connection to something else or their own mystical experiences. One chaplain likened connection to "the yoga idea of union versus separation or isolation"; the latter, to them, was a form of suffering. Other chaplains interpreted connection as a byproduct of interdependence or emptiness. We are able to connect with others because we are, in fact, not separate from them. Any sense of separation is actually a delusion that perpetuates suffering. In this respect, connection had a soteriological function for several of the chaplains I spoke with. One described it as being "beyond words," a phrase often used to describe prajñā, or wisdom. Connection takes on an aspect of wisdom when viewed as a function of interdependence or emptiness. One chaplain talked about connecting with careseekers on the basis of a shared buddha-nature, of not being fundamentally different from others, and therefore being interdependent.

Connecting was a common concept, though not ubiquitous, in the data. Ten of the thirteen chaplains spoke about connecting with careseekers; two more spoke about connecting with teachers and 'the sacred,' but not careseekers; and the remaining chaplain did not explicitly reference connection, but did talk about being present. It is probable that presence and connecting with careseekers as a chaplain are learned skills, though it may come more naturally to some than others based on diverse life-experiences and temperaments. Some chaplains talked about having strong connections with people in their past, particularly teachers and spiritual friends, and attributed some of their ability to connect to careseekers to this prior experience. In most other cases, a sense of connection could be inferred from how chaplains spoke about the process of soliciting and receiving feedback from others on their reflections. Sharing did not always lead to connection, but it certainly could and often did. Both being present and connecting rely on traits referenced by the chaplains in this study. These traits include character virtues, as well as aspects of personality or temperament, emotional self-management, and authenticity. Some of these traits, such as love, compassion, and openness, have already been described in relation to the intentions one holds when being present with careseekers. These can be categorized as virtues. Other traits relate to personality and temperament. Some chaplains spoke about being naturally introverted and reflective, "not very emotional," or sensitive, while others were outgoing with a deep love for people's stories, but no patterns applied to most or all chaplains.

Whether introverted or extroverted, many chaplains spoke about the necessity of emotional self-regulation. They realized it was important to remain calm and equanimous with careseekers, especially when careseekers themselves were experiencing turbulent emotions. They empathized with those emotions, laughed and cried with careseekers, but not to the degree where it might distract the careseeker or cause additional distress. One chaplain explained, "[My practice] helped me to stay calm, because you hear pretty incredible stories from people, and I can't be reacting to, you know, everything. I think I should be the calm existence in...people's chaotic situations." Emotional self-management was important both during encounters and afterward to ensure effective self-care and long-term sustainability. Another chaplain specifically researched "compassion satisfaction," which is "the inherent pleasure that is experienced in being compassion [sic]. So it's a *vedana*, it's a *vedana* of feeling, and for me it's been really valuable to notice it and to cultivate it...[as one of the] mitigating factors for compassion fatigue and burnout." *Vedana* is a sensation that accompanies consciousness and one of the five aggregates that make up what we misperceive as 'self.' This is an example of a chaplain explicitly engaging in praxis, that is a theory-laden practice with engaged reflexivity. All chaplains relied on their Buddhist practice, particularly meditation, for emotional self-regulation, as well as other coping methods, including setting healthy boundaries, self-care routines, appropriate consultation, and therapy.

The final trait that several chaplains repeatedly cited is authenticity. Several chaplains reported anxiety over navigating the new role of Buddhist chaplaincy within a predominantly Christian country and profession. Not only did they deal with all of the same fears of inadequacy, 'feeling fake,' or 'doing it wrong' that I have observed in all chaplains, but they were also uncertain whether their religious background would be a help or hindrance, welcome or unwelcome by careseekers and peers. However, as chaplains progressed in their spiritual care practice, they reported overcoming these insecurities and developing a sense of confidence and sufficiency rooted in authenticity. The more they grew into their identities as Buddhist chaplains, the better they felt about their spiritual care practice and the better the outcomes they reported. Some chaplains reported that supervisors and peers helped in this process. For example:

> I made a verbatim presentation on that encounter. The responses from my peer and the supervisor were very supportive. Yeah, and encouraging, because at that time it happened, like almost three years ago, I think. At that time, I was still struggling how to be, say, authentic. Be myself and be a Buddhist at the same time being a chaplain. So, I think, I believe the responses were kind of encouraging me.

This was not universally the case, though it did represent most chaplains' experiences with support from their CPE cohorts leading to greater authenticity. Even those who struggled with their CPE experience developed a sense of authenticity over time based on responses from careseekers. One such chaplain talked about leaving graduate school with a sense of confidence that was then slowly eroded in CPE, where they had to instead "develop [an] essentially Christian theology for chaplaincy, in order to just function in that environment," only to rediscover their confidence after working for several months beyond CPE residency. They said:

> **Researcher**: What do you think does have a relationship to the quality of the care afterward?
> **Participant**: Being a Buddhist in the encounter. [laughs] Like, practicing in the encounter. Yeah, I think I've had many instances, especially earlier on, where I felt like really armed with some sort of very sound analysis and plan of care, and confidence maybe, and realized like, "None of this is relevant now. They're in a totally, this person's in a totally different place, and I need to adapt to that, and be willing to let go of all of that." And that, I think, is just practice coming in.

This chaplain rediscovered a sense of authenticity as a Buddhist as a result of the positive response they received from careseekers. Overall, the concept of 'authenticity' came up twenty-two times in the initial thirteen interviews, making it among the most common values for chaplains.

In addition to character traits and intentions necessary for spiritual care, chaplains identified numerous behaviors they engaged in during spiritual care. These behaviors were categorized in the interview and reflection data first in relation to processes or actions. The most common chaplain actions were assessment, contemplation, spiritual practice, interpreting traditions, support, raising ethical concerns, being present, consulting, observing, reflexivity and meditating. These were the most common behaviors chaplains described doing while providing spiritual care. This does not mean these were the most common behaviors *performed* while providing spiritual care. Repeated psychological studies have demonstrated the unreliability of self-reports for documenting actual behavior. Rather, self-reports tend to document behavior that is meaningful to the actor, which is therefore memorable. In my study, meaningfulness was prioritized above frequency. Therefore, self-reports were suited to capture this data. Observation would be the best way to capture a more realistic picture of chaplain behaviors overall, but this was not an aspect of my study.

Assessment emerged as a surprisingly common activity. The term 'assessment' is not meant formally, as in conducting a written spiritual assessment of a careseeker, although chaplains reported doing this occasionally. Rather, 'assessment' here captures instances in which chaplains made a judgment or employed discernment, to use a more Buddhist term. This is reflected in statements such as "My sense is that…," "The key issue is…," or "It is best to…" Here we see chaplains making value judgments, not in the sense of judging the careseeker's intrinsic or moral worth, but in the sense of employing their expertise to determine a course of action or predict its effect. The frequency with which chaplains engaged in this behavior may surprise them, given the emphasis they also placed on being nonjudgmental, open, and maintaining a mindset of not-knowing. I do not perceive this as a contradiction, but rather evidence of expertise and wisdom. So long as judgements are held lightly and adjusted as needed, they pose no problem. However, I believe that being able to recognize when we do make judgements is essential to being able to adjust them. I was not able to test and see if a chaplain's perceptions of how often they employ judgment are aligned with how often they believe they are making judgments. This may be a fruitful area for future research.

Contemplation was another key behavior that was frequently cataloged in the interviews and written reflections. This behavior is reflected in statements such as, "After this visit, I continued to contemplate…," "…really distill what I think…," or "Contemplating the Four Thoughts that Turn the Mind…" From these examples, we find that this behavior includes components of cognitive reflection and meditative practice that are more analytical in nature. (Meditative practice to develop calm, concentration, and mindfulness were cataloged under 'meditation.') Chaplains engaged in this kind of contemplation in reference to encounters with careseekers. Thus, this behavior has the hallmarks of reflection, particularly as it relates to recollection and spiritual formation. Meaning-making was sometimes an outcome of contemplation, but not always. Contemplation was almost always carried out through cognitive, affective, and/or meditative tasks; in other words, thinking, getting in touch with one's emotions, or meditating, which can also include thinking and emotional awareness through formal exercises. One may write about one's contemplations or share them with others later, but that would not itself be considered contemplation. I believe the category of contemplation is larger than and actually includes the category of reflection, as well as other categories, such as meditative exercises. This may be a uniquely Buddhist contribution to our understanding of reflection in spiritual care.

The chaplain's own spiritual practice was also important to their ongoing work as a spiritual caregiver. Chaplains described their spiritual practice as "Really living it [the Dharma] more fully or coming back into balance…," "Allow[ing] me to cultivate…," or "It is best to practice Dharma prior to such transitions as a way to…" Practices were listed specifically, such as particular types of meditation, *kōan* practice, retreats, yoga and tai chi, and the cultivation of virtues. The term 'practice' was also used more generally with the connotation of living one's life in accordance with the Dharma, especially the Noble Eightfold Path, the Five Precepts, refuge vows, bodhisattva vows, and, for the monastic participants, the *vinaya*, or rules of conduct for monks and nuns. The dual connotation of the term 'practice,' both specific and general, can lead to a broad category of behaviors designated as practice.

In analyzing the data, I tended to categorize specific practices, such as meditation, separately from general statements about practice (such as those above) to capture what their practice *means* to the chaplains I interviewed. In the latter respect, chaplains often had both utilitarian and soteriological understandings of their practice. For example, one chaplain wrote in their reflection:

> As a chaplain, I find that my practice of zazen meditation and moment-to-moment mindfulness are ways that I enact the Dharma. These practices allow me to cultivate equanimity (*upekkha*), compassion (*karuna*), loving-kindness (*metta*), generosity (*dana*) and the other *pāramitās*. My aim is to, like Avalokiteshvara, hear the cries of the world, and thus relieve the suffering of the people I encounter. I see this as a way to live out my Bodhisattva Vows to work for the liberation of all beings.

In this sense, practice is both utilitarian – a means of cultivating virtues that assist in their work as a chaplain – and soteriological – a means of liberation for all beings. This view of practice is aligned with the Dharma, particularly with the parable of the raft. This simile compares the Dharma to a raft constructed for crossing turbulent waters. After crossing, the Buddha asks:

> [Buddha:] "Having crossed over to the further shore, he might think, 'How useful this raft has been to me! For it was in dependence on this raft that, making an effort with my hands and feet, I have crossed over to safety on the further shore. Why don't I, having hoisted it on my head or carrying it on my back, go wherever I like?' What do you think, monks: Would the man, in doing that, be doing what should be done with the raft?"
> [Monks:] "No, lord."
> [Buddha:] "…In the same way, monks, I have taught the Dhamma compared to a raft, for the purpose of crossing over, not for the purpose of holding onto. Understanding the Dhamma as taught compared to a raft, you should let go even of Dhammas, to say nothing of non-Dhammas." (MN 22)

Likewise, one's practice is utilitarian and soteriological; it is for the purpose of crossing over into liberation. Some practices are provisional, to be abandoned when one achieves certain attainments, or to be progressively replaced with other practices. Some practices are ongoing. Even the Buddha continued to meditate after his enlightenment, one presumes to maintain the health of mind and body until they were transcended at the body's death forty years later.

My exploration of these themes and concepts is preliminary and charts the broad shape of Buddhis spiritual care. The following two chapters present a more formal Framework and model. Before proceeding, readers have another opportunity to improve their knowledge and skills in relation to reflection. The chaplains I interviewed had different ways of perceiving reflection and practicing reflexivity in their work, but some clear patterns emerged that can help us understand various aspects of reflection in the same way the prior section has outlined various aspects of spiritual care.

Conclusion and Reflection

The Buddhist chaplains I interviewed understood reflection or the act of reflecting in various ways. One participant said of the interview process itself, "I'm reflecting as we speak." Reflecting had the following meanings and connotations to the chaplains. First, it involved an aspect of recollection, or looking back at what had previously happened. Often, this is to understand the connections between causes and effects. Chaplains compared what had just occurred to other prior events to look for broader patterns. Mindfulness, including awareness of one's inner experience, was an important tool in being able to later recall with accuracy what had happened. In this respect, it is about being present – one's own experiences of being with another. Sometimes reflection is about understanding an experience, and sometimes it is about letting go of a difficult experience one cannot change (or even understand), which leads into the next connotation of reflection.

Second, reflecting is a way to make or find meaning in events and activities. Sometimes this was described as achieving clarity, wisdom, integrity, or understanding. Chaplains would explore or reconcile multiple perspectives, clarify and articulate their own intentions, and learn how to better act on those intentions, either in relation to cultivating virtue (i.e., *pāramitās*) or skillful means (i.e., *upāya*). One participant said, "As chaplains, [if] we can't reflect on what we're doing and how we're helping people, and, you know, how we're sometimes, how sometimes we're not helping people, then we are less effective, and we are less capable of dealing with the issues that come up, dealing with the challenges everyone faces." Reflection was much more powerful and memorable when chaplains had a personal interest in making meaning of something, versus when reflection was simply assigned. In the latter case, some chaplains described just going through the motions to please others (including during CPE), not necessarily to contribute to their own growth. At other times, reflecting at the behest of someone else, specially someone the chaplain respected, could lead to meaningful growth.

Third, reflection contributes (or should contribute) to our spiritual formation. It helps us process our emotions, especially in relation to past and present suffering, trauma, illness, injury, death, and grief. It also helps us understand the nature of self/nonself and deal with our own ego and identity. Chaplains spoke about how their work enriched their meditation and overall spiritual growth and that reflection helped them derive meaningful insights from their work. This is where chaplains most often reported coming into conversation with the Dharma. Some chaplains found the process of reflection, especially when shared, to be affirming and empowering, especially as it related to their identity and authenticity as Buddhist chaplains. Finding language to describe our experiences and communicate them to others assists with both achieving clarity or insight and with reconciling to our own personal narratives about who we are in relation to others. One chaplain said, "You know, we can just be so lonely and alienated in our experiences that having reflection and developing language can offer so much connection," so the themes of reflection and connection are linked.

Fourth, reflection can be carried out through various mechanisms, including cognition, emotion, meditation, conversation, writing, and rereading what one has previously written to consider it again. Reflection utilizes many of the same skills cultivated through meditation, such as mindfulness, awareness, and concentration, but it also uses other skills, especially when one is constructing a reflection to be shared with others. In this case, chaplains reported that the process of writing and sharing reflections during CPE helped them improve their ability to clarify and articulate meaning. It also forced them to really dedicate time to thinking about issues, which is not always easy in the midst of busy lives. Sharing reflections, whether in CPE or elsewhere, was a powerful process for learning and growth. Sharing provided chaplains with access to viewpoints they would not be able to achieve on their own. Feedback was also a topic of later reflection.

Fifth, a few chaplains were concerned that the reflection process could lead to fabrication of meaning "that wasn't there" or to discursiveness, a mind that wanders unskillfully from subject to subject. I myself had a visceral experience of this during an exercise in my first CPE unit when my cohort was asked to speculate as to why a careseekers was behaving in a particular way. I felt it was impossible to know and any story we constructed about the careseeker would hinder our ability to remain open to who they actually were. However, I later came to understand that, as an exercise about a fictional careseeker, it was a helpful activity for generating empathy and connecting theoretical knowledge with practice to embody reflexive praxis.

Likewise, some chaplains were concerned that reflection may have the connotation of *auddhatya*, or restlessness (of mind), one of the five hindrances to attaining *jhana*, a state of meditative absorption on the path to awakening. One chaplain in particular seemed very concerned with avoiding fabrication and discursiveness, to the point where they were reluctant to engage in any interpretation of spiritual care encounters and tended to describe their reflections as journalistic reports, detailing only what 'actually' happened in the encounter. (As a researcher, I am well aware that all description contains some amount of interpretation, however much we try to avoid it.) This predisposition was influenced by a particular form of Buddhist practice, the Zen study of kōans with a teacher. Kōan study is the study of short cases or stories that are often similar to riddles or have a nonintuitive outcome. This participant related the experience of being with a careseeker to the experience of kōan study and their teacher's guidance:

Participant: I was always like, you know, trying to take in the moment [during a spiritual care encounter], as is, just raw state. And just notice when I might be wanting to interpret something. And I think there's like a moment of like interpretation, but, you know, I guess what I was scared of was like trying to make something out of something that it wasn't. You know, I guess, my meditation teacher is like, you know we work on these kōans and I had these answers and he'll be like, you know, "You're interpreting still. You're still interpreting and still looking at this conceptual thing."...[During kōan study] I'd have to go to my teacher and I'd have to present my understanding, but present it like a non-conceptual way, knowing that the kōan is in my body, or it's in my bones. It's kind of a saying in Zen, like, "Know the kōan so well that it's in your bones." And he would often say like, "You're still interpreting." You know? He's like, "If you're watching your mind really closely, like it will just keep on…" You know, just the slightest little interpretation and you're like all the way off. You miss it. And he was like, "Concentrate! You need to concentrate more." And I was like, "Well, I don't know? Like what is concentration then? Maybe I don't know." And he was like, "Just be there. Just be there in the moment, fully, with no hang-ups."

[Later in the interview] I was experiencing it in my mind a lot, especially on reflection, but, you know, giving someone spiritual care, it was a vivid experience. It was a vivid, visual experience, especially someone who is like actively dying. You know, I'd be like, "Okay, well, they're

like at the old age and death part of birth, old age, sickness, and death." But see, that was just something that went across my mind and that's really not getting at it, you know? That was just like a…I would say like there is interpretation. That's uh, I don't want to say that's discursive, but….
Researcher: But it's an interpretation.
Participant: Yeah, it's an interpretation, where birth, old age, sickness, and death, um…when I look, I could experience birth, old age, sickness, and death in a single moment in my mind…That's still interpretation, whereas like, you know, feel it. Feel birth, old age, sickness, and death. Do you feel it in your bones? Do you feel it in your bones?

When I inquired about this viewpoint among other chaplains to see how prevalent it might be, some affirmed that it could align with certain Zen tenants and practices, while others questioned the extreme nature of the viewpoint. One responded:

Well, I mean, I would say kind of Middle Way, too. That seems a little bit of one extreme, of saying, "No, not concepts. We're not gonna talk about concepts." Like, well, but actually in practice, the *shikantaza* [Zen meditation], you know mindfulness or other practices it's, you actually do label in a way. I mean, at some level you're noticing what is arising. You don't have to cling to it and keep it small, but you can notice what's there. I think it's pretty important because if we're not reflecting on what's happening, we're not able to, then we're kind of, we're maybe perpetuating some unconscious stuff that maybe is not so helpful. So, I would worry about

that on the other end. Right? I respect that view of not knowing, and we can never really know. I mean, what can we ever know? How can we ever know the true Dharma?

The last statement refers to the nature of ultimate truth as beyond language and concepts. As with all things Buddhist, the Middle Way between extremes seems preferable. Overall, while chaplains found reflection helpful and an important aspect of their spiritual lives and practice of spiritual care, some were averse to the over-emphasis on meaning-making (as one aspect of reflection) they perceived to be a result of the Christian origins of 'theological' reflection methods.

I speculate this may be related to a faith-based commitment to the world as created by an omniscient, omnipotent God whom, one presumes, meant to create the world in a particular way. Thus, God means all things in the world for some purpose. Therefore, from a monotheist perspective, learning one's purpose or the meaning of an event would help one better understand or draw closer to God. Whereas in Buddhist cosmology, the universe has always existed (its origin is one of the questions not to be speculated upon lest it drive one mad), and phenomena rise and fall through cyclical patterns of becoming and dissolution, humans included. Meaning is not imparted by any outside force, only momentarily constructed by finite beings. As such, any meaning we may assign to an event may be useful, but ultimately empty, just as all language and concepts are ultimately empty of inherent nature. In the Christian paradigm, meaning is ontological and serves a soteriological function. In the Buddhist paradigm, meaning is purely heuristic and may or may not serve any soteriological function. While meanings may be upaya (skillful means) in the present, it must ultimately be abandoned to achieve awakening, the final goal of practice. Therefore, Christians and Buddhists may frustrate one another over these topics. Christians seem quick to 'fabricate' meaning that may or may not be there, and Buddhists seem reluctant to ponder the meaning of particular events. These are only my own musings and not the point of the present section but serve to illustrate how Christians and Buddhists may reflect on the same topic and come to different conclusions. Let us return to the topic of reflection itself.

Sixth, one chaplain pointed out that reflection is not universally positive:

> Yeah, and you know, obviously sometimes I think it's very valuable to reflect on what I've done. Like, purely from a professional standpoint. Like, okay, I was really in a very intense emotional situation, so it can help to critically reflect on what I did and think about like, was I, you know, cognizant at the time?...But I guess my main point is like, I don't think reflection on chaplaincy from a spiritual perspective has a direct relationship to the quality of the care afterward. Like, or, it doesn't have a predictable relationship. It's not always positive. It's not always negative.

Sometime what we call reflection may stray into the territory of speculation or rumination. It is important to avoid 'pigeon holing' the careseeker or judging too quickly who they are or what they need. Likewise, rumination or repetitive discursive thinking on topics, particular with a negative emotional valence, is a common source of stress among chaplains. This chaplain provided an example of working with a patient whom the rest of the care team had trouble communicating with, but with whom the chaplain had formed a strong connection:

> I don't think that [reflection] was helpful. I don't think the reason we connected in the first place, and I don't think the spiritual care that I was providing that was valuable, was aided by that reflection. I think I became kind of appropriated by the rest of the care team and their agenda, and I kind got caught up in this sense of like some sort of salvific goal of spiritual care, as opposed to just companioning people in their experience, whatever it is. And I think I lost touch of where I usually stay in my practice of chaplaincy where I'm just present and hold a certain motivation. So, in that way, I think the reflection, it added too much fabrication.

This is another example of how the concepts clustered around reflecting relate to the concepts clustered around spiritual care, particularly ideas about connecting and being present for careseekers. Reflection can both aid that process and hinder it. This is aligned with the Buddhist concepts of Right Intention and Right View. It is not helpful to reflect with wrong intention (i.e., malice) on wrong views. It is helpful to reflect with Right Intention (i.e., goodwill) on Right Views, which is primarily about understanding the nature, causes and cessation of suffering, or the Four Noble Truths. Many chaplains noted that their ability to reflect in helpful ways did improve over time. The Dharma is quite clear that reflection is a tool and as such it can be used in both 'right' and 'wrong' ways.

Seventh, reflection is a skill that improves over time. As the interviews progressed, I developed better methods for eliciting information from chaplains about the processes by which they learned to practice reflection in relation to their spiritual lives and spiritual care as chaplains. A narrative of change and growth in their reflection methods began to emerge as well. As my questions became more focused, I inquired specifically about what chaplains might expect from someone who had done a lot of reflection compared to someone who was just beginning to reflect on spiritual or religious themes. This was essential for developing the Framework presented in the next chapter and may be useful to new chaplains in charting their own trajectory in relation to reflection. While we can use reflection both skillfully and unskillfully, there is no reason to expect that we will start out being entirely skillful at it. Like anything, reflection must be learned and we become more skilled over time through repeated practice. Our skill is refined through sharing our reflections and receiving feedback from peers and supervisors.

During the initial interviews, chaplains characterized their earlier attempts at reflection as naïve and uncritical, easy or lazy, fearful, skeptical, unnecessarily critical, feeling insufficient, and full of struggling, confusion, and self-doubt. In contrast, they characterized their reflections now as more sophisticated and nuanced, more refined, softer, more open, confident, less judgmental, more comfortable with not-knowing, more intentional and structured, feeling more authentic as a Buddhist, developing a natural habit of pausing, thinking, and reflecting that is intentional, being emotionally open with others, clear, and articulate, more attuned, skilled, and effective, based in habitual writing and sharing, wise, and well-directed. I remember this process myself. For example, it was feedback from peers that prompted me to understand that I communicate emotion through action verbs. "But how did you feel about what he said?" they would ask and I would think "I told you how I feel!" A detailed review of my reflection would reveal that I had written "I wanted to smack him upside the head," which *meant* – to me – I was frustrated by the careseeker's foolishness. "I wanted to jump up and leave the room" *meant* I was deeply uncomfortable with the situation. Based on this feedback, I learned to name my emotions as such – frustration, discomfort – and, through the process of naming them, began to recognize and work with them in a deeper way. This method of communicating about my emotions (through action verbs) is cultural and familial, and I can always return to it in those contexts, but does not necessarily convey the same meanings in all groups. Over time my reflections became more clear and direct, which also forced me to look more closely at my own experiences and helped me become a more reflexive chaplain.

One chaplain characterized this growth process as one in which, at an early stage, they were still very much discovering new insights, while now they were working to digest those insights and live them fully. For many, the process of living one's insights led to more confidence and clarity over time as the Dharma was affirmed through their direct experience, which is precisely what the Dharma calls on practitioners to do. Many chaplains described starting from a place of confusion and seeking answers to help them with their lives. Mature reflection was characterized by a change in what one seeks, becoming less about seeking answers and more about seeking to live with virtue and integrity – to put the answers one had found into practice (or to become comfortable with the not-knowing, which is another sort of practice). This affirms the order of the Three Prajñās, which move from developing wisdom from listening, then contemplating, then practicing.

Finally, correlations between Christian literature on theological reflection and the ways in which the chaplains I interviewed discussed reflection demonstrate the parallels and distinctions. For one thing, the chaplains I interviewed also described reflection as a process, rather than a product, even when it resulted in written work. For many, the written reflections were only one stage in a longer process of reflection. This aligns with Graham, Walton, and Ward's description of theological reflection as "An activity that enables people of faith to give an account of the values and traditions that underpin their choices and convictions and deepens their understanding" (2005, p. 5-6). Likewise, the chaplains in this study affirmed that reflection enabled them to clarify and articulate why they acted in certain ways and how they understand the world. Graham, Walton, and Ward (2005) further posit that reflection enables connection. In their case, as Christian theologians, this connection is between the person and "divine horizons," (p. 6) whereas the chaplains in this study were more likely to make connections between cause and effect, between their situation and the Dharma as an interpretive lens, and even between people. Both groups, the chaplains and academics, would agree, "At the heart of theological reflection, therefore, are questions about the relationship of theory to practice."

I tracked the questions chaplains ask themselves, many of which are about the theory-practice relationship, including simple questions, such as, "What did I say to a patient and why did I say it? And what's my sense of their spirituality and spiritual state? And why is that my sense?" Some chaplains asked more nuanced questions:

> You wanna understand suffering? You wanna understand suffering of marriage, of kids, of pain from both physical, psychological, emotional pain? Look at your life. Look at other people, and, oh, look at the way you prac- of not living up, not abiding to the five precepts, and what that leads you to. And does it bring you more happiness or does it bring you more suffering? And if it brings you more suffering, what do you intend to do about it? What are some of the teachings out there that tells us this, and what are some of the practices out there that allow us to grapple with some of these issues?

This chaplain is asking directly for a theory to understand suffering and practices to deal with suffering, two of the most common topics in Buddhist literature. Another chaplain humorously (but seriously) asked about the practice of meditation, "What's the value of sitting on your butt anyway?" Questioning plays a major role in both Christian theological reflection and reflection by Buddhist chaplains.

Whereas Graham, Walton, and Ward "connect theological discourse to discourse about the nature of God," the chaplains I interviewed connected their reflections to many other things, including the Dharma. However, it is not sufficient to simply replace Christian teachings with Buddhist teachings in the process of reflection. While both types of reflection are, as these authors state, "A critical, interrogative enquiry into the process of relating the resources of faith [or religious teaching, or wisdom derived from direct experience] to the issues of life," (p. 6) this is only Graham, Walton, and Ward's (2005) most general description of theological reflection. Nevertheless, it is sufficient to assert that the methods of reflection the Buddhist chaplains employed are on a par with the kind of theological reflection described by Graham, Walton, and Ward. However, I believe the role of reflection itself occupies a significantly different context within the Buddhadharma, which will be explored more in the next chapter in relation to the Three Prajñās, or wisdom derived from listening, contemplating and meditating.

At this juncture, I encourage readers to reflect on this chapter in relation to its three sections. First, consider your own sources of Dharma that infuse your spiritual care practice. Consider where you feel 'called' to provide care. While the notion of a 'calling' or 'answering a call' is a Christian concept, we Buddhists are nevertheless often asked to describe our 'call' when applying for CPE and paid positions (as though this was a universal concept). While the notion of receiving a 'call' from an outside deity may be uncommon to Buddhists, we can still relate to a sense of feeling drawn to one context over another for the purposes of our work. Reflecting on why that is the case will enable us to answer these questions when they are asked of us, in whatever form they come. Finally, consider the various concepts discussed in relation to effective spiritual care and the practice of reflection itself. The following questions may serve as helpful prompts:

1. What is good 'spiritual care'? What passages from the Dharma immediately come to mind in relation to this question or when you consider your work as a chaplain? Where did you first encounter those words and what was your earliest understanding of them?
2. Find a passage in a sutta, sutra, or Buddhist scripture that seems to apply to your work as a chaplain. What is the context in which it was delivered? How does it apply to your work? What are its implications and limitations for working in an interfaith context?
3. What resources from your lineage, teacher, or sangha support you in your work (or future work) as a chaplain? Does your teacher and sangha understand what a chaplain is and, if not, how does that affect the support they offer?
4. Where do you feel drawn to practice as a chaplain and why? Do you have prior experiences in that context? What do you think might suit you to work in that sector? What will make it challenging for you to work in that sector?
5. Which of the concepts discussed in the sections above seemed most relevant and important to the practice of spiritual care? Why is that?
6. Did any of the concepts discussed above surprise you and, if so, why? Or was there anything missing that you expected to find but did not? What would you add?
7. Recall to mind a past experience in which someone provided 'spiritual care' to you. They may or may not have been a chaplain or religious person at all. Write a short narrative about this experience, including what each person said, and what you thought and felt at the time. Then reflect on that encounter. What can you learn from it in relation to your own practice of spiritual care?

3

THE THREE PRAJÑĀS FRAMEWORK

The Three Prajñās Framework for Spiritual Care is both 1) an 'interpretation' of what Buddhist chaplains have described doing in their work and 2) 'interpretive' because it can serve as a guide by enabling us to look at the behavior of future and present Buddhist chaplains and place it within the Framework. The Buddhadharma contains many such frameworks, including the Four Noble Truths, the Three Hallmarks of Existence, and the Three Unwholesome Roots. Like any good map, they both describe the terrain and help us orient ourselves in relation to it so we can get where we want to go. Likewise, the Framework does not reinvent the three Prajñās. It merely applies them to a modern context: Buddhist chaplaincy. The Framework originated from an effort to describe how Buddhist chaplains develop and provide spiritual care. In describing how several Buddhist chaplains behave, it can also prescribe how other Buddhist chaplains might behave if they wanted to achieve similar results. We can learn from example.

The Framework includes four iterative stages: self, student, chaplain, and kalyāṇamitra, or spiritual friend. At each stage, one proceds through the three Prajñās of gaining wisdom by listening, contemplating, and practicing at in successively more refined ways. Buddhist chaplains who have developed wisdom by listening, contemplating, and practicing through the earlier stages of the Framework are better able to exemplify the model of kalyāṇamitra, the fourth and final stage. This is especially true when the chaplains themselves have been accompanied by kalyāṇamitra during their spiritual formation. At each stage, the three Prajñās are cumulative and recursive. When at a later stage, the chaplain relies on wisdom developed in (and through ongoing practice of) the earlier stages as well.

At this point, I must remind both the reader and myself that the Three Prajñās are not synonymous with the *acts* of listening, contemplating, and practicing. Rather, the Three Prajñās are the wisdom derived from those acts, the results of those acts. They are the outcomes of having listened, contemplated, and practiced well and toward a specific purpose: awakening. Although the Three Prajñās may be described in shorthand as listening-contemplating-practicing, we must remember that this is in reference to wisdom developed through that act, not simply the generic act.

This chapter includes a description of how the Framework emerged from the 'data' – that is, the interviews and reflections I collected from the thirteen Buddhist chaplains I interviewed. Some parts of the framework were referenced explicitly by several chaplains and referred to implicitly by others. A literature review summarizes the three Prajñās according to the Buddhist scriptures, compendiums, and modern literature. As we will see, the three Prajñās are a relatively minor concept in the otherwise massive and highly detailed literature of Buddhism and in relation to the topic of prajñā, wisdom, itself. However, the concept is notable in its ubiquity in all three major branches of Buddhism and across many extant schools. During the course of this work, I was deeply immersed in a dialectic between my interview data and the Buddhadharma. It seemed natural then to write my first draft of the theory in the literary style of a Pāli sutta, presented below. As with any good sutta, the remainder of the chapter contains a complete exegesis of this more succinct presentation.

Sutta on Learning and Practicing Spiritual Care

Listen well, noble friends! Thus, I have heard (in the data). There are three types of wisdom that must be developed in learning the Dharma, considering the Dharma, and coming to know the Dharma for oneself if one wishes to be a spiritual friend to others. One must develop wisdom by listening, by contemplating, and by practicing. These three tasks to develop three types of wisdom follow a four-fold path.

Regarding wisdom based on listening, first, one listens to the Dharma for one's own edification. Second, having developed interest, one dedicates oneself to listening as a student guided and accompanied by a spiritual friend in the form of a teacher, mentor or other learned person. Third, having developed compassion, one listens to learn to be of service to others. Finally, having developed wisdom based on listening, one listens to others to serve them along their own spiritual paths as a spiritual friend.

Regarding wisdom based on contemplating, first, one contemplates what one has heard to make sense of it for oneself. Second, having developed some ideas, one contemplates in companionship and dialogue with others, particularly one's spiritual friends. Third, having refined one's understanding, one contemplates in what way to best serve others in light of their varied circumstances. Finally, having developed wisdom based on contemplating, one aids others in contemplating to make sense of their own circumstances, as a spiritual friend.

Regarding wisdom based on practicing, first, one practices meditation and other spiritual exercises for the sake of one's own awakening. Second, having developed concentration, one practices meditation, chanting, ritual and other forms under the guidance of a teacher, mentor, or spiritual friend. Third, having developed some attainments, one practices caring for others, having seen one's own awakening is bound up with theirs. Finally, having developed wisdom based on practicing, one accompanies others to better aid them in their liberation, as a spiritual friend. Thus, one has developed wisdom through listening, contemplating, and practicing following a four-fold path.

One proceeds in this manner of developing wisdom based on listening, contemplating and practicing because one realizes, through the process of listening, contemplating and practicing, that one's own suffering is inextricably bound up with the suffering of others. One realizes that compassion, the will toward freedom from suffering for all beings, is inextricably bound up with wisdom. One realizes that self is other and other is self; self is no different from other and other is not separate from self. One realizes that one cannot proceed on the spiritual path alone, without spiritual friends and that, through proceeding on the spiritual path, one becomes a spiritual friend to many.

When, through developing wisdom by listening, contemplating, and practicing for oneself, these realizations occur, one seeks out a spiritual community and a teacher with whom to develop further wisdom by listening, contemplating, and practicing. When one is surrounded by spiritual friends in the form of a community and teachers, one may then apply oneself towards liberation from suffering for all beings. This may be done in various ways and involve various new skills, which must be learned through listening, contemplating and practicing. When, through developing wisdom by listening, contemplating and practicing in service to others, one comes to know that others also listen, contemplate and practice, in various ways, toward their own liberation from suffering, one then gains the skill to facilitate and accompany them on this journey as a spiritual friend. This skill improves if one has also had the experience of being accompanied on one's own journey and encouraged to develop wisdom by listening, contemplating and practicing by a spiritual friend, such as a mentor, teacher or peer. While one is accompanying others, one continues to develop wisdom by listening, contemplating and practicing for one's own awakening, as part of a community with a teacher, and to improve one's skill in serving others. One may also continue to be accompanied by spiritual friends who support one's growth towards awakening.

When these practices become widespread, we form a community of spiritual friends, a sangha, all mutually concerned with one another's awakening and the liberation from suffering of society at large. Sangha, or community, is the third refuge of Buddhist practice and vital for liberation from suffering. When we serve others, and accompany others in these ways, we support the development of a worldwide sangha of spiritual friends, regardless of religious affiliation or belief. In this way, the overall suffering of the world is reduced and each individual's access to enlightenment is improved. Thus, I have heard (in the data), and the world, with its numerous beings, chaplains, careseekers, teachers, and spiritual friends, rejoiced!

Emergence of the Framework

We can connect the Framework to the Noble Eightfold Path. The Path's three aspects are prajñā, sīla and samadhi, or wisdom, moral behavior and concentration or meditation. Prajñā is dealt with in detail and its two aspects, Right Intention and Right View, are developed in the sections below. Samadhi is included in the Framework as part of wisdom based on contemplation (at its initial stages) and wisdom based on meditation (at its more-developed stages), though I have made no effort to align its constituent aspects, Right Effort, Right Mindfulness and Right Concentration, with the Framework. Finally, sīla, comprised of Right Speech, Right Action, and Right Livelihood, is implicit in the behavior and ethical standards of the chaplain and in the model of the kalyāṇamitra as a moral exemplar, explored further in the final chapter. Further comparison could yield useful theoretical connections but is not the focus of this work. Instead I chose to stay closer to the data collected from the chaplains in this chapter.

The three Prajñās were referenced explicitly by some chaplains I interviewed for the 2017 study, such as during this exchange:

> **Researcher**: And I'm wondering if you remember when was the first time you were introduced to the idea of practicing reflection in relation to your spiritual or religious life?
>
> **Participant**: …So, one is the Three Prajñās, right? So, hearing, contemplating, and meditating. And, so, you know, hearing teachings, yada-yada, retaining information, and then contemplating, which is like wrestling with information. And I think I learned that formally when I took my vows, refuge vows, in college. Like engaging in reflection in an active way, like, "I don't understand what generosity really is," and "What does it mean to have ultimate generosity?" and, "How does that apply to my life or this particular moment in which I felt that person was being thrifty?" or, you know, whatever. So, this sort of active cognitive process. And then there's maybe, what you can say is a different kind of reflection, which is meditating. Just actually being present to what's there, and tracking it and following it, and being flexible and willing to just follow what's there. Which isn't traditionally reflection, but, in some ways, it's like…uh, maybe more often what I do. When

people say, "Oh! When you reflect on that, what do you think?" And I usually actually just watch, like, "What is happening right now when I'm angry or when I'm grieving?" And then just track what's there...then I'll also say that retreat is a big part of my life. Um, formal retreat practice. So, you know, multiple days to weeks of time set aside for hearing, contemplating, and meditating. So, there's a very intentional push to deepen my reflection about my understanding of my tradition, my behavior, how it interfaces with my profession. You know, moral reflection is part of that, too.

This Buddhist chaplain, after naming the Three Prajñās, elaborated on the relationship between the final two – contemplation and practice – in a manner that typified many of the interviewed chaplains. While reflection was understood by most as a cognitive (or even discursive) process, Buddhist reflection also employs awareness and other mental skills gained from meditation. Buddhist chaplains report that meditative awareness of their own inner thought processes, emotional and physical states, assumptions, and unspoken responses to others provided primary material for later reflection (e.g., reflecting on why I was so angry when I was with that patient or reflecting on why my shoulders tensed when he said that). Moreover, the chaplains in this study all employ meditative awareness for active listening in conversations with careseekers, as well as with themselves. Thus, we see that for Buddhist chaplains, reflection can take on the same kind of meditative flavor as formal, on-the-cushion meditation. As we shall see in the literature review below, this aligns with the explanation of the Three Prajñās found in the earliest Buddhist texts.

Another chaplain referenced the Three Prajñās implicitly in their written reflection, stating: "The issue [the careseeker faced], more or less, has been intuited through study, contemplation and practice of the Dharma." It is not entirely clear if the chaplain is using the Three Prajñās, but "study" is one possible translation of the first type of wisdom (by listening), and the threefold typology does otherwise align. However, even if they did not mean it as an explicit reference, this quote provides evidence that the chaplain may have been exposed to the framework implicitly, as part of the way Buddhism is taught and practiced throughout the world. These two chaplains represent Vajrayana and Theravada perspectives respectively, while the third chaplain, below, represents a Mahayana perspective.

In the first follow-up interview (prior to the development of the Framework), a Buddhist chaplain explicitly described wisdom derived from listening-contemplating-practicing using a Japanese compound term for it:

Participant: At least for myself, my experience, of course, the CPE supervisors emphasize action-reflection-action. But my experience, my interpretation is that Buddhist tradition of, in Japanese, *monshishu*. *Mon*, three Chinese characters. The first one is listening or hearing. The *shi* is thinking or contemplation. And the *shu* is the practice. So, I found that this fits better to me, of course, I've been doing action-reflection-action but in addition, action means a practice, to practice. Reflection is a kind of contemplation. I needed the third one or the first one, listening and learning. It's like learning, studying. So, I've been thinking on reading, rereading Buddhist text to find out their guiding principle, guiding teaching for me as a chaplain. And I've just finished the residency at the end of the August, and I did nine CPE units.
Researcher: Wow. Congratulations!
Participant: Yeah but I found myself...I'm comfortable with myself as

I am now. And at the beginning I was struggling, how can I be a Buddhist at the same time a chaplain? But I'm very much comfortable being a chaplain and a Buddhist.

This chaplain clearly described the Three Prajñās and consciously employed them in response to discomfort with the action-reflection-action model commonly practiced in CPE.

I strongly empathized with this chaplain's statement as I, too, felt uncomfortable with the action-reflection-action model of learning in spiritual care. To some extent, I am still uncomfortable with it. I felt, as this chaplain did, that a period of learning, study, and contemplation needs to precede action. I occasionally reversed the model in my mind, from action-reflection to reflection-action. I wondered if the learning and study that preceded the first action were simply implicit, as though a religious person would naturally study before stepping into the role of a chaplain (or chaplain intern) for the first time. However, this was not my experience in CPE. Some of my peers were first-semester chaplaincy students, starting their rounds as chaplain interns before completing any coursework. I internally questioned this practice at the time, from the vantage point of one who had completed three full years of MDiv curriculum before beginning my CPE training. I felt far more prepared than my peers beginning their own graduate programs. However, I cannot objectively say that, because of my education, I made fewer missteps or that I was any better of a chaplain than they were. Though I had no effective response to the action-reflection-action model at the time, I continued to experience a vague sense of discomfort in its use. I was also extremely thankful that I had studied so long prior to offering spiritual care to others. This chaplain's description of a similar discomfort with the action-reflection-action model and his own accommodation with it through the substitution of monshishu, or wisdom based on listening-contemplating-practicing, struck me almost with a sense of relief. Here was the comfortable formula I had been seeking all this time. It sparked my curiosity in the three Prajñās, which I had formerly taken for granted, and that curiosity led to the work below.

Literature Review of the Three Prajñās

The earliest known appearance of these three terms listed together is in chapter thirty-three of the *Dīgha Nikāya* (Walsche, 1995, p. 486). It appears as a passing reference in a list of threefold concepts intended to be chanted as a mnemonic device retained from the original oral tradition (one presumes). This reference is expanded upon in the *Abhidhamma* (in the *Vibhanga*, ch. 16, section 3, p. 181), but again, only briefly. The *Visuddhimagga*, or "Path of Purification," a fifth-century CE text by Buddhaghosa, includes the threefold framework (Buddhaghosa and Ñāṇamoli, 1999, p. 433-434), but does not expand on it in any significant way beyond the *Abhidhamma*.

It is not until we leave the Pāli texts, which were originally compiled in Sri Lanka, and move north to the Sanskrit *Sarvāstivāda Abhidharma* compiled in northern India, that we find a lengthier treatment of the Three Prajñās within a highly structured soteriological system. The *Sarvāstivāda* school, or "Teaching That All Exists," developed one of the most complex system of Abhidharma in Sanskrit no later than the first century CE, in Sanskrit. Although no longer an extant school of Buddhism, the Sarvāstivāda had a lasting impact on later Mahayana and Vajrayana schools in large part due to the spread of their *Abhidharma* along central Asian trade routes. It is this formulation of the Three Prajñās upon which later Mahayana and Vajrayana authors, including Gompopa (Ray, 2011, p. 49) and Tsongkapa (Gyatso, 2007, p. 207), appear to rely. Modern teachers from all three branches of Buddhism, including Reginald Ray, Padmasiri De Silva, Bhikkhu Bodhi, Geshe Kelsang Gyatso, and others, continue to reference the Three Prajñās when explaining how to learn the Dharma and how meditation relates to study and reflection.

As we can see, the Three Prajñās concept dates to the earliest Buddhist texts, persisted throughout the ages in all three major branches, and remains relevant to modern teachers. Nevertheless, I still characterize it as a 'minor' concept within the Dharma, both in terms of the amount of time most teachers dedicate to exploring it (usually no more than a paragraph or two), and also in terms of its simplicity. I surmise that teachers need only briefly convey the Three Prajñās due to this simplicity. They are easy to understand and apply, which may have also contributed to their broad appeal and longevity.

But what precisely are the Three Prajñās that I repeatedly reference? This literature review will examine the Pāli and Sanskrit roots of the terms, present their earliest explications in the *Dīgha Nikāya*, *Abhidamma*, and *Sarvāstivāda Abhidharma*, cover the minor disagreements in their use, and then summarize how they are employed by modern Buddhist teachers. This literature review, and the one on kalyāṇamitra in the next chapter, can also serve as examples of how to exegete, integrate and apply Buddhist teachings to the new profession of Buddhist chaplaincy. For this reason, I include both literature reviews in their entirety, at the risk of being pedantic. This kind of detailed explication has not been possible in the shorter form publications (i.e., journal articles and book chapters) on Buddhist chaplaincy to date. Nevertheless, it reflects the depth of study many others have previously completed and that many more will complete in years to come.

Defining the Three Prajñās

According to *The Princeton Dictionary of Buddhism*, the Three Prajñās are *śrutamayīprajñā*, *cintāmayīprajñā*, and *bhāvanāmayīprajñā* in Sanskrit, commonly translated as the "wisdom derived from hearing or learning," the "wisdom derived from contemplation or analysis," and the "wisdom derived from meditation or generated from cultivation," respectively (Buswell and Lopez, 2014). In Pāli, they are *sutamayā paññā*, *cintāmaya paññā*, and *bhāvanāmaya paññā*. There is no single common translation for the three terms, as we can see from the table below.

The translations of these terms have commonalities, but little consistency in the literature; even the tenses and forms (ending in -ing or -tion) are inconsistent from one use to the next, though this may be a result of the author's choice of sentence structure. Both Sanskrit and Pāli use compound words, leading to the same middle and ending for all three compounds, *-mayīprajñā* and *-maya paññā*, respectively. (The use of spaces or hyphens between the three terms of the compound is inconsistent across authors in both Sanskrit and Pāli. I have chosen the most commonly used forms.) The middle part, *mayī* or *maya*, is regularly translated as "based on," "derived from," "generated by," "consisting in," or "by means of," indicating a dependent relationship between the first term and the last.[22]

---

22 For the sources of these translations, see *The Princeton Dictionary of Buddhism* (2017); the *Pāli-English Glossary*

Term	Translation from Sanskrit	Translation from Pāli	Modern Usage
śruta / suta ...	Hearing, learning, or study	Learning or heard	Hearing or listening
cintā ...	Reflection or analysis	Reasoning or thinking	Contemplating or reflecting
Bhāvanā ...	Cultivation or meditation	Development, mental development, making be	Meditating or cultivation

Prajñā and *paññā*, Sanskrit and Pāli respectively, are very common words within the Buddhadharma and most frequently translated as "wisdom." However, *The Princeton Dictionary* (2017) points out that this term is perhaps "closer to 'gnosis,' 'awareness,' and in some contexts 'cognition'; the term has the general sense of accurate and precise understanding, but is used most often to refer to an understanding of reality that transcends ordinary comprehension" (p. 655). As such, prajñā is a multivalent term that is deeply explored in a vast array of Buddhist literature. Moving forward, I use Sanskrit when referring to the original terms and the English words "listening, contemplating and practicing" as my preferred translation. Let us examine each compound in turn.

According to *The Princeton Dictionary* (2017), the compound term śrutamayīprajñā is:

> "wisdom derived from hearing [viz., learning]," the first of the three types of wisdoms, which refers to understanding derived from listening to (and, by extension, reading and studying about) the dharma. This type of wisdom provides a grounding for the development of mental attention and concentration, which is crucial for meditative calmness (śamatha). (p. 856)

(1883); glossary of *Ancient Buddhist Texts* at http://www.ancient-buddhist-texts.net; *Understanding the Mind* by Geshe Kelsang Gyatso (2002); Reginald A. Ray, "How to Study the Dharma," *Lion's Roar* (blog) May 1, 2004, https://www.lionsroar.com/how-to-study-the-dharma/; Eric Rainbeau, *Basic Sobriety: Shambhala Buddhism and the Twelve Steps* (2016); and Jamgon Kongtru Lodro Taye, *The Treasury of Knowledge: Book Seven and Book Eight, Parts One and Two, Fundamentals of Buddhist Study and Practice*, trans. Richard Barron (2013); Jew Chong Liew, "The *Sarvāstivāda* Doctrine of the Path of Spiritual Progress" (2009); Buddhaghosa and Bhikkhu Ñāṇamoli, *The Path of Purification*; Gotama Buddha, *Vibhanga: The Book of Analysis*, trans. U. Thittila (1969, repr., Rangoon, Burma: Pali Text Society, 2010)

In other words, it encompasses knowledge gained at an intellectual level from hearing or reading an explanation provided by someone else. This would be analogous to reading in a book that Paris is the capital of France without ever having been to Paris oneself. In the case of the Pāli suttas and Mahayana sutras, the historical Buddha is the purported source. Therefore, when the Buddha states that craving is the cause of suffering, one may accept this statement initially on faith in the awakened wisdom of the Buddha. However, it is not sufficient for one's own awakening to 'know' this truth on the basis of faith alone. One must also investigate it within one's own experience, which brings us to the second type of wisdom.

According to *The Princeton Dictionary* (2017), the meaning of the compound term *cintāmayīprajñā* is:

> "wisdom derived from reflection [or analysis]"; the second of the three types of wisdom…. Building upon what one has learned through Śrutamayīprajñā, the practitioner deepens that knowledge by reflecting upon its significance and its application in understanding the nature of this world and beyond. This reflection may involve a certain level of mental attention and concentration, but not yet full meditative calmness (śamatha). (p. 193)

In other words, this encompasses both reasoned belief and, to some extent, introspection. It would be analogous to reading in several books that Paris is the capital of France, verifying this in conversation with a French citizen, and comparing it to other facts about France. Through this sort of analysis, one develops confidence that Paris is indeed the capital of France, even though one has not yet personally travelled there. One also fully understands the significance and application of this knowledge. If, for example, one wanted to visit the French capital or petition the French government, logically, one might travel to Paris, not to another city. One can recognize images of Paris and would, in theory, also be able to recognize Paris if one suddenly found oneself there. However, this is still an intellectual form of knowledge integrated within a system of knowledge on other topics, some intellectual and some experiential. It still lacks full verification and is prone to error and bias.

Finally, *The Princeton Dictionary* (2017) explains *bhāvanāmayīprajñā* as being:

> lit. "wisdom generated by cultivation"; often translated as "wisdom derived from meditation"; the third of the three types of wisdom.... Although the general understanding is that this third and final manifestation of wisdom comes after, and is largely dependent on, the previous two types, *bhāvanāmayīprajñā* is considered to be the highest of these three because it is the culmination of one's efforts to cultivate the path (*mārga*) and the product of direct spiritual experience. This third type of wisdom is a form of *vipaśyanā*, an understanding of reality at the level of śamatha—profound concentration coupled with tranquility. (p. 113)

This is wisdom derived from a direct experience of truth, experiences primarily achieved through advanced meditation and marked by calm and clarity. In other words, one has now travelled to Paris. One can, with complete confidence and clarity, say that Paris is the capital of France based on first-hand knowledge.

Likewise with the Dharma. It is not enough to memorize the teachings handed down in sacred texts or from learned teachers. Nor is it sufficient to come to a reasoned conclusion through analysis and contemplation. One must test all truths against one's own direct experience. However, this should not be confused with perception. The ancient Buddha and modern epistemologists, philosophers, and psychologists can describe many ways in which our perceptions routinely fail us. Rather than just seeing, hearing, and smelling Paris, one directly experiences Paris through a mind (which is a perceptual filter) purified of all biases (in the forms of craving, aversion and delusion). As a spiritual exercise, meditation plays a primary role in this purification and direct experience. The Buddha achieved enlightenment while meditating under the bodhi tree in India. Meditation has thus been the vehicle for enlightenment for Buddhists for access to ultimate truth for over two thousand years.

The Three Prajñās in Ancient Texts

We can see in these three definitions a clear progression from wisdom based on listening, to contemplating, to practicing. However, in the Pāli literature (*Dīgha Nikāya*, *Abhidhamma*, and *Visuddhimagga*), this order is slightly different, starting with wisdom based on contemplating, then listening, then practicing. The present order, which is ubiquitous in modern Theravada, Mahayana, and Vajrayana literature first occurs in the *Sarvāstivāda Abhidharma*. (In theory, Theravada authors might draw more on the Pāli literature, thus referencing the contemplating-listening-practicing order, but this does not appear to be the case. My survey of contemporary Theravada authors was not exhaustive.) Its prevalence in contemporary literature demonstrates the ongoing impact of the now-extinct Sarvāstivāda school. The order of the terms is important because the terms themselves make epistemological distinctions, document the most prevalent approach to learning the Dharma, and inform normative assumptions about how one ought to progress on the path of awakening.

The Three Prajñās appear in chapter thirty-three of the *Dīgha Nikāya* as follows:

(43) 'Three more kinds of wisdom: based on thought, on learning [hearing], on mental development [meditation] (*cintāmayā panna, sutamayā panna, bhāvanāmayā panna*).

No further explication is found in this chapter, nor do these terms appear elsewhere in the *Nikāya*s.[23]

They are explicated in chapter sixteen of the *Vibhanga*, or "Book of Analysis," part of the Pāli *Abhidhamma*, or compilations of doctrines. (The *Visuddhimagga*, or "The Path of Purification," a later compilation of important Pāli texts by Buddhaghosa, includes this same passage, p. 433-434). This book first summarizes the list of three-fold things as found in the *Dīgha Nikāya* and then explicates each in turn. Per an English translation by U Thittila, for the Three Prajñās it states:

> 768. Therein what is 'wisdom by means of thinking'? (The wisdom) In the spheres of work invented by ingenuity or in the spheres of craft invented by ingenuity or in the branches of science invented by ingenuity or (knowledge that) action is one's own possession or (knowledge that) in conformity with truth matter is impermanent; feeling; :P: perception; :P: mental concomitants; [325] :P: or consciousness is impermanent; that which is similar, inconformity, ability (to comprehend), view, choice, opinion, seeing, ability to apprehend (these) states, is acquired without hearing from others. This is called wisdom by means of thinking.
>
> P = Is impermanent. [sic]
>
> Therein what is 'wisdom by means of hearing'? (The wisdom) In spheres of work invented by ingenuity or in the spheres of craft invented by ingenuity or in the branches of science invented by ingenuity or (knowledge that) action is one's own possession or (knowledge that) in conformity with truth matter is impermanent; feeling; :P: perception; :P: mental concomitants; [325] :P: or consciousness is impermanent; that which is similar, inconformity, ability (to comprehend), view, choice, opinion, seeing, ability to apprehend (these) states, is acquired by hearing from others. This is called wisdom by means of hearing.
>
> All wisdom of one who has attained, is, wisdom by means of development. (*Vibhanga*, p. 424-425)

Here we can see the basis for the reversal of the order of the first two terms. Wisdom developed through contemplation is explored first, perhaps on the assumption that individuals have already given thought to these matters prior to seeking teachings from the Buddha or his disciples. Moreover, it seems that wisdom can arise from reflecting on one's own experience prior to hearing the Dharma from another. Indeed, the Buddha's own life story indicates this is possible. His observation of impermanence, aging, illness, and death spurred him to seek out teachers on the spiritual path. Though he benefited from listening to learned teachers, ultimately, he left them to achieve awakening on his own. The Dharma he discovered was never explained to him by another. Thus, he achieved

---

[23] I am by no means an expert on the Pāli language or the Pāli Buddhist canon. I make this assertion based on a digital search of the *Tripitaka* for the terms "*cintāmayā panna*," "*sutamayā panna*," and "*bhāvanāmayā panna*" and their starting roots, "*cintā*," *suta*," and "*bhāvanā*" in the Wikipitaka database, http://tipitaka.wikia.com/wiki/Main_Page, via Google, and via Google books. I found no other instances of the "*-mayā panna*" construction or the grouping of "*cintā*," "*suta*," and "*bhāvanā*." If other scholars are aware of further instances in the Pāli canon, I urge them to contact me.

it through contemplating and practicing, and he then transmitted it to others, who listened. As a result, many Buddhist scriptures begin with the classic words, "Thus, I have heard [from the Buddha]…"

Moreover, in the *Abhidhamma*, we see the first explanation of what the wisdom gained by contemplation, listening and practicing actually is: the wisdom of the ownership of one's actions (*kamma*) and the wisdom of impermanence (*anicca*). Action, more commonly known by the Sanskrit term 'karma,' follows the laws of causation. That is, through one's own actions, one sows seeds from which one must reap the fruit, primarily the fruit of birth and death in an endless cycle of becoming (*samsara*). The cycle of becoming is understood to both include literal birth and death and also the metaphorical birth and death of various phenomena from moment to moment. The person I am in this moment predicates the person I am in the next moment, but they are not the same. Thus, the cycle of action also exists within an ongoing flow of impermanent phenomena, always rising and falling away based on causes and conditions. That which is impermanent – matter, feeling, perception, mental concomitants, and consciousness – are known as the five aggregates (*skandha*s) that make up a person, that which is constantly changing. The Buddha uses the five aggregates to demonstrate that nowhere within any one of them, nor in their combination, can be found a self (*ātman*), thus demonstrating the doctrine of nonself (*anātman*). Therefore, wisdom is the apprehension of *karma*, impermanence, the compounded nature of phenomena (*pratītyasamutpāda*), and nonself.

While this wisdom can be apprehended for oneself through contemplating one's direct experience (impermanence being the most obvious example in daily life), it is often necessary to learn about them from listening to others, particularly in relation to their subtler concepts, such as nonself. However, to really grasp them, to turn intellectual knowledge into gnosis, one must achieve wisdom through mental cultivation. In both the original order[24] and the later ordering of these terms, we see that wisdom developed through practice comes last and is fundamentally different from wisdom gained through either listening or contemplation.

By the time the Sarvāstivāda school formed (no later than the fifth century CE) and recorded their *Abhidharma* in Sanskrit, the order of the Three Prajñās had become established in the form they are typically presented in today (although it could have been in this order all along) by lineages in all three branches of Buddhism: wisdom derived from listening, contemplating and practicing. Perhaps more important, however, is that the Three Prajñās found a place within a well-defined, systematized five-part path to enlightenment. They were no longer merely mentioned within a list of things, unrelated to other aspects of the Dharma.

The five-part path includes 1) accumulation of prerequisites, 2) preparation, 3) vision, 4) cultivation, and 5) the stage of no further learning.[25] The second stage of the path, *prayoga-mārga*, or preparation, includes the Three Prajñās. I base my understanding of the *Sarvāstivāda Abhidharma* on two dissertations completed at the University of Hong Kong in recent years, one by Liew Jew Chong (2010) and the other by Stephen

---

24 That the order found in the *Dīgha Nikāya* and the *Abhidhamma* is the 'original' order cannot be definitively asserted. The Pāli canon was first written down in Sri Lanka around the same time as the canon was being recorded in Sanskrit in northern India. Both are based on earlier oral traditions. Many parts of the two canons correspond. However, parts of the Sanskrit canon have also been lost or exist only in Tibetan or Chinese translations. The *Sarvāstivāda Abhidharma* could be based on works even older than the Pāli canon, but this cannot be verified. The Sarvāstivāda writing that survives is believed to be younger than the oldest versions of the Pāli *Tripitaka*, however.

25 Though extinct, the (pre-Mahayana) Sarvāstivāda school's influence is still felt, most keenly in the writings of the Madhyamaka scholar Nagarjuna, whose teachings on emptiness (*sunyata*) were most likely a direct refutation of the Sarvāstivāda's intrinsic dharmas, and in the Yogacara school, who adopted the five-part path in their theory of the bodhisattva.

Suen (2009). The former provides the most detail on the Three Prajñās, and the later corroborates Liew's interpretations and explanations. This is some of the only English-language literature to explore the minor concept of the Three Prajñās in detail in relation to the Sarvāstivāda canon. Scholars fluent in Chinese and Sanskrit are invited to verify its veracity for themselves.

In his dissertation, "The Sarvāstivāda Doctrine of the Path of Spiritual Progress: A Study Based Primarily on the *Abhidharma-Mahāvibhāṣā-śāstra*, the *Abhidharmakośa-bhāṣya* and Their Chinese and Sanskrit Commentaries," Liew Jew Chong outlines the path of preparation as the last "worldly" stage before the aspirant enters into the "supramundane" stages of the path. Liew describes how,

> through intensive meditation, he will come to progressively obtain three types of understanding: those derived from hearing (*śrutamayī-prajñā*), reflection (*cintāmayī-prajñā*), and cultivation (*bhāvanāmayī-prajñā*) respectively. The perfection of these understandings culminates in the termination of this stage, marked by the direct-comprehension of the four Noble Truths (*satya-abhi-samaya*, also called the path of seeing '*darśana-mārga*'). (p. 47)

Liew cites a passage from the *Abhidharma-Mahāvibhāṣā-śāstra* describing the Three Prajñās in their ascending order in relation to particular mental and meditative practices:

- *śruta-mayī-prajñā*: the analysis and establishment of the intrinsic and common characteristics of dharma-s, destroying the delusion with regard to existent entities and cognitive objects (*ālambana*)...
- *cintā-mayī-prajñā*: contemplation on the impure, mindfulness of breathing, etc.
- *bhāvanā-mayī-prajñā*: 'warmed-up,' 'summits,' 'receptivities' and the 'worldly supreme dharma-s.' (p. 57-58)

Liew points out that while developing the first type of wisdom, a student is expected to learn from a teacher and study the sacred texts, it is nearly impossible to memorize these texts as they are both abstract and numerous. The Sarvāstivāda school recommended mnemonic devices and mental exercises for summarizing key points in the Dharma and making connections between them. At this stage, understanding is characterized as 'veiled' knowledge, rather than direct comprehension (*abhisamayā*). We see that while meditation is often considered a part of wisdom derived from practicing ('meditation' and 'practice' are often used synonymously in western Buddhist circles), some types of meditation and mental exercises actually occur earlier.

Interestingly, both *śamatha* (tranquility) and *vipaśyanā* (insight) meditation are included in the second type of wisdom, not the third (Liew, 2010, p. 59), though the *Princeton Dictionary* places *vipaśyanā* in the third. Liew states clearly, "The first three [*śamatha* and two-part *vipaśyanā*] of the seven stages of the Path of Preparatory Effort pertain to the understanding derived from reflection" (Liew, 2010, p. 59). Liew provides a useful overview of śamatha and vipaśyanā meditation, which I will not fully explore here. Suffice it to say that śamatha is generally translated as 'calm-abiding' meditation and focuses on the breath to develop steady concentration, while vipaśyanā is generally translated as 'insight' meditation and contemplates different objects, starting with the body, then sensation, thought, and phenomena to understand the nature of things. These two types of meditation are often practiced intermixed, with the meditator going back and forth between them as needed, just as a weightlifter might shift between exercises in a single workout. In the early stages, it is better to cultivate śamatha until the mind is stable, clear, and able to focus for longer periods. The texts Liew studied also note that temperament may contribute to a preference for one over the other. Those who mostly practice śamatha "delight in solitude and shun noisiness...and constantly dwell in quiet places," while those who mostly practice vipaśyanā "delight in studying and reflecting" on the texts (Liew, 2010, p. 62).

Thus, the wisdom derived from contemplation includes the earliest meditative techniques, while the wisdom derived from practice relies on more advanced meditative techniques. The basis of the third wisdom is associated with four advanced meditative techniques, known as 'warmed-up' or *ūṣmagata*, 'summits' or *mūrdhan*, 'receptivities' or *kṣānti*, and 'worldly supreme dharmas' or *laukika-agra-dharma* (Liew, 2010, p. 56). Together, śamatha, two-part vipaśyanā, warmed up, summits, receptivities, and worldly supreme dharmas, make up the seven stages of the path of preparation. The *Abhidharma-Mahāvibhāṣā-śāstra* contains a sort of FAQ section in which the questions of students and the responses of learned masters were recorded. One such question-and-answer states that the meditative stage of 'warmed-up' is not derived from listening or contemplating, but rather from practicing. Another FAQ passage of the *Abhidharma-Mahāvibhāṣā-śāstra* (Liew, 2010, p. 218) relates the Three Prajñās to the *jñānas*, or stages of insight:

> (Question:) Which mundane knowledges are also known as *jñāna-parijñā*? (Answer:) [In the case of] one whose wisdom is derived from listening (*srutamāyi-prajñā*), [this includes practices] like the contemplation of the unique and common-characteristics of the eighteen *dhātu*-s, etc; [in the case of] one whose wisdom is derived from thinking (*cintamāyi-prajñā*), [this includes practices] like sustaining mindfulness of breathing (*ānāpāna-smṛti*), the [cultivation of] the four foundations of mindfulness, etc; [in the case of] one whose wisdom is derived from cultivation (*bhāvanāmāyi-prajñā*), [this is] like the warmed-up (*ūṣmagata*), the summits (*mūrdhan*), receptivity (*kṣānti*), the worldly supreme *dharma* (*laukika-agra-dharma*), etc, and this (ie, the cases of hearing, thinking and cultivation) [together] with *anāsrava-jñāna* are known as *jñāna-parijñā*. (Liew, 2010, p. 177-178)

This passage explains that through listening, one can come to understand the characteristics of the eighteen dhatus, which are elements of sensory experience. Collectively, the eye, ear, nose, mouth, skin, and mind that perceive visual forms, sounds, smells, tastes, touches, and thoughts that produce the mental representations of vision, hearing, smelling, tasting, feeling, and thinking, equaling eighteen elements. In other words, the sense organ, the object, and the subjective perception, times the six sense bases. Understanding how human perception functions is the fundamental basis of Buddhist psychology. Through Buddhist psychology, we can better grasp how the mind interprets (and misinterprets) lived experience. Meanwhile, knowledge gained through contemplation is linked directly to the contemplative techniques of śamatha and vipaśyanā meditation.

Here, we may need to dispense with a common misconception about these types of meditation, which is that they are about "not thinking" or "stopping thoughts." The misconception that meditation is about not thinking or is different from thinking comes about through popular culture and secular repurposing of meditation for stress relief and improved coping skills. In its earliest forms, meditation can indeed provide these benefits. However, this is a little akin to saying the purpose of going to the gym is to get out of the house and see people (rather than becoming healthy and fit). In the long run, if one remains diligent in one's practice and continues to progress, other experiences begin to arise. Not all of these experiences are relaxing or pleasant, but the Dharma holds that they are ultimately beneficial. After all, the Four Noble Truths are the truths of suffering. Looking squarely at the nature of our own suffering and the suffering of others is generally not an exercise in stress relief. However, cultivating this ability through meditation is integral to the Buddhist chaplain's ability to provide spiritual care and self-care, as the chaplains I interviewed affirmed.

Rather, meditation at these stages is about training one's cognition to behave in a certain way. In becoming thoroughly familiar with the patterns of one's thoughts during these forms of meditation, one learns how to focus and direct their thoughts towards particular objects of contemplation, such as the Four Noble Truths and other teachings of the Dharma, in order to 'penetrate' them fully and gain direct insight into their nature. This is accomplished through advanced forms of meditation, including the jñānas, which are part of contemporary Buddhist teachings. (I do not recall hearing about the other four types of meditation in modern teachings, though they may be related to some stages of jñāna; I am not an expert in these forms of meditation, which are quite complex.)

Liew sums up the Sarvāstivāda treatment by stating:

> Having cultivated sufficient merit in the Path of Requisites, the practitioner in the Path of Preparatory Effort practices (1). 'hearing,' (2). 'reflecting' and (3). 'cultivation,' attaining understanding (prajñā) by means of (a) analyzing and categorizing the true dharma-s, (b) non erroneous contemplation relying on this analysis, and (c) cultivation based on this non-erroneous contemplation respectively. ...The culmination of this process is a qualitative transformation of this prajñā to intuitive insight or 'direct comprehension' (abhisamaya), which marks the point of entry into the Path of Seeing. (Liew, 2010, p. 295-296)

We thus see that listening-contemplating-practicing is all for the sake of prajñā, or wisdom. This is understanding beyond words and through direct comprehension. This is going to Paris. The paths that follow are about living in Paris and, when possible, guiding others to Paris.

Stephen Suen, having also focused on the *Sarvāstivāda Abhidharma* in his dissertation, affirms that the primary purpose of listing-contemplating-practicing, which he translates as "listening, reflection and cultivation (*śruta-cintaā-bhāvanā-mayī prajñā*)" [sic], is also the development of pure prajñā, or wisdom – that is, prajñā with no 'outflow' or that which no longer contributes to the generation of karma that holds a being in samsara, the cycle of suffering. Purity can only be reached by passing through impure wisdom; in other words, experiences of ultimate truth must be reached through conventional truth (Suen, 2009, p. 16). It is not clear if this is causal, as in relative truth is a necessary condition for ultimate truth, or if the relationship is simply temporal, as in, one dwells in relative truth prior to the attainment of ultimate truth. Suen verifies the understanding of these terms provided by Liew's dissertation; both works focused on the particular texts in which the wisdom developed by listening, contemplating, and practicing are referenced in the *Sarvāstivāda Abhidharma*, which is easily as massive as the Pāli *Abhidharma*, if not more so. The *Sarvāstivāda Abhidharma* is the last of the ancient texts surveyed in this literature review.

Modern Authors and the Three Prajñās

Many modern authors reference the Three Prajñās, though few provide much detail on them. This section summarizes some contemporary portrayals, though it is not meant to be exhaustive. Tibetan teacher Geshe Kelsang Gyatso refers to the Three Prajñās as methods for "dispelling ignorance," which is the basis of "all mistakes, delusions, and incorrect actions" (Gyatso, 2002, p. 207). Jamgon Kongtru Lodro

Taye, another Tibetan teacher, refers to it as developing "sublime intelligence" (2013, p. 261). Most other contemporary teachers refer to them for developing wisdom. The contemporary teachers surveyed all used the order of the wisdoms as they appear in the *Sarvāstivāda Abhidharma*, rather than the earlier Pāli texts – wisdom based on hearing, contemplating, and practicing.

One of the most straightforward and detailed articles on the topic is by Tibetan teacher Reginald Ray published in May 2004 in *Lion's Roar* magazine, a popular Buddhist monthly. Ray translates the Three Prajñās as wisdom based on "hearing, contemplating and meditating." The first wisdom involves the intellectual study of teachings to develop "a precise and detailed knowledge of traditional doctrines." One 'hears' or reads to learn what the tradition has to say on a topic (Ray, 2004). According to Tsongkhapa, an ancient Tibetan teacher, listening sheds light on the path (Gyatso, 2002, p. 207). Taye draws on the work of Vasubandhu, a central Asian monk of the fourth or fifth century CE who wrote extensively on the *Sarvāstivāda Abhidharma*, to describe how, when hearing the teachings, one "has only the words" as the object of one's study (Taye, 2013, p. 261), suggesting memorization and systematization. Ray's characterization is not passive; he includes discussing, debating, and academic activities such as exams under the first prajñā (Ray, 2004).

Bhikkhu Bodhi, an American teacher in the Thai Forest (Theravada) tradition, refers to this as 'learning' that provides a basis for wisdom by clarifying the principles into which one develops insight through mental training (Bodhi, *Dharma Reflections*, 2016, p. 160). Here, Bodhi is saying that not all topics are equal in relation to developing wisdom from listening, contemplating, and practicing. Indeed, when we hear what is unwise, contemplate in ways that are unwise, and practice in ways that are unwise, we develop the very opposite of the goal. This is much more likely if we are attempting to develop wisdom based on listening, contemplating, and practicing entirely on our own. Likewise, Taye (2013) advises that one who wishes to develop wisdom must "mentally distance themselves from inappropriate trains of thought and other distractions" (p. 261). For this reason, Gyatso, Ray and others advise finding a teacher and a sangha to guide one's practice of listening, contemplating and practicing. Thus, in The Three Prajñās Framework for Reflection in Spiritual Care, stage two: student plays a critical role in developing one's ability to provide spiritual care and act as a spiritual friend to those in need, and one's ability is improved through the company of spiritual friends.

Modern teachers are clear that wisdom developed from listening precedes that developed from contemplating, although this process may be iterative rather than linear. Ray states, "Once the mastery of the literal teachings has been attained, the practitioner progresses to the second prajñā, 'contemplating.'" I wonder how literally he means this linear progression. The Buddhist teachings are vast. Even after over a decade of serious study, including two graduate degrees, I could scarcely claim mastery over the teachings, although I do consider myself to possess a level of fluency with them. It is for this reason that the Sarvāstivāda recommend various mnemonic devices, mental exercises, and particular topics of focus (i.e., the eighteen dhatus) as helpful in developing wisdom based on listening. Here also, a modern teacher can start a conversation about the nature of pedagogy.

Another common pedagogical tool, Bloom's Taxonomy of Learning, orders various cognitive processes from the starting point of first obtaining information, through intermediate stages such as analysis and application, into the so-called highest forms of cognition, including synthesis and creation (Anderson and Krathwohl, 2001, p. 27-29). Bloom's Taxonomy has been criticized as being artificially linear. Experienced teachers point out that students must often apply a skill before they fully understand it or before they can evaluate its implications and limitations, although application comes further along on the taxonomy than understanding or evaluation (Stratton, 2000, p. 40).

Likewise, we could wonder how one could possibly 'master' all of the teachings prior to contemplating them. Is contemplation not an integral step towards full understanding? I suspect Ray may agree, though the short nature of an article in a magazine for general audiences, including those new to Buddhism, may have precluded this level of nuance. The Pāli texts also implicate a reversed order, or perhaps, when considered together with the Sarvāstivāda texts, we can infer a back-and-forth between the first two Prajñās in the development of wisdom. Regardless, most modern teachers list wisdom based on contemplating second.

In his article, Ray characterizes contemplation as seeking the meanings of the teachings in one's life and reflecting on how they relate to daily experience. Taye refers to two different schools of thought on the second prajñā, one of which, the 'Particularists,' characterizes it as understanding both the words and their meaning, while the other, per Vasubandhu, holds that one cannot simultaneously grasp both the words and the meaning, as the latter is beyond words and concepts. Rather, wisdom based on contemplating uses "reasoning to arrive at a definitive conclusion concerning the meaning of what one has heard," before proceeding on to grasp the meaning itself in the third prajñā (Taye, 2013, p. 261).

Ray sees this as a progression from abstract concepts to the "felt meaning" of psychologist John Welwood (incidentally, another example of the 'psychologization' of American Buddhism documented by David McMahan in his book, *The Making of Buddhist Modernism*). This difference is akin to learning individual dance moves then combining them into a ballet. Ray (2004) writes, "With the second prajñā, we begin to see that terms and ideas that we had at first understood only on a conceptual level hold deep and far-reaching meaning for us." In some cases, we already possess deep knowledge of insights conveyed by the Dharma, as the Pāli *Abhidhamma* conveys. Through listening, we often experience recognition and gain a new vocabulary for something we have already observed. This is precisely the beauty of the Dharma – it describes a reality we all experience (or so it claims) and one that we may have been contemplating for quite some time before hearing our first Dharma talk. This is particularly true in the case of suffering, which every living human knows from the day of their birth (if not before). In other cases, Ray is entirely correct. With less intuitive concepts such as śūnyatā (emptiness) or anātman (non-self), we must first learn them and then look for them within our own experience. Even with suffering, which we all know, it may take years or decades to fully understand its pervasive subtleties. "Consider the teachings about death," Ray (2004) encourages us:

> We read over and over that death is real and that comprehending this is an important inspiration and motivator to practice. Although we are continually exposed to this idea, our understanding tends to remain purely conceptual and we resist really letting it "hit home." Then some external circumstance intervenes – someone close to us dies or we ourselves receive a real scare.

In Ray's description of the wisdom derived from contemplation, I hear affinities with Richard Osmer's writing about episodes of being "brought up short" that often spur processes of practical theological reflection (Osmer, 2008, p. 43). This is often the case with our careseekers, many of whom are directly dealing with issues of illness, injury, aging, and death. Although none are ignorant of these realities, many have somehow managed to go much of their lives without giving serious thought to the fact that these things will happen to them or those they hold most dear. They have listened, but they have not contemplated.

Buddhism, according to Ray, does not wait on circumstance to spur contemplation of difficult topics. Rather, one actively encourages contemplation of these painful truths using "various tools and techniques to help us penetrate the superficiality of our own ignorance and resistance." While we have used the term 'contemplation' in a generic sense to this point, as in 'reflecting,' 'thinking about,' 'pondering' and 'observing,' we can also use it in a more technical sense. Ray refers to specific contemplations or meditative exercises used within Buddhism to integrate certain spiritual insights, such as teachings on impermanence, death, and non-self, in ways that result in wisdom. The chaplains in this study directly referenced some of these contemplations. For example, one chaplain referred to contemplating the "repulsiveness of the body," which is designed to reduce clinging to the body and help realize non-self. Ray points out that many of these exercises can be uncomfortable, if not painful, but nevertheless beneficial, even necessary for spiritual progress. Many chaplains meditated on mettā (loving-kindness) or karuna (compassion) on behalf of careseekers, which are also specific contemplations. The second prajñā includes contemplation in both senses, as in general reflection and as in specific meditative exercises designed to integrate understanding or cultivate certain skillful beliefs, virtues, attitudes, and habits.

This could create some confusion with the third prajñā, which I have translated as 'practicing,' but which many Buddhist teachers translate as 'meditating.' Bhāvanāmayīprajñā is not meditation itself or a particular type of meditation, but rather a wisdom that develops *from* meditative practices. Gyatso (2002) refers to this as the wisdom that "eradicates" ignorance, while the previous two Prajñās only "weaken" ignorance (p. 207). Taye (2013) describes how, at this stage, one "meditate[s] one-pointedly on the meaning of what one has [previously] contemplated" (p. 261).

In general, the earlier forms of meditation are considered prerequisites for stabilizing the mind so that more advanced forms of meditation can cultivate this wisdom. Śamatha is a prerequisite to stabilize the mind prior to vipaśyanā, or insight meditation, and other advanced practices. One way to distinguish whether or not a meditative practice belongs to the second or third prajñā depends on the aspects of the mind it engages – a dualistic, conventional mind or a nonconceptual, ultimate mind. Contemplative meditation focuses on particular concepts and teachings rather than the breath or body. Concepts, such as compassion, when repeatedly contemplated begin to evoke feelings within the body and certain thoughts such as "May all beings be free from suffering" become habitual. This distinguishes when wisdom based on contemplating becomes wisdom based on practicing. Contemplating during meditation is still in the realm of concepts, words, and languages, while practicing during meditation transcends the realm of concepts, words, language, and dualism to approach direct apprehension of 'true reality.'

Thus, the third prajñā is not 'meditation' (if it were, enlightenment would be much more commonplace), but rather "an experience of unconditioned reality, the ultimate nature of our own awareness that undergirds and holds all relative knowledge and experience," per Ray, that is reached through meditation, during meditation, or as a result of meditation. When this happens, everything with which we previously struggled falls away. True insight results in lasting changes in attitudes and behaviors. The very way we are in the world is altered. However, we need not wait until that moment of insight to change our behavior. Change will be slower and more incremental without it, but in the interim, we can still practice or act in accord with the more enlightened nature we all possess, but seldom glimpse.

In the traditional understanding of the Three Prajñās, the primary thing we practice is meditation itself, just as the Buddha practiced meditation before, during, and after his enlightenment. Ray continues, "The practice of the third prajñā is to rest and remain in the meditative state at ever-deeper levels and for increasing periods of time. One lives one's life ever more fully as an expression of unbounded awareness." He thus implicitly affirms that the third prajñā is not only a matter of meditation. It affects every aspect of one's life.

Ray concludes his article by saying, "Each of the three prajnas [sic] is necessary to the others; none can be skipped or short-changed." This is true, as I explore further below, but it does not mean the Prajñās are simply linear. Rather, they are both cumulative and recursive. Just listening and being able to repeat back what one knows can lead to an intellectual pride devoid of fruits. Contemplating without listening to knowledgeable sources can result in mistaken views, rumination, or going around in circles, especially when trapped in negative thought processes such as greed, hatred, and delusion. Practicing ungrounded by listening or contemplating can often lack a sense of motivation, discipline, or direction. Any one by itself will not result in wisdom. Thus, all three are necessary and generally proceed in order from listening to contemplating to practicing.

Yet, one cannot simply satisfy oneself with listening once, then contemplating once, then practicing once. For example, having read the *Way of the Bodhisattva* by Śāntideva at different points in my life, I gain new understanding each time. When I first read it, years ago, I glossed over some of the sections I now find to be the most profound because I had not yet sufficiently practiced and did not yet possess the kind of direct experiences that would help me understand them. Reading it again now (and probably again in the future), I am fascinated by the same passages as though they were entirely new and engage in renewed contemplation for their meaning in my life – which further energizes my practice. Thus, I know from my own experience that the Three Prajñās are, as Ray asserts, integral to one another. However, I experience them as more recursive than linear.

Likewise, the chaplains in this study continue to read, study, and listen to Dharma talks, while also reflecting on their meanings for themselves and as part of a sangha with teachers and peers, while also continuing their meditative practices, both on a daily basis and through more intensive retreats. Therefore, the Three Prajñās Framework for Spiritual Care is further classified into four stages, described below. Briefly, these are self, student, chaplain, and kalyāṇamitra. In the culminating stage, one has developed the wisdom to aid others in listening, contemplating, and practicing through the recursive process of doing it in various contexts.

The Three Prajñās Framework of Spiritual Care

The Three Prajñās Framework of Spiritual Care is comprised of wisdom developed through three tasks: listening, contemplating, and practicing. Each task is enacted at four different stages, each an application of the same principles to a more specific context than the previous. These stages have been abbreviated to self, student, chaplain, and kalyāṇamitra. The first stage, self, is concerned with the chaplain-to-be's own spiritual practice as an individual. The second stage, student, places their spiritual practice in a relational context with others, particularly teachers, guides, mentors and spiritual friends. The third stage, chaplain, is concerned with the chaplain's ability to provide spiritual care for others and grow in skill and capacity. The fourth stage, kalyāṇamitra, is concerned with the chaplain's ability to facilitate spiritual growth and theological reflection for careseekers of various worldviews and contexts; essentially, the kalyāṇamitra helps careseekers advance on their spiritual path. Each stage corresponds to a role described by the Buddhist chaplains I studied. Various roles predominate at different times of life, but they generally tend to progress in this order. No previous stage is ever fully left behind, and all chaplains in the study, who ranged from interns in their first unit of CPE to board-certified chaplains, demonstrated all four stages to some degree.

Movement through this matrix is both from left to right and from top to bottom. The first and second levels may also be reversed or intermingled, as many come to their spiritual or religious practice through others, such as being raised within a religious community. In the case of at least one participant in this study, it was not until deciding to become a chaplain that they also began serious religious practice in service of that goal, though they had been nominally Buddhist their entire life. In most cases, however, the third stage is a natural outgrowth of progressing through the first two stages, and the fourth stage is a culmination of the previous three.

It is worth noting that while these stages all reference the roles of the chaplain, they can be traversed by anyone. In an earlier study (Sanford, 2013), I collected many examples of spiritual care being provided by non-professional spiritual caregivers (e.g. nurses, parents, friends, but not chaplains or clergy). One is more likely to receive quality spiritual care from a trained chaplain, just as one is more likely to receive a quality meal from a trained chef, but spiritual care is something anyone can do and many frequently provide without labelling it as such.

Likewise, the chaplain experiences a role reversal in relation to their own spiritual mentors, teachers, and supervisors, in which the chaplain becomes the careseeker for whom spiritual growth and reflection is facilitated by another. The table below describes these levels in relation to the chaplain and the careseeker, but one could easily substitute any two parties. This framework may also be applicable to other forms of Buddhist-inspired care, such as therapy or social work, though the

Stages	Tasks of the Three Prajñās of Spiritual Care		
	Listening	Contemplating	Practicing
Self	Listening, reading, studying, learning on one's own	Considering, analyzing, reflecting on one's own; learning śamatha and vipaśyanā	Meditating, including jñāna practice; realization of the Four Noble Truths and Noble Eightfold Path
Student	Listening, reading, studying, learning as directed by a teacher or formal course of study	Considering, analyzing, and reflecting through dialogue with others, especially spiritual friends; working with a meditation teacher	Communal meditation and practice; Three Refuges (Buddha, Dharma, Sangha)
Chaplain	Actively listening to careseeker(s) and one's own responses while providing spiritual care	Considering, analyzing, reflecting, and learning to provide spiritual care; using meditative skills in caregiving	Practicing spiritual care and self-care; applying compassion and wisdom, esp. non-self
Spiritual Friend	Inviting careseeker(s) to share and facilitating the careseeker's ability to 'listen' to the sources of their own wisdom	Inquiring to help careseeker consider, analyze, reflect, and learn about their situation	Assessing careseekers and implementing appropriate spiritual care interventions; Spiritual friendship

implications would need to be carefully evaluated by professionals in those respective fields.

In the following descriptions, each prajñā at each stage is examined three ways: 1) the intention that motivates the chaplain, 2) the nature of the task undertaken, and 3) the wisdom that develops as a result. This follows another classic Buddhist framework – ground, path, and fruition. When developing wisdom based on listening at the stage of 'self,' what is the intention of the participant, what do they do, and what is the outcome? Likewise, I explore wisdom developed from contemplating and practicing at that stage, and with wisdom based on listening, contemplating, and practicing at the stages of student, chaplain, and kalyāṇamitra. Each stage is explicated with quotations from the chaplains I interviewed, including some longer passages to provide thick description.

Intention (centanā), or why someone does something, is an important factor in the development of wisdom (or any action, as per the Buddhist theory of karma) and can also be understood in relation to Right Intention, an aspect of the Noble Eightfold Path. Intention documents what chaplains are trying to do and why. This is the 'ground' on which we stand. Task documents how chaplains described what they are doing. This is the 'path' we walk. The outcomes or 'fruition' documents what wisdom they report developing as a result, either explicitly (because I did X, I realized Y) or implicitly (I did X; later, I realized Y). Fruition attempts to capture the nature of the wisdom developed, in respect to both its conventional (i.e., practical) and ultimate aspects. Intention, task, and outcome define each prajñā at each stage.

Stage One: Self

At this stage, the participant's spiritual journey begins with the intention to seek meaning in their life, sometimes in response to a particular circumstance or event and often for the purpose of alleviating a specific form of suffering; at other times, the participant stumbles across a book or idea at sparks their interest. The tasks they undertake include listening and reading, consuming articles, books, magazines, podcasts and audio recordings, attending talks and meditation training, or taking classes (though not as a formal course of study). One participant shared a particularly poignant story of finding a book that helped her at a critical point in her life:

> I became very, very ill a number of months later, and it was at that time that I began just practicing on my own in Nicaragua…. I found a book by Thich Nhat Hanh and, you know, I just started meditating on my own, listening to Dharma talks, um, from like Gil Fronsdal and other people, you know, like podcasts.

Chaplains I interviewed discussed all kinds of topics from the content of these books, articles, podcasts, and talks, including suffering (dukkha), interbeing, death, grief, pain, illness, anxiety, anger, fear, diversity and race/ethnicity, identity, and how to be "a Buddhist in a Christian-centric environment." Reading and listening helped the not-yet-chaplains "see [reality] for yourself," "grapple with questions," "transform that grief," "alleviate human suffering," and "informed me [in a way] relevant to my work." They also read books on religious traditions other than Buddhism or books comparing Buddhism with other religious traditions, as well as secular works (e.g., psychology, medicine, etc.).

The outcomes of listening at this stage includes strengthening Right Intention (the intention to do what is wholesome, beneficial, and skillful) and Right View (to know what is wholesome or not wholesome, beneficial or harmful, skillful or unskillful), often based in a burgeoning sense of curiosity as to the beneficial effects of various ideas. Wisdom based on listening at this stage gives the chaplain a vocabulary to start talking about suffering and problems within their lives (though they may yet lack direct comprehension of the full meaning), which is helpful for the next task: contemplating.

Through contemplating, the not-yet-chaplains intend to understand what they have heard or read and, more importantly, verify it against their own experiences, make sense of their lives, and use this knowledge to bring relief to themselves or others. One participant said, "My problems had to do with my thought processes," and pursued Buddhism as a solution. With this intention, they go about contemplating through four primary tasks: thinking, writing, conversing, and learning meditation. One participant shared how a lifelong journaling practice evolved as they encountered Buddhist teachings:

> I've had an off and on journaling practice, or journaling was one of the ways I reflect and I, so you know, before I was Buddhist, or spiritual, I guess, or meditating, or reflecting, I was living. And then, let's say, the age of eighteen, maybe my journaling starts to be more spiritually reflective, you know. That would include looking back at when I was, let's say, fifteen and in high school. So there were some amount of retrospective considering. I think that, I mean, I'm thinking back to when I was seventeen and eighteen and journaling and thinking about how the world worked and why there was poverty and why there were insiders and outsiders. That was some of the first, kind of like, late-adolescent content of my reflection, I suppose. Maybe that was where existential and strictly spiritual overlap…I might've, I think I felt in my early twenties that when I would journal there were these kind of new realizations and important things, and more new learning, and I suppose thus, from, from early to mid-twenties or late twenties I might've been discovering [the Dharma], and maybe from late twenties to late thirties now I'm more like digesting things.

The chaplains-to-be also began meditating to cultivate focus, stability, and the clarity of mind necessary for the other tasks. The outcomes of contemplating at this stage are characterized as development or self-development, awareness or self-awareness, and mindfulness. In other words, having gained a new vocabulary to understand suffering and various other phenomena, chaplains now become aware of how those phenomena appear in their lives. Wisdom at this stage is still largely conceptual, and the interviewees described dualistic subject-object relationships between "I/me/mine/my practice" and "the Dharma/Buddhism/the teaching." Through being able to name and understand their relationships with other forms of phenomena and experience, they start to gain insight into causes and conditions, outcomes and effects that will, in the next stage, transcend names and labels.

Chaplains-to-be begin practicing with the intention of alleviating suffering in their own lives and those of others. They described this as a process of "living more fully" or "coming back into balance." Practicing includes meditation, chanting, services, yoga, and integrating the mental skills and viewpoints generated by these activities (e.g., focus, awareness, compassion) into daily life. One chaplain said, "Practice is everyday life." Chaplains-to-be implemented the other two aspects of the Noble Eightfold Path, śīla, or moral behavior, and samādhi, or concentration developed from meditation. Śīla is an important foundation for all forms of prajñā and also an outcome of prajñā, as moral behavior is a hallmark of the wise. While the details of what and how the chaplains-to-be practiced at this stage are few (interview questions focused more on later stages; this could be a useful area for further research), the fruits of this practice were described as integral to their later work as chaplains, especially in relation to understanding suffering. One chaplain said:

> So, uh, I've been meditating in my, nowadays in my own way. It's kind, um, sometimes casually, like mindfulness, and sometimes, um, śamatha, ...the meditation practice has helped me a lot to being [sic] present and especially it's interesting that the chaplain's training, based on western Christianity or Judaism, emphasizes a presence. Nonanxious and nonjudgmental presence. Just like, it just like Buddhist practice of nonattachment. So, the being mindful helps me a lot as being a chaplain, in sometimes difficult situation... meditation is the core.

The chaplains developed wisdom into the pervasive and interconnected nature of suffering, including the interrelation of human suffering.

For most (including both Asians and Asian-Americans raised with Buddhism), the first stage began during the teenage years or adulthood (for some, as late as their fifth decade). Two chaplains I interviewed (of the thirteen) were raised by devout Buddhist families in predominantly Buddhist countries and became students of the Dharma as children; for them, this stage was brief or practically indistinguishable from the second stage. For both, at some point, listening, contemplating, and practicing resulted in formal renunciation to become monastics.

To summarize, during the stage of 'self,' one experiences the framework as shown in the table below.

Stage Two: Student

Chaplains-to-be enter stage two with the intention of learning from others, through others, and with others. For those who were raised by a Buddhist family or in a Buddhist culture, this may mean either engaging more deeply with their root tradition or exploring other Buddhist traditions before finding a sangha and teacher with whom they feel comfortable. For others, this may mean going directly to graduate school and only later finding a sangha and teacher. One chaplain described how, after years of practicing with a particular sangha, they needed more:

> I just felt like it wasn't enough. Like going to temple on a Friday night wasn't enough. I felt like it was just socializing for me, so I sought out,

The Three Prajñās Framework of Spiritual Care experienced as 'self'			
Phase	Intention	Task	Outcomes
Listening	Seeking meaning, esp. in relation to distressing life events	Reading books and articles; listening to podcasts and talks	Developing Right Intention and Right View
Contemplating	Understanding the meaning; comparing to one's own experiences	Thinking, writing, conversing, and learning meditation	Development of awareness and/or mindfulness
Practicing	Alleviating suffering for self and others	Integrating with daily life (e.g., meditation, chanting, services, yoga, or virtues); the Noble Eightfold Path	Understanding suffering and other Dharmic concepts

so I took some classes to learn about basic Buddhism again. I went to different monasteries to learn about meditation. I felt like it, there wasn't enough depth at the center that I was at. It was more like a young adult, you know like a young adult ministry group, you know? So…I had a lot of deep questions about meaning and purpose and I think that a lot of, uh, the sutra, the teachings answer some of my questions.

Though they may not have yet realized it, chaplains-to-be were seeking spiritual friends to help them on their journey. Tasks performed at this stage include both sangha-based and college-based education, either sequentially or simultaneously. Their course of study was directed and progressive. It was aimed toward designated pedagogical goals and included material the student might not otherwise encounter on their own. One chaplain narrated how they developed wisdom based on listening as a student:

> I think it was that first semester in divinity school and I started practicing with a Tibetan lama who was there in Cambridge and kind of immersing myself in the text, in the reading, in the sutras. No, you know, I think it was my second, I think it was my second semester at that point. Anyway, it doesn't matter, but…because I was studying with, you know, Janet Gyatso and Charles Hallisey and some really just amazing scholars who are also deep practitioners, and really kind of teaching the Dharma, you know, and that was amazing and it was totally a deep dive into Buddhist study.

The fruition of listening as a student includes deeper knowledge of the Dharma, as well as wisdom derived from listening and being listened to in relationships with others. This wisdom takes the form of confidence, diligence, and a sense of welcome and identity within the Buddhist communities. One participant described this as being "part of the living tradition" that is "passed down face-to-face." They continued:

> There's really something kind of incredible that can happen in that face-to-face transmission with another human being and that, you know, being very powerful. There's something else that can happen there. The retreat [with my teacher] a couple years ago was on Prajñāpāramitā and one thing that he said that was kind of interesting was that Prajñāpāramitā is intimacy.

The perfection of wisdom, prajñāpāramitā, is intimacy with another human being. This is the wisdom developed from listening to and with others, which is not available merely from reading and listening to podcasts or teachings delivered by a teacher with whom one has no relationship.

The intention of contemplating at this stage is also relational; it is primarily to check one's understanding against the understanding of others to further develop Right View that aligns both with the Dharma and with the nature of one's own experience, including the parts of one's experience that are not self-evident and need the assistance of spiritual friends to be brought to one's attention.

The tasks involved included reflecting, writing, journaling, and sharing on assigned topics with defined groups (e.g., classmates); working in assigned dyads; talking with friends, spouses and teachers; participating in group meditation and retreats; participating in communal services, chanting, and other practices; participating in "process groups"; and receiving feedback and direction in relation to one's meditation, chanting, or kōan practice from a teacher. Topics for contemplation in this stage include fundamental Buddhist topics such as suffering, aging, illness, and death; questions about one's identity, intention, hope, impact, habits, learning, fear, "edges," and other "stuff that I might sift through and work through from [a] Buddhist place"; how to pause, meditate, transition, process emotions, maintain equanimity or peace; how to cultivate awareness, receptivity, openness, maturity, insight, and compassion; how and why a particular lineage or tradition practices in a certain way; how the teachings were systematized, understood, and passed down; the history of a lineage; and also how to relate to other religious traditions, including how to understand their perspectives and how to explain or "translate Buddhist perspectives to non-Buddhists.

The fruition of contemplating with others was particularly rich for the chaplains and many were eager to share them. One chaplain described an aspect of their graduate studies that involved unstructured peer group discussion:

> Well, part of the MDiv training that we went though, the, the training we went through for the Masters of Divinity was a little thing called process group. They've saved my bacon so much, during that whole process, …getting that whole degree. That, it's something that, 'til this day I've tried and tried and tried to get my peers [after college] to start working on…. In a lot of cases, yes, it was very humbling, and it was very changing. It changed how I operated and how I looked at things because I was able to take in perspectives that I didn't have. You know, because my vision is what it is, I don't get to see what other people see. So, having that perspective, you know, the multiple perspectives that were not mine, allowed me insight I otherwise would not be able to obtain.

The critical aspect of developing wisdom based on contemplating in stage two is that it is dialectical. It is based on discussion, debate, and even challenge. The primary results of this dialectical process were: 1) stronger and more articulate understanding, and 2) clearer awareness of one's own biases, patterns, and various subconscious mental and emotional phenomena, as pointed out by others.

At this stage, practicing both deepens and takes on a communal element. The intention at this point is to find a common identity and to establish oneself authentically within something larger than the self. Many tasks help forge a sense of shared identity, including services, chanting, group meditation, volunteer work at temples and centers, and discussion. Retreat practice was prominent for several chaplains. More than one chaplain discussed the power of vows, including refuge vows and bodhisattva vows. The vow itself is a form of practice, regularly recited, chanted, or reaffirmed, particularly in a communal setting. Other practices referenced included yoga, tai chi, kōan practice, and various forms of meditation. At least one chaplain referred to the practice of communal living as part of an intentional community and others implied it in reference to living in various Buddhist communities on either a short- or long-term basis.

The fruition of wisdom developed from practicing at this stage is twofold. First, it imparts awareness of the lineage and context for practice and place within that lineage. One chaplain described the relationship between practice and one's spiritual community as that of receiving:

> In the Insight meditation practice, it seems that the lineage, I mean the lineage is one of receiving. Not so much receiving the lineage, but receiving your own practice and your own understanding as the lineage. I mean the lineage itself is the practice of self-understanding. So my own

experience is intimately tied to practicing and being authorized to teach within that lineage.

Practicing does not occur in a vacuum. Even among eclectic practitioners, each practice exists within particular lineages. In stage one, one may be almost unaware of the lineage while starting to practice. In stage two, they are aware of the origins and reasons behind those practices.

Second, the fruition of practicing at this stage deepens one's understanding of Dharmic principles. While insights in stage one focused on the pervasive nature of suffering in their own lives, at this point, chaplains-to-be began to describe insights associated with prajñā, including the interconnectedness and interrelation of all beings, including people; the realization of emptiness and dependent co-arising, the Two Truths (discussed further below); an awakened mind, bodhi, and bodhicitta, the cultivation of virtues such as equanimity and compassion; understanding the deep commitment necessary for ongoing practice; a deeper understanding of suffering and the ways to alleviate suffering individually, relationally, and socially; and deeper understanding of one's own moral and ethical behavior (śīla) in relation to others and the world. One chaplain described the relationship between practicing and virtue:

> Well, being a Buddhist and specifically practicing the Buddhist divine abode of equanimity is kind of really key to what I do. It allows me to operate in...which I show compassion to all people, to all beings as equally as I possibly can while, you know, kind of being in this milieu of stuff going back and forth, and people arguing and I utilize the equanimity that Buddhism, you know, kind of trumpets. I use that to build bridges between people. That's probably the key way in which I'm utilizing my faith in my practice.

The Three Prajñās Framework of Spiritual Care experienced as 'student'			
Phase	**Intention**	**Task**	**Outcomes**
Listening	Learning from, through, and with others	Formal education, sangha- and/or college-based with formal student-teacher and classmate/sangha relationships	Deeper understanding of Dharma; confidence and identity in relationship to community; intimacy
Contemplating	Checking one's understanding and gaining insight from others	Dialectical learning through reflecting, writing, journaling, sharing, and receiving feedback	Stronger and more articulate understanding; awareness of one's own biases, patterns, and subconscious phenomena
Practicing	Build common identity within something larger than self	Dharma services, chanting, group meditation, volunteering, discussion, retreats, vows, and/or communal living	Awareness of lineage and history; understanding of interconnectedness/emptiness, awakened mind, and relational morality

At this stage, the wisdom that develops from practicing involves both deeper and more direct insight into many of the basic teachings – insight at a nonconceptual level, a level of ultimate truth beyond words. This imparts confidence in the teachings through direct experience. It becomes an unshakable faith that needs no further explanation or justification, nor does it need to be explained to others.

To summarize, during the stage of 'student,' one experiences the framework as shown on the facing page.

Stage Three: Chaplain

At stage three, chaplains and chaplain interns listen with the intention of serving others, but perhaps more critically, they listen with the intention of learning *how* to serve others. This involves both listening to others and listening to themselves (skills honed during stage two) within the new context of spiritual caregiving. Their first task is to listen to the situations and stories of careseekers. Their second task is to listen to themselves, to their reactions and responses while working with careseekers. They also practice listening with multidisciplinary teammates, CPE supervisors, and peers, gaining valuable feedback on their work and listening to their own responses as they receive that feedback. For example, one chaplain shared the conceptual mechanisms that allowed them to reflexively listen to others and self at the same moment:

> Understanding the five aggregates gave me a method for identifying and being helpful in the face of my coworker's intense and fluctuating thoughts, feelings and sensations. This model of self-experience is also helpful in tracking and attending to my *own* constellation [sic] of experiences in caregiving encounters. For example, I noticed that after talking to my coworker at length, I started to feel sleepy and have physical sensations of heaviness in my chest, which then limited my energy for patient care. This awareness prompted me to set boundaries regarding the duration of time spent with my coworker, and also helped me attend to my own grief surfaced by our conversations.

In instances such as these, it may be difficult to distinguish between listening and contemplating. One chaplain referred to a method from meditation that may be helpful in this regard. When listening inwardly, they simply listen and "note" what is happening, without getting caught up in analyzing why it is happening. "Noting" or labeling fleeting thoughts and feelings is a common technique in śamatha and vipaśyanā that several chaplains deployed. One chaplain described it as:

> It's called basic attendance for keeping a, um, keeping a consistent attention on the person in a non-judgmental and like loving way…you know, staying present…watching my mind. That's a, might have to suspend somethings, I don't know. I might have like an internal monologue going on, like, "Oh, I remember I have to go here and I have to go do this thing. Talk to this person and remember to hand this thing in." Meanwhile, this person's talking, so you're learning to just like notice that and just kinda suspend it, being able to come back to it. Make the mental note.

This is but one ability employed during listening with careseekers that is based on a skill honed through meditation.

The fruition of wisdom developed by listening includes "ministry of presence." Chaplains repeatedly described the qualities of presence necessary to listen to careseekers well, including to "see things as they are," being "comfortable being silent with someone," "be aware of my emotions," "notic[ing] what's there," having unconditional positive regard, and being nonjudgmental, loving, compassionate, and without agenda were all repeatedly mentioned (and explored further in Chapter 7). They cultivated their ability to listen through all manner of suffering and to remain present, grounded, and emotionally, mentally, and physically healthy without getting "hooked" or caught up in the careseeker's distress or their own analysis. Wisdom that comes from listening at this stage involves active (even joyful) engagement with the work, while also being nonattached to the outcome.

The intention of contemplating at stage three is to learn from past experiences how to become a better chaplain and accompany careseekers as a spiritual friend. This intention is twofold. First, chaplains intend to seriously reflect on their work in order to provide better spiritual care to those in need. Second, chaplains intend to integrate their work as spiritual caregivers with their own path to awakening. When asked if anything about the work surprised them, one participant shared:

> **Participant 010:** Um, actually the emphasis on one's own awakening. That's been the most like, "Oh, right! Shit, that's important!" [laughs]
> **Researcher:** [laughs]
> **Participant 010:** ...so much of the work is like, "How do I offer myself? How do I be responsible? How do I develop this skill set? How do... transformation into a certain kind of person that can do certain things or sustain certain kinds of care?" Um, but really getting to a place where I was so depleted and felt like I could have all of the community's support and training and mentorship and self-care in the world, and I'm still a confused being, and I'm still flawed, and I still make mistakes, because I don't even know what the right thing to do is. And it's just like coming up again and again against my own suffering, and realizing that that really is, like, you know, the tradition says that all the time, like, you know, "How do I become enlightened first to then be of service?"...Yeah, that sneaks up on me over and over. Oh, yes. I really, I really do need to attend to my own, my own sanity. That's so foundational.

Tasks for developing wisdom through contemplation at stage three include formal exercises as part of CPE training, including writing weekly essays, reflections, verbatims, assessments, and other assignments; sharing with peers and supervisors and receiving feedback; and sharing thoughts and concerns via interpersonal reflection (IPR). Chaplains contemplated various questions, such as "How did that go? What did I say to a patient and why did I say it? What's my sense of their spirituality and spiritual state? And why is that my sense? What are my biases, potentially?" "Why is this so important to you?" "Could it [the encounter] have been better? If what I'm doing is not useful, why am I doing it? Am I doing the right thing here? I think I am, am I really though?" "Like how much am I paying attention? How much anxiety am I bringing to the room, or distraction, or whatever? Like, what is the quality of my presence?" "How much is my mind being discursive about it? How much is my mind being like triggered? Am I triggered by something?" "What is it that they're holding that's so important? What is it that they can't integrate or bear to encounter? Why can't I help them? How do I offer myself? How do I be responsible? How do I develop this skill set?" Sometimes questions were imposed by others in ways the Buddhist chaplains in this study did not appreciate. For example, one chaplain reported:

There was such a structure, institutional structure I felt pressuring me to think about my spiritual life in relationship to my work in a particular way. Like the pressure was, "What is your definition of God and how does this impact your human relationships?" Um, and so I was constantly like, "How does that translate to what I'm doing, or thinking, or how I'm engaging with the work." Like the, there was just incredible attention around that, how to translate my assigned reflection with my actual reflections. Um, so I think that's given me a lot of insecurity, maybe, at the beginning of my career.

In the case of this chaplain, they reported repeated pressure from both their CPE supervisor and cohort to focus on God and away from concepts more spiritually meaningful to the chaplain, delaying their own spiritual formation (which the chaplain experienced once freed from the structure of that particular CPE program). For the most part, however, this process of questioning was beneficial, especially when chaplains were empowered to explore questions important to their professional and spiritual needs.

Fruition in contemplating one's work as a chaplain includes many insights into: motivation, identity, authenticity, confidence, self and ego, and selflessness; peace, balance, compassion, empathy, equanimity, love, joy, calmness, clarity, and spiritual strength; a relationship with mystery and the unknown, not-knowing, open-mindedness and openheartedness, ideas about God/gods, miracles, faith, devotion, surrender, and other interreligious concepts; the Two Truths, emptiness, interdependence, dependent co-arising, impermanence, change, and other Buddhist concepts; aging, illness, injury, death, grief, struggle, suffering, and trauma; transference and countertransference, addiction, abuse, mental illness, and other psychological factors; family, institutional, and social dynamics; racism, sexism, and other forms of bias and discrimination; and ministry of presence – how to be with others who are suffering; how to suffer alongside them; how to accompany, guide, and support; how to be with one's own suffering while with others; and how to cope with one's own suffering and the suffering of others in order to be of service to them. These insights into how to accompany were some of the most valuable and poignant of all those related during interviews and in reflections. One chaplain reported:

> During this encounter, I was mindful, particularly when hearing about how Elena was abused by Derek, that I can't fix family dynamics that go back generations, but I can be here with compassion. I am part of causes and conditions, but I don't have control over a complex situation. This allows me to be less enmeshed in the situation and more spacious, which ultimately does more good than the anxiety that accompanies feeling one has to "fix" or "rescue" each careseeker.

In contemplating this situation, the chaplain reached a mental and emotional accommodation that enabled them to accompany the careseeker, recognize the causes and conditions of the situation, and not over-identify with or become overinvested in changing a situation beyond their control. As one chaplain put it, this wisdom is "The importance of not knowing what will happen, not fearing change amd [sic] learning to remain open to the unexpected, bringing oneself to the moment, assessing and responding anew to circumstances as they actually arise."

The intentions of practicing at stage three derive from compassion, loving-kindness, goodwill, acceptance, and a willingness to connect, even with nonresponsive patients. This is a direct application of Right Intention through the cultivation of many Buddhist virtues or "perfections" (pāramitā),[26] such as generosity, morality, patience, effort, concentration, wisdom, skillful means, vows, renunciation, honesty, determination, loving-kindness, and equanimity.

Tasks involved in wisdom developed from practicing at stage three including basic skills such as introducing oneself, saying prayers with and for careseekers, reading and writing charts, consulting with multidisciplinary team members, leading brief meditations, chanting, etc. Most importantly, however, being present was the primary practice of chaplains and chaplain interns, described as "diving in," awareness, "being openhearted," staying calm during "quick and chaotic" situations in emergency departments and intensive care units, being mindful of difference, listening (as a practice) to peoples' stories, and being genuinely interested in them. Being present also includes a quality of being fully engaged while being nonattached, nonjudgmental, having no agenda, or accepting the careseekers and the situation as they are. One participant quoted Joan Halifax's statement, "Strong back, soft front," to describe this approach. Several chaplains acknowledged times when they were unable to be present or when even being present failed to benefit the careseeker. A third type of task involves self-care, which includes one's own meditation practice; compassion and loving-kindness for oneself; chanting and religious services; reaching out for appropriate support and talking about difficult cases with team members, supervisors, and peers; setting healthy boundaries; processing one's own emotions, especially negative emotions, around careseeker visits; practicing gratitude and appreciation; going on periodic retreat; and, when needed, therapy or counseling.

The fruition of wisdom based on practicing at stage three includes a sense of confidence

---

26 The pāramitās involve both an intentional component and an action component (see the tasks described below). The intentional component is critical during the "training" phase of an aspiring bodhisattva or arhant's spiritual development. While one cannot always accurately predict or control the outcomes of one's actions, one can purify one's intentions and learn from each failure. Purity of intention provides motivation to try again.

The Three Prajñās Framework of Spiritual Care experienced as 'chaplain'			
Phase	Intention	Task	Outcomes
Listening	Learning how to provide spiritual care and serve others	Listening to careseekers & listening to self-in-relation	Engaged "presence"
Contemplating	Learn from past experience and improve spiritual caregiving; integrate experiences with own awakening	Formal training exercises, such as via CPE or ongoing professional development; questioning oneself and others	Insights into oneself; cultivation of virtues; deeper Dharmic insight; esp. engagement in the work while being nonattached to outcomes beyond one's control
Practicing	Application of virtues such as the brahmavihāras or pāramitās (e.g., compassion)	Being present; pragmatic caregiving skills; ongoing self-care	Sense of connection and pragmatic wisdom for different situations; confidence

and sufficiency in one's identity as a Buddhist chaplain. This usually manifested in a sense of connection with careseekers, including a "connection across difference." Building a sense of connection is the first step toward accompanying others as a spiritual friend.

Chaplains also acquired pragmatic wisdom for dealing with careseekers, teammates, and themselves, such as how to recognize and respond to various situations, including trauma, dying, death, grief, and bereavement; preparing for, a family's anxiety during, and recovering from surgery; domestic abuse and family conflict; addiction and recovery; mental health issues, including personality disorders, psychosis, and suicidality; and loss of agency, transitions, aging, and other significant life changes. While it is the sense of connection that provides meaning and motivation for chaplains to continue their work, this pragmatic wisdom developed from the practice of spiritual care also gives them confidence that they can do the work and will continue to improve over time.

The role of the chaplain at this state is summarized in the table on the facing page.

Validating the Framework

I validated the Framework against two primary criteria: verisimilitude and the Dharma. In other words, is the Framework 'true to life' or, at least, true to the qualitative data collected in the 2017 interviews? And is the Framework true to the Dharma or, at least, our understanding of the Dharma today according to various traditional and modern sources and not just my personal interpretations of it? The first criteria of verisimilitude raises another issue which I call the 'normative paradox.' This is a paradox also explored within the Dharma, particularly via the simile of the raft.

The normative paradox is that in describing what is, we imply what *ought* to be. In setting out upon this research, I sought to describe and interpret what Buddhist chaplains do, why they do it, and how they understand it. I identified a reflective progression common to the chaplains I interviewed, one that may also be common to other Buddhist chaplains. I then carefully reviewed my interview data to see if all four stages were, at some point, described by all the chaplains I interviewed and found that indeed they were. The chart on the next page illustrates that all chaplains demonstrate all four stages of the Framework to a greater or lesser degree. (Note: The chart should not be read as an assessment of each chaplain or an attempt to diagnose what 'stage' they exemplify. It merely demonstrates that all four stages appeared in our conversations based on the questions I chose to ask. I should also note that interviews were not conducted in the same order that participant numbers were assigned.)

As we can see, the majority of the data pertained to stage three, which is not surprising, given the focus of the questions on reflection in spiritual care. Some chaplains spoke very little about reflection in relation to their earliest spiritual practice, and some chaplains rarely described attributes or behaviors related to spiritual friendship as part of their chaplaincy. When chaplains described very little of a stage, I carefully re-examined their materials to ensure that the data was coded appropriately. I sought to ensure that I was not simply categorizing statements in the data according to my own normative assumptions about what ought to be there. I can never be entirely certain I was successful, which is why others must critically examine this Framework and why I must continue to collect data and conduct analyses related to this and other topics relevant to Buddhist chaplaincy.

I also validated the Framework via follow-up interviews with five of the thirteen chaplains who participated in the research. The Framework was not yet fully developed during the first three follow-up interviews. Rather those interviews tested five theoretical hypotheses. The Framework developed in response and was explained in full during

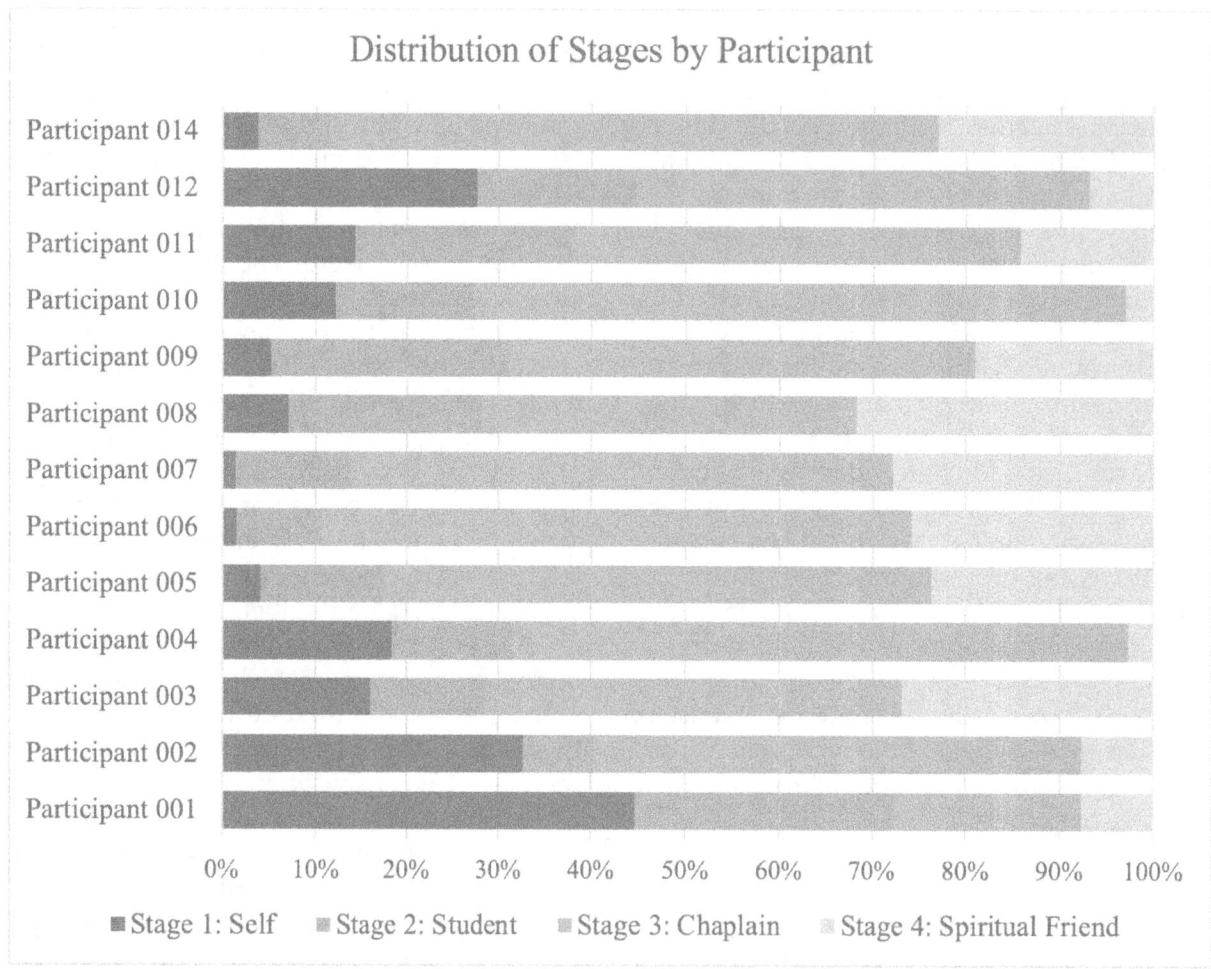

Distribution of Stages by Participant
Stage 1: Self ■ Stage 2: Student ■ Stage 3: Chaplain ■ Stage 4: Spiritual Friend

the final two interviews (along with the five hypotheses). Buddhist chaplains were shown an early draft of the Framework (via video conference screen share) and asked for their feedback. Did the Framework look 'right?' Did it reflect their experiences? Both chaplains affirmed that the Framework aligned with their experiences and validated it as a useful heuristic. The first chaplain's response could be characterized as strongly affirmative, with useful and appropriate critique demonstrating strong comprehension. The second chaplain's response could best be characterized as moderately affirmative, with some mixed statements and limited critique. The first participant said:

This is beautiful, Monica. I think it's a real, um, I haven't seen anything this well thought out at all in the literature and it seems dead on to me. I like the way that you reframed to me cintāmayīprajñā. I have heard it in terms of analysis and reasoning before. But, as you know, Pāli and Sanskrit have paragraphs worth of meaning put into one word. I'm 100 percent sure that contemplating fits into that paragraph. ...I mean, I'm looking more carefully at the text right now to see if there's anything I can think of that doesn't make sense, that I might challenge. ...In the 'assessment' process, so I almost feel like you might consider adding under the practicing column in addition to chaplain assesses, chaplain responds. Because, to me, those are actually tightly interrelated and integrated things, but they are slightly different.

The interview continued with a careful dialogue about the terms and behaviors as they were categorized into the three tasks of the three Prajñās, especially as it related to the work of the chaplain with careseekers. This follow-up interview was both validating and generative, adding additional layers and nuances to the Framework. Furthermore, the chaplain affirmed the thesis of this work, which is that Buddhist chaplains who have sufficiently traversed the earlier stages are better able to embody the fourth stage and act as kalyāṇamitra and that this ability is especially enhanced when they themselves have been accompanied, at some point, by spiritual friends of various religious traditions.

The second follow-up interview chaplain had less feedback to offer in relation to the Framework, saying that it looked, "great," but, "Yeah, just never thought of it in this way" and that they needed time to consider it. Through further discussion, the chaplain elaborated on how they saw the process of employing the Three Prajñās as recursive depending on context, being used both internally (for self-reflection) and externally (with careseekers). This affirmed a major characteristic of the theory and showed the participant saw it operating on various levels. Overall, the follow-up interviews validated the framework (two) and thesis (all five). All five follow-up interviews also offered enriching critique and expressed difference or disagreement at other points in the interviews, leading me to believe in the basic reliability of their responses. (In other words, they didn't always tell me what I expected or wanted to hear, which leads me to believe they would be willing to point out where I might have gone wrong.)

Having validated the data for faithfulness to reality to the best of my ability, I conclude that if these stages are not universal, they are at least fairly common. Of course, this can lead to the assumption that what is common is normative. I must warn against this assumption. If history is any teacher, it is dangerous to assume what is 'ought to be.' Many morally reprehensible practices have been justified this way. While I cannot believe the Framework could be as dangerous as some historical mistakes, it is also a product of its context. As Cheryl Giles reminds us, our present context remains rife with white, male, cisgendered, heteronormative, and able-bodied privilege and socioeconomic exploitation of the poor, working classes, people of color, and other marginalized groups (Giles in Giles and Miller, 2012, p. 43-45). Moreover, the Framework may very well be at the mercy of a western bias towards individualism. There is no reason to assume this work is immune from these and other influences, though I have tried to be aware of them. They could appear within the data themselves via statements provided by the chaplains I interviewed; in my analysis of the data and choices to privilege certain themes, topics, codes, and categories over others; and in my explanations here. While almost half of the chaplains who contributed to the Framework's development were Asian or Asian-American, the interviews, their questions, and theory itself were developed by someone (myself) with a strong form of American individualism. Sangha and the role of personal relationships are given places within the Framework, but this theory fundamentally applies to individuals. There may be less individualistic interpretations of the three Prajñās or other Dharmic topics to which I am blind. I welcome the contributions and critiques of other authors on this question. The next task was to validate the Framework against the Dharma, which requires a longer discussion.

To determine if the Three Prajñās Framework of Spiritual Care is aligned with the Dharma, I must say more about prajñā itself. The literature review above covered the three Prajñās and briefly alluded to the nature of prajñā, naming and noting some of its qualities without elaboration. The Buddhist chaplains also listed many of those qualities in their interviews and reflections. Now, I must contextualize the Three Prajñās and the Framework within a broader constellation of concepts that make up the expansive Buddhist literature on prajñā, or wisdom. It is important to note that my viewpoint is primarily Mahayana. As such, there is some overlap with Theravada teachings on paññā (Pāli for 'wisdom'), but also significant development on the topic of emptiness (śūnyatā) and the role of the bodhisattva path that are unique to Mahayana. In general, the Mahayana teachings are included within the Vajrayana, though they may be expanded on or reinterpreted according to uniquely Vajrayana practices.

The concepts treated below include impermanence (anitya), interdependence (pratītyasamutpāda), nonself (anātman), emptiness (śūnyatā), and the Two Truths (satyadvaya). Emptiness is a Mahayana concept that includes the characteristics of impermanence, interdependence, and nonself. Briefly, "Emptiness is the lack or absence of intrinsic nature (svabhāva) in any and all phenomena, the final nature of all things (dharmatā), and the ultimate truth (paramārthasatya)," per the *Princeton Dictionary of Buddhism* (2017, p. 871-872). Meaning that because all phenomena are impermanent and interdependent (not independent), they are 'empty' of intrinsic nature; this includes the 'self,' which is nonself.

In summation, all the previous concepts describe the ultimate truth (paramārthasatya) that one apprehends directly via meditation. However, they belong to the conventional truth (saṃvṛtisatya) because they are only words on paper. The ultimate truth to which the words point is itself beyond words – is nonconceptual – and can only be known through direct experience. The Framework of wisdom via listening, contemplating and practicing is also a conventional truth, including its relation to the practical wisdom of spiritual care. Yet, while practicing in the later stages, it can also lead to apprehension of the ultimate truth, as spiritual friendship aids the chaplain in transcending the self. The soteriological purpose of the three Prajñās in the Buddhist literature is to attain ultimate truth via bhāvanāmayīprajñā, or the wisdom derived from practicing. However, one passes through conventional truth during śrutamayīprajñā, the wisdom derived from listening, and cintāmayīprajñā, the wisdom derived from contemplating. All Buddhist concepts can be understood with reference to these Two Truths, the ultimate and the conventional. Wisdom (prajñā) itself can also be understood via conventional and ultimate truths.

Wisdom is a multivalent term for acquiring the insights or truths named above. One can understand the differences between truths as the appearance and reality using the analogy of a mirage. While looking at a mirage in the desert, the statement, "I see water," would be true, though no water is present. The Two Truths points to the notion that although we can make true statements about our perceptions as the perceiver, our perception of reality is not the same as reality itself (Dalai Lama, 1994, p. 122). It is important to note that so-called conventional truth, though sometimes describes as 'illusion,' is also factual, true and an important vehicle for liberation. The term 'illusion' points not outward, but inward. The problem is not with the world, but with our minds. Our perceptions and our minds must be purified through meditation to achieve direct experience of ultimate truth. All forms of language function at the level of conventional truth inasmuch as they are contextual and conditional. Likewise, religious statements also fall into the paradigm of conventional truth. Thus, the Buddhist adage, "Do not mistake the finger [pointing at the moon] for the moon," advises us to not mistake the written or spoken Dharma for the ultimate truth. Thus, what one hears, reads and contemplates, being bound up in language, belongs to the realm of conventional truth. It is the raft that carries us to the other shore. We could not make the journey without it, but once standing on the opposite bank, we have no further need for the raft.

Spiritual experiences, on the other hand, may provide one with a direct apprehension of ultimate truths. Prajñā is insight into ultimate truth. When teaching complex concepts, such as prajñā, the Buddha would often preface the ultimate with a conventional truth, just as bhāvanāmayīprajñā is prefaced with śruta- and cintāmayīprajñā. For example, before describing śūnyatā, or emptiness, a concept difficult to grasp, the Buddha would explore the feeling of the unsatisfactoriness of things, which is easy to relate to one's own direct experience. In the *Training Anthology*, Śāntideva quotes an earlier Buddhist text called the *Meeting of Father and Son* (*Pitā-putra-samāgama*), which is purportedly a discourse of the Buddha explicating the unsatisfactoriness of existence, as experienced through the 'three poisons' of attachment, aversion and delusion, and their relationship to the cultivation of wisdom of emptiness (Goodman, 2016, p. 234-244). The Dalai Lama states that the ultimate truth "cannot be perceived by the intellect." This is because, as the eighth-century Buddhist teacher Śāntideva points out in the *Bodhicaryāvatāra*, the intellect itself exists on the level of conventional truth, but humans possess another type of intelligence that can perceive ultimate truth (Dalai Lama, 1994, p. 118-119).

The Three Prajñās and the Framework, as concepts, also belongs to conventional truth, but this makes it flexible. Anything that exists conditionally can also change as conditions change. As a concept, it can be repurposed and applied to mundane activities in service of practical goals, such as reducing suffering in oneself and others short of complete liberation.

Ultimate truth, meanwhile, remains unchanging, nondual, and cannot be perceived by a mind that still conceptualizes subject and object (Dalai Lama, 1994, p. 120). Multiple chaplains in my 2017 interviews referenced this important principle. One described what some might call a mystic experience and what Zen Buddhists refer to as a moment of kenshō, or momentary knowledge of the true nature of oneself and, by extension, all things. The chaplain reported:

> I was thinking of the popular phrase from the *Avatamsaka Sutra*, "one is all, all is one." And I was walking in the, in the park, in the woods of the park, in downtown Tokyo, when I was walking to my office. One day, one morning, I suddenly realized that I am here now thanks to the innumerable relationships with other, others beyond time and space. I suddenly felt something warm in my heart and started to cry. I realized that kind of, uh, glimpse, glimpse of reality, my, my encounter with something big. And now I think that phrase is kind of the guiding post for me. And the "one is all" means the wisdom, or emptiness, because in one small grain of sand of the river Ganges, whole universe is there. That's means [sic], one consists of the inference from all the other. That means, one is perfect, but in one grain, there is nothing eternal, or nothing, kind of inherent to that existence. Nothing is me, but it's okay. And uh, "all is one," I've been thinking that is not simple, but now I understand that means love and compassion.

Other chaplains referred to similar experiences more in passing, rather than by offering a detailed narration of a direct experience of ultimate truth, however brief. These references were frequently in relation to an interview question about what commonly arises within the chaplain's own reflections.

For example, when I asked, "Do you find there are particular ideas, concepts, terms, or teachings from the Dharma that tend to come up over and over?" one chaplain responded, "Certainly, and 'emptiness' is the biggest of those. Not, obviously, the nihilistic version, but the notion of phenomena as being compounded, interdependent, conditional, comes up a lot. Um, there's also the ultimate and the worldly, sort of understandings that comes up." Another chaplain related the nondual view of emptiness directly to a worldview that helps them cope with the impermanence of their own role as a spiritual caregiver:

> I mean emptiness teachings. I feel like it's so easy to get really deep into this idea of like, "I'm the helper, and I'm helping others," or "Now I feel helpless and I need help." But just the emptiness of and the transitoriness [sic] of these roles. Like how, how to have good professional boundaries and personal boundaries, while also realizing that all of these identities are transitory and empty of an inherent nature. Just holding that.

Chaplains also reported difficulty explaining these glimpses of ultimate reality and the concepts Buddhists commonly use to describe this truth, such as emptiness, nonself, etc., to peers and supervisors. One chaplain related, "I guess the hardest thing for me always is feeling like I wasn't understood necessarily by my peers or where I was coming from. It was this like, 'Okay, well let me now explain, you know, emptiness or…' you know, it's just, that's not easy to do."

These concepts also arose in the chaplains' written reflections, which included explicit references to the Two Truths, emptiness, interdependence, seeing reality, nonself, wisdom, and various spiritual or mystic experiences. In response to the question, "Is there a theme or pattern connecting this issue to other spiritual care experiences?" one chaplain wrote, "Another theme is that of upāya, or skillful means. This is tied directly to the acknowledgment of relative and ultimate levels of reality/understanding that is spoken of throughout all of the vehicles of Buddhism I'm aware of." The chaplain then explored their careseeker's Christian worldview as they understood it and concluded by stating, "In my own experience and reading, what looks like emptiness or equanimity from one perspective may well manifest as love or compassion from another (the two wings [wisdom and compassion] teaching and the relative and ultimate teaching)." Another chaplain pointed out in their reflection, "The Dharma is the truth of reality and suffering. It has been expressed through the sutras written by buddhas and ancestors, and it is also intended to be practiced with and realized for oneself," which is exactly what one attempts through the practice of meditation. These statements also serve as evidence of the verisimilitude of the Framework, as the Dharma matches the real-life experiences of these Buddhist professionals.

Bhāvanāmayīprajñā describes the mind's capacity to move beyond concepts of subject and object through proper training. Absolute truth is sought through a "positive way" of practicing, and it cannot be achieved through "negation" or "gained by analysis," though some people may spend many frustrating hours on the latter (Dalai Lama, 1994, p. 122). Most descriptions of ultimate truth follow this latter route (using analytical language), but it is important to remember that they are only descriptions, not the truth itself. It is only through the direct practice of meditation that ultimate truth can be seen by the mind and, "Once it has been experienced, it is not necessary to demonstrate it again," according to the Dalai Lama. "Its existence is true, and one does not have to rely on argument to prove that it exists" (Dalai Lama, 1994, p. 122-123). But if one seeks emptiness analytically, using words, we cannot find it. "What has been found by experiencing [emptiness] through listening, reflecting and meditating cannot be found through such analysis."

When one seeks it through analysis, "there is nothing that exists," (Dalai Lama, 1994, p. 123) because analysis is based in language, and language itself can only convey conventional truth. This kind of switching back and forth between considering conventional and ultimate truth is common within Buddhist literature and has been demonstrated by the Buddhist chaplains in this study, per their quotes above. Moreover, it may be an area for significant future research among Buddhist chaplains.

As we have seen from the study chaplains' quotes, the nature of the self can be understood within this paradigm of conventional and ultimate truth. Although, conventionally, I can say that 'I' exist, that the person 'Monica' exists, that a Buddhist chaplain exists, ultimately, this person is just a construction of ever-fluctuating aggregates, causes, and conditions giving rise only to the momentary perception of 'I' and not to any fixed identity. The *Bodhicaryāvatāra* affirms:

> 9.10
> As long as the conditions are assembled,
> Illusions, likewise, will persist and manifest.
> Why, through simply being more protracted,
> Should sentient beings be regarded as more real?

Verses such as this in the *Bodhicaryāvatāra* proclaim all things are empty of inherent existence, including ourselves, to which we cling more fiercely than any other illusion. According to Śāntideva, this is because our perception of 'I' is rooted in the vehicle of that perception, our body. The central part of chapter nine of the *Bodhicaryāvatāra* analyzes each portion of the body and even the faculties of the mind to find the root of this 'I' and comes up empty:

> 9.59
> The flesh and skin are not the "I,"
> And neither are the body's warmth and breath.
> The cavities within the frame are not the "I,"
> And "I" is not accounted for in sixfold consciousness.

The *Bodhicaryāvatāra* not only refutes the existence of any 'I,' it decries this delusion as the source of all suffering. Humans suffer from birth, old age, sickness and death, which are prominent themes among our chaplains, especially those working in healthcare settings. Humans also suffer to feed, cloth, house and safe-keep this body. Worse yet, people suffer for the sake of pride, for the sake of acquiring that which we desire, and from the delusion that satisfaction of our desires will lead to lasting happiness. Freedom from this suffering comes when one experiences the truth of emptiness and through this insight, releases all attachment to the 'I,' along with its cravings and desires. (At this point, it is important to note that even enlightened bodies are still subject to aging, sickness, old age and death; still need be clothed, housed, fed, etc. In letting go of attachment to the 'I,' we simply relinquish any worry about these events, and negative emotions associated with these processes will cease to arise. It is said that the Buddha, old and ill, experienced pain, but no suffering during his death, as relayed in the *Maha-Parinibbana Sutta: Last Days of the Buddha* DN 16.) The Dalai Lama (1994) asks:

> Why do we need to realize emptiness? We do not wish to suffer and we know that the root of suffering is the untamed mind. Because the mind perceives and understands things mistakenly, negative emotions arise and the mind is never at peace. (p.122)

Because we perceive incorrectly and are deluded, "We should not accept our perceptions just as we experience them...We should ask ourselves what our perceptions are masking. If we do this, an understanding of the two truths will arise in our minds" (Dalai Lama, 1994, p. 123). This is the goal of cultivating wisdom both in oneself and, when appropriate, in careseekers who suffer from many of the same causes.

So how does the Buddhist chaplain, a spiritual caregiver, cultivate this wisdom? Through listening, contemplating, and practicing spiritual care, Buddhist chaplains deepen their insights into the relationship between prajñā (wisdom), śūnyatā (emptiness), and anātman (nonself). The chaplains in this study affirmed these insights in their interviews and reflections, referenced above. Let me say a little more about the relationship between these concepts to place the chaplains' quotes in context.

Wisdom is insight into the ultimate truth, which is that all phenomena are empty or śūnyatā. In his book, *Mapping the Bodhicaryāvatāra: Essays on Mahāyāna Ethics*, Pabitrakumar Roy explains, "Śūnyatā is an adjectival quality of all dharmas [phenomena] – not a substance...rather, it refers to reality as incapable of ultimately being pinned down in concepts" (Roy, 2011, p. *xvii*). Because śūnyatā is beyond all concepts, ultimate truth can only ever be misconceptualized in language. Yet it remains critically important on the Buddhist path, especially for Buddhist chaplains who wish to practice nonattachment to views, agendas, and 'fixing' things. For Buddhist chaplains, this practical wisdom is reinforced by teachings on nonself and emptiness, which can be observed in one's direct experience of bhāvanāmayīprajñā, or the wisdom derived from practicing spiritual care with careseekers. Roy reminds us, "Lest there should remain traces, subtle and potent, of egoity, talk of emptiness in intended as the antidote. The discourse is a spiritual therapy to help liberate people from constricting viewpoints" (Roy, 2011, p. *xvii*). The practice of virtues such as compassion and equanimity, epitomized in the work of a spiritual caregiver, are part of that antidote because they reduce self-clinging.

Moreover, the various Buddhist virtues "become pāramitās [perfections] only as and when they are informed by prajñā," according to Roy's understanding of Śāntideva's classic text (Roy, 2011, p. *xvii-xviii*). We have previously seen how the perfections (i.e., virtues) are both intentions and outcomes of practicing at each stage of the Framework. Only when the chaplain has experienced śūnyatā do they truly understand the scope and best practice of compassion, because only then do they fully experience the suffering of all beings as their own – or rather, having fully abandoned the concepts of 'I' and 'other,' can they fully identify 'I' *with/as* 'other,' seeing no distinction between the two (not seeing them as two at all). This is referenced in the *Sutra on Reflection in Spiritual Care* earlier in this chapter. In fact, seeing neither 'I' nor 'other,' they see only suffering or not suffering and, with clear insight into suffering's causes, also gain clear insight into the means for its cessation, no matter where (or in whom) it occurs. Perfect wisdom possessed by the historical Buddha allowed him to lead many beings to direct experiences of enlightenment and liberation from suffering. Even imperfect wisdom, if it is a fraction of true insight, can aid Buddhist chaplains in easing the suffering of careseekers and themselves.

The Buddhist chaplains in this study, or at least those of Mahayana traditions, reported that, through listening and contemplating, or śruta- and cintāmayīprajñā, they realized intellectually that 'I' am empty. Yet, as we've seen, intellectual understanding is not sufficient, so at this point, they are still walking the path of faith. When they practice exchanging the 'I' with the 'other' to diminish the ego as part of spiritual care, they engage bhāvanāmayīprajñā. These practices can take the form of meditative exercises either done as preparation for or during a caregiving visit, by cultivating altruistic virtues and behavior (the perfections), and directly through their work as a spiritual caregiver. Ultimately, however, Buddhist chaplains realize that the 'other' is also empty. Creating a temporary hierarchy of 'I' and 'other' is upāya, skillful means, part of the conventional truth, but not the ultimate truth. Exchanging 'I' with 'other' benefits the aspiring bodhisattva by training the mind to release attachment to the self, which is, by its nature, the strongest source of attachment in one's life and the deepest root of clinging and, thus, suffering. Alleviating suffering and aspiring for nirvāna are the ultimate soteriological goals of the chaplain.

However, this exchange of 'I' with 'other' still reifies a dualistic relationship. The Buddhist chaplains in this study report that their best work is accomplished when the concept of 'I' dissolves entirely, when the distinctions between self and other disappear, and when the chaplain can be fully present to the experience of providing care within the moment. (Descriptions of these experiences are akin to descriptions of 'flow' states, in which self-awareness recedes in favor of full engagement with the task. 'Flow' is studied in psychology, particularly in the work of Mihály Csíkszentmihályi. I cannot fully compare the two states here, but this would be an interesting project.)

We can see that the interviews affirm that prajñā and its associated constellation of concepts, including emptiness, interdependence, impermanence, nonself, and the Two Truths, are important to Buddhist chaplains and regularly reflected in their work as spiritual caregivers. These concepts are also complex, and while they do show up in chaplains' reflections, they are often difficult to explore for both chaplains and their CPE supervisors and peers. From this review of the literature on prajñā, I conclude that the Three Prajñās Framework of Spiritual Care is a 'Dharmically' appropriate application of an existing concept – the Three Prajñās – to a specific situation faced by practicing Buddhist chaplains: providing and reflecting on spiritual care. Moreover, the Framework is not a new invention, but rather a descriptive interpretation of what Buddhist chaplains are already doing, some of them explicitly and others implicitly.

Conclusion and Reflection

We can now consider how this framework might apply to our own work as chaplains. The Framework falls within the category of 'praxis,' which can also be understood as 'theory-laden practice' or 'practice-informed theory,' as one prefers. It is the synthesis of theory and practice that serves as the basis for change, expressed in the Framework as movement from task to task and stage to stage. The Framework can be used for several purposes:

- Pedagogy: guiding the education of future Buddhist chaplains
- Spiritual Formation: assessing or guiding the development of future and current chaplains
- Spiritual Care: offering a method for practicing spiritual care, including techniques for interacting with careseekers in relation to each of the three tasks
- Reflection: a method for structuring one's own reflections and facilitating reflection for careseekers
- Wisdom: developing insight on the path to awakening

In most applications, the Framework is only loosely visible, with one exception: reflection. The Framework was originally developed as a tool specifically related to reflection. Most of data collected as part of the original research was focused on that topic. Of course, in asking about reflection, chaplains naturally shared the subject material of their reflections, including their own spiritual journeys and careseeker encounters, enabling the development of a larger theory. Nevertheless, one of the major criticisms of the Framework is that of scope-creep.

In 2017, I interviewed thirteen Buddhist chaplains about how they reflect and facilitate reflection for others. The Framework that developed from the data is arguably broader than just applying to reflection. The central concept, cintāmayīprajñā, or wisdom derived from contemplation, clearly includes the practice of reflection. However, it is also broader than just reflection. If reflection occurs *after* action, that is, based on recollection, then contemplating is broader than reflection because it can also include consideration *prior* to action (cintāmayīprajñā coming before bhāvanāmayīprajñā). The earlier and latter concepts, śrutamayīprajñā and bhāvanāmayīprajñā, wisdom derived from listening and practicing respectively, provide information and experiences upon which to reflect (and skills with which to reflect, i.e., concentration), but are also even broader than reflection. The Buddhist chaplains I interviewed did not merely listen to tradition, reflect on its meaning, and then apply any insights they derive from this to spiritual care. They listened, developed wisdom based on listening, contemplated, developed wisdom based on contemplating, practiced, developed wisdom based on practicing, and then listened again with new insights. Each task includes both the application of particular skills and the apprehension of particular understandings. The emphasis on the development of wisdom in each area makes this Framework uniquely Buddhist and distinct from Christian forms of 'theological' reflection.

Application of the Framework to reflection is fairly straightforward because the 'data' collected on this topic was sufficient to validate the theory. However, data saturation was not achieved in all theoretical categories, and so these categories are not yet fully and accurately explicated. In layman's terms, we need more information before we can prove the Framework is applicable to all the areas listed above. Thus, the Framework is only loosely applied to topics such as pedagogy (although it is arguably pedagogical in its original description, per the literature review on the Three Prajñās), spiritual formation, spiritual care and wisdom (again, see the literature review). Nevertheless, I maintain my thesis: Buddhist chaplains who have developed sufficient wisdom from listening-contemplating-practicing as self, student and chaplain are then better able to accompany others through listening-contemplating-practicing as a kalyāṇamitra. They further benefit from having themselves been accompanied by spiritual friends, especially if some of that experience was interreligious.

You can assist in judging whether the Framework applies broadly to spiritual care or not through your own practice as Buddhist chaplains. For now, it may be helpful to explore the Framework as a template for reflection on your own path of spiritual formation. You can use the tables from the preceding sections that outline the intention, tasks, and outcomes of development of each prajñā at each stage. Briefly fill in the template on the facing page for yourself (as outlined in the previous tables) and then compose a reflective essay related to each stage.

You can also use the following prompts for your reflection, if that is easier.

1. Before you became a student/after you formally became a student/when you first began to practice as a chaplain or chaplain intern, how would you describe the quality of your listening? What intention did you have? How did you listen? What came from listening? Did anything change about the way you listened over time?
2. Before you became a student/after you formally became a student/when you first began to practice as a chaplain or chaplain intern, how would you describe the quality of your contemplation? What intention did you have? How did you contemplate, whether through formal meditation or informal thinking? What came from contemplating? Did anything change about the way you contemplated or thought about things over time?
3. Before you became a student/after you formally became a student/when you first began to practice as a chaplain or chaplain intern, how would you describe the quality of your practice? What intention did you have? How did you practice? What came from practicing? Did anything change

about the way you practiced over time, especially in relation to how your practice became integrated with your life or work?

You can also apply the Three Prajnas Framework to reflecting on a particular experience or spiritual care encounter. Again, use the table on the following page or one of these prompts:

1. Consider an experience you have had of receiving spiritual care (or any form of care) from another person. What was the quality of their attention like? How is this similar to or different from the kind of attention we are used to receiving? What did they do or say that helped you in that moment? Afterward, what came out of that experience that leads you to remember it to this day? What did you learn, about yourself or others, if anything?

2. Consider an experience you have had in attempting to do something difficult (related to spiritual care or not). What was your intention in undertaking that experience? What did you do during the process? What was the result? In what way do you think your intention was related to your choice of action and the result (or not)?

3. Consider an experience you have had as a student attempting to learn something challenging. What was the quality of your listening, reading, or watching like? How did you contemplate or process the information? And how did you put that knowledge into practice? Did you get stuck at any particular point along the way (hard to listen, hard to understand, or hard to do) and, if so, why?

4. Consider an experience you have had in providing spiritual care to another person. What was your intention before entering that interaction and during the interaction? What was the quality of your attention like? What did the careseeker do or say and what did you do or say in response? What emotions were present in the room, for yourself and the careseeker? How do you understand the careseeker's situation in relation to the Dharma and your own knowledge? How did the careseeker understand their situation within their own worldview? What was the outcome of that encounter for the careseeker and yourself? What might you do differently with the wisdom of hindsight? What would you do if you were to encounter that careseeker again?

Stage: _____			
Phase	**Intention**	**Task**	**Outcome**
Listening			
Contemplating			
Practicing			

4
Kalyāṇamitra, or Spiritual Friendship

The most commonly cited scripture on kalyāṇamitra is in chapter five of the *Saṃyutta Nikāya* of the Pāli Canon (SN45.2), the *Upaddha Sutta*:

> Thus have I heard. On one occasion the Blessed One was dwelling among the Sakyans where there was a town of the Sakyans named Nagaraka. Then the Venerable Ānanda approached the Blessed One. Having approached, he paid homage to the Blessed One, sat down to one side, and said to him:
>
> "Venerable sir, this is half of the holy life, that is, good friendship, good companionship, good comradeship." "Not so, Ānanda! Not so, Ānanda! This is the entire holy life, Ānanda, that is, good friendship, good companionship, good comradeship. When a bhikkhu has a good friend, a good companion, a good comrade, it is to be expected that he will develop and cultivate the Noble Eightfold Path.
>
> "And how, Ānanda, does a bhikkhu who has a good friend, a good companion, a good comrade, develop and cultivate the Noble Eightfold Path? Here, Ānanda, a bhikkhu develops right view, which is based upon seclusion, dispassion, and cessation, maturing in release. He develops right intention ... right speech ... right action ... right livelihood ... right effort ... right mindfulness ... right concentration,[27] which is based upon seclusion, dispassion, and cessation, maturing in release. It is in this way, Ānanda, that a bhikkhu who has a good friend, a good companion, a good comrade, develops and cultivates the Noble Eightfold Path.
>
> "By the following method too, Ānanda, it may be understood how the entire holy life is good friendship, good companionship, good comradeship: by relying upon me as a good friend, Ānanda, beings subject to birth are freed from birth; beings subject to aging are freed from aging; beings subject to death are freed from death; beings subject to sorrow, lamentation, pain, displeasure, and despair are freed from sorrow, lamentation, pain, displeasure, and despair. By this method, Ānanda, it may be understood how the entire holy life is good friendship, good companionship, good comradeship."

Good friendship is essential to the Buddhist path. Two of the three things in which Buddhists take refuge are spiritual friends: the Buddha or one's teacher and the sangha or one's spiritual community. In scripture, kalyāṇamitra act as both wise teachers and compassionate companions on the spiritual path. In

---

[27] Where ... is found, the passage from the first item on the list repeats. This repetition is frequently edited from the print editions of Pāli texts for brevity and replaced with ellipses (...).

the notes on the passage above, Bhikkhu Bodhi clarifies that the three Pāli terms *kalyāṇamittatā*, *kalyāṇasahāyatā*, and *kalyāṇasampavaṅkatā*, or 'good friendship, good companionship, and good comradeship,' are synonyms. The triple repetition adds emphasis.

Bhikkhu Bodhi's note also adds context to the passage by clarifying Ānanda's thinking behind the question: "This practice of an ascetic succeeds for one who relies on good friends and on his own manly effort, so half of it depends on good friends and half on one's own manly effort" (2000, p. 1980). The Buddha clearly refutes this idea. It is an easy thought to have when one is contemplating in seclusion, as Ānanda was at the time. We forget what others do on our behalf so that we are able to contemplate in seclusion. One's practice succeeds not at all through one's own efforts (manly or otherwise), but rather depends entirely on the support of good spiritual friends. This understanding is upāya, or skillful means, as it cuts through our habits of egotism and defeats spiritual pride in one's so-called accomplishments.

While this passage is the most famous, the topic of spiritual friendship receives a more detailed treatment in the *Aṅgutarra Nikāya* or *Numerical Discourses of the Buddha*. The *Aṅgutarra Nikāya* is a detailed compendium of topics, concepts, lists and similes, and often lacks the narrative flow of the other nikāyas. This chapter explores what the *Aṅgutarra Nikāya* tells us about friendship, including the benefits of good friendships and drawbacks of bad friendships, the kinds of persons to associate with or avoid, and how to maintain good relationships with one's friends. Friendship also appears in Mahayana and Vajrayana literature. The collective sources are too vast for an exhaustive survey, but I review some primary texts, including the work of Buddhaghosa, Śāntideva, prajñāpāramitā (perfection of wisdom) literature, and lojong (mind training) literature. Finally, I summarize modern research on the topic, both historical/textual and applied.

I take a note of caution from anthropology and cultural studies that 'friendship' is not universally understood to be the same in every culture at every time throughout history. To understand the applicability of kalyāṇamitra in our work, we must reflect on the way modern Americans understand friendship in comparison to ancient Indian and other Asian cultures where it is referenced. Therefore, I prefer the Sanskrit term kalyāṇamitra to the English translation of good or spiritual friendship because this relationship is distinct. It is important to distinguish this model for care from mundane behavior towards one's personal friends.

Following this literature review, this chapter explicates the model of kalyāṇamitra that emerged from the research with practicing Buddhist chaplains. It describes how a chaplain as kalyāṇamitra thinks and behaves towards their careseekers within the framework of the Three Prajñās for spiritual care. The chapter then compares existing Buddhist spiritual care literature with the research findings. Thus, the kalyāṇamitra model is based on a robust foundation of 1) scripture, 2) modern interpretation and teaching, 3) qualitative research, and 4) the collective wisdom of the field of Buddhist chaplaincy.

In the academic field of pastoral care, there is a long history of using models and metaphors as the basis for chaplain identity and behavior. Many of these models have been collected by Robert C. Dykstra in the book *Images of Pastoral Care: Classical Readings*, which includes the shepherd, the living human document, Samaritan, healer, clown, wise fool, coach, midwife and storyteller. Kalyāṇamitra is distinct in two ways. First, it is an entirely Buddhist model, not reliant on either Judeo-Christian teaching or western sociological, psychological, or philosophical theories (though we may compare it to both at various points). Second, unlike many (but not all) of these models, it is not metaphorical. The Buddhist chaplain is not a metaphorical healer of theoretical souls or metaphorical herder of metaphorical sheep. The Buddhist chaplain is a genuine spiritual friend to those in need. (This distinction is not meant as a criticism. Buddhist teaching uses its fair share of metaphors. All metaphors require a certain amount of interpretation to implement. What it means to a clown in the context of chaplaincy requires recognition and imaginative interpretation of the metaphor. The paradigm of kalyāṇamitra skips this cognitive step. As we shall see below, the Buddhist scriptures are very direct in their descriptions of kalyāṇamitra.)

Literature Review of Kalyāṇamitra

Defining Kalyāṇamitra

Kalyāṇamitra is a compound term that literally translates as 'good friend.' The base of the compound is *mitra* (*mitto* in Pāli) and means a friend, companion, ally or associate, as well as the relationship of friendship. *Mitra* can be used at both the start and end of a compound term. In this case, at the end of the term, it serves as the noun. For example, *pāpamitra*, a term also found in the scriptures means 'friend of sin' or, more commonly, 'evil friend' or 'friendship with the wicked.' Alternatively, *laghumitra* means "a slight or weak friend, an ally of little power or value," *kulamitra* means a either a family friend or a friendship among equals, and *mitrāmitra* means a relationship with one who is both friend and foe simultaneously ('frenemies,' in the modern idiom). *Mitra* can also appear at the beginning of a compound, in which case it serves as an adjective modifying another noun, such as in *mitrabhāva* or "a state of friendship, friendly disposition" or *mitradroha* or "injury or betrayal of a friend." The list of *mitra* compounds available in Sanskrit is extensive, reflecting the importance and complexity of social relations in ancient India. These definitions are available at *sanskritdictionary.com*.

Kalyā is a noun that most directly means either 'praise' or 'eulogy.' When combined with -*ṇa*, it becomes an adjective and is used frequently as a positive modifier to other nouns. On its own, *kalyāṇa* can be translated as 'beautiful,' 'agreeable,' 'virtuous,' 'excellent,' 'good,' 'beneficial,' 'salutary,' 'auspicious,' 'happy,' 'prosperous,' 'fortunate,' 'lucky,' 'well,' and 'right.' (See sanskritdictionary.com for more.) Thus, it seems as versatile as the all-purpose positive idiom 'cool' in the English language. *Kalyāṇa* is most commonly used as the start of a compound term, such as *kalyāṇadharman* or "of virtuous character or conduct," or *kalyāṇakīrti* or "having a good reputation." Rarely, it comes at the end of a compound when being modified by an adjective indicating degree, such as when something is very or not very beautiful (*pravarakalyāṇa* and *nātikalyāṇa*, respectively), for example. Both *kalyā* and *mitra* are also used frequently in names of people.

The Sanskrit Dictionary online translates kalyāṇamitra as "a friend of virtue," "a well-wishing friend," "a good counselor," and as a name for the Buddha. Kalyāṇamitra in our context more accurately refers to "a spiritual companion or mentor (sometimes, though rarely, referring even to the Buddha himself) who encourages one in salutary directions and helps one to remain focused on matters of real religious import," according to the *Princeton Dictionary of Buddhism* (2013, p. 410). Therefore, I have chosen to translate it as 'spiritual friend' or 'spiritual friendship' throughout this text. I could equally have chosen 'religious friend,' though in the context of interreligious spiritual care, I believe 'spiritual' to be the more applicable term. (Given that neither 'religion/religious' nor 'spiritual' have direct translations in most Asian languages, including Sanskrit and Pāli, scholars could spend a long time arguing over which is more accurate. I have simply chosen that which is more practical for my purposes.) *The Princeton Dictionary* elaborates:

> Association with a kalyāṇamitra is said to be one of the foundations of religious progress: it is one of the seven things conducive to the welfare and weal of monks and one of the indicators that a monk will perfect

the seven constituents of awakening (bodhyaṅga). In the absence of "good friends," it was thought preferable for monks to lead the solitary life of the rhinoceros (see khaḍgaviṣāṇa; khaḍgaviṣāṇakalpa). Three kinds of kalyāṇamitra are described in the literature: an instructor, a fellow practitioner, and a lay supporter (dānapati). The Tibetan title "geshe" (dge bshes), referring to a monk who has successfully completed the scholastic curriculum of the dge lugs sect, is a contraction of the Tibetan translation of kalyāṇamitra. (2013, p. 410)

Though Sanskrit is also the canonical language of many ancient Hindu and Jain texts, the term kalyāṇamitra has become so synonymous with the Buddha and Buddhism that the compound *kalyāṇamitrasevana* means "becoming a disciple of the Buddha" and *kalyāṇamitratā* means "to perfect the life of Buddhism," per *The Sanskrit Dictionary*. Thus, to become a Buddhist and practice the Noble Eightfold Path to its pinnacle is to become a good friend to all.

Kalyāṇamitra in Ancient Texts

This survey reviews scriptures and commentaries from the Theravada, Mahayana, and Vajrayana traditions, starting with the *Nikāyas* of the Pāli Canon, from which we have already read the most famous sutta on the topic. I now briefly review a few sections of the *Aṅguttara Nikāya* (relying on Bhikkhu Bodhi's translations from Wisdom Publications) which provides far more detail on what constitutes spiritual friendship, and a section from the *Dīgha Nikāya* that references the topic in relation to laypeople. Then, from the Mahayana traditions the *Aṣṭasāhasrikā Prajñāpāramitā Sūtra* (Edward Conze's 1994 translation) and the works of Śāntideva, both the *Śikṣāsamuccaya* (Charles Goodman's 2016 translation) and the *Bodhicaryāvatāra* (the Padmakara Translation Group's 2008 edition)

are consulted. These texts are also important to the Vajrayana traditions, from which lojong or mind training texts (Thupten Jinpa's 2014 compilation and translations) are also reviewed. This demonstrates the pervasiveness of the concept of kalyāṇamitra through each major branch of Buddhism, and the commonalities and distinctions within those traditions. As I reviewed each text, I mentally related their content to the work of a chaplain based both on my own experiences and those of colleagues. However, the process of explicating each text for its value to spiritual care led to a tediously long chapter. Instead, I condense and confine most comments on the application of this wisdom to the sections after the literature review. Choosing one of the cited texts (or finding another) and composing a written reflection on what it means to your practice as a Buddhist chaplain would be a worthwhile exercise for any reader. Let us start with the Pāli, which are generally acknowledged as the oldest Buddhist texts.

Kalyāṇamitra appears repeatedly in the Pāli suttas most frequently in the *Aṅguttara Nikāya* or *Numerical Discourses of the Buddha*, a compendium of lists and typologies. The term 'friend' appears in dozens of chapters, often combined with positive and negative adjectives. The Buddha gives a great deal of advice about friends, how to identify them, whom to associate with or not, the advantages of good friends and disadvantages of bad friends, as well as instructions on how to maintain good relationships with others. Related lists of virtues, typologies of speech and action, and the role of friends on the path to enlightenment are all contained within the numerical chapters. Some of the content repeats. A list of virtues founds in the chapter on threes, for example, may also be found in the chapter on fives, with two new virtues included. Some may see these as inconsistencies, but the Buddha was known throughout his forty years of teaching to give different lessons to different people, each according to their ability, and to build on earlier teachings with latter ones of increasing complexity, just as we do today in modern pedagogy. By compiling all that the Buddha, or, in a few cases, his most eminent monks, has said about friendship, we can develop a comprehensive model of the spiritual friendship described as the "entirety of the holy life" in SN45.2 and discern what qualities we should adopt as chaplains acting as kalyāṇamitra toward careseekers.

This survey cannot be exhaustive; I have chosen only to cover three themes from the *Aṅguttara Nikāya*. For a listing of locations where advice on friendship appears, see the appendices. Instead, this section focuses on three themes and builds upon those themes as they appear in other canonical texts and later commentarial literature. First, I examine the qualities of good friends. These qualities are primarily listed to help the novice monk find and attach himself to good friends. We can also use them as a guide to our own behavior and spiritual development, just as the novice would hope to do. Second, I examine the role of friendship within the spiritual journey. In the *Aṅguttara Nikāya*, the spiritual path is conceived in a prototypically Buddhist way, so we must carefully consider the implications of these passages for our current interreligious context where spiritual paths have various means and various ends based on diverse worldviews. Third, I examine how we may know good friendship from bad friendship by its fruits – that is, what outcomes we observe in ourselves and others when surrounded by good friends. These observations can guide us to choose our friends wisely and amend our own behavior skillfully.

The qualities of a good friend include numerous character virtues and right conduct. Overall, good friends are virtuous, faithful, generous, and wise (AN8.54), and these qualities are enumerated throughout the *Aṅguttara Nikāya*. The Buddha explores four primary sets of qualities for a good friend. First, as the Buddha instructed Ananda, one should associate with those who successfully follow the Noble Eightfold Path with two added characteristics: right knowledge and right liberation (AN10.155). Second, one should abide by the ethical precepts to preserve life, to not take that which is not given, to not commit sexual misconduct, to not lie, speak divisively, harshly, or indulge in idle chatter, have few desires for ourselves, goodwill towards others, and right views (AN10.199). The precepts are intended for both lay followers and monastics and provide explicit guidance for how to enact the ethical portion of the Eightfold Path (right speech, action and livelihood). Third, spiritual friends demonstrate seven qualities that lead to non-decline – that is, that lead one towards liberation and away from suffering, towards wisdom and away from ignorance, towards wholesome qualities and away from unwholesome qualities. These seven qualities are reverence for the 1) teacher, 2) Dharma, and 3) Sangha, also knowns as the Three Refuges or Three Jewels, as well as reverence for 4) training (ethical precepts), 5) concentration, 6) being easy to correct, and 7) good friendships. To display proper reverence towards these things one speaks in praise of them, encourages those who do not have them to find them, and, at the proper time, praises those who have them (AN7.35). As chaplains, we can cultivate these seven qualities in ourselves and demonstrate them to others implicitly through our behavior. Fourth, good friends in the Buddha's time display many of the qualities we would expect in friends today. They give what is hard to give, do what is hard to do, patiently endure what is hard to endure, reveal secrets to you, preserve your secrets, and do not forsake you in times of trouble (AN3.135, AN7.36). In relation to this list, we should remember that the Buddha's teachings were often contextual, and this teaching is concerned with peers, that is, friends who are on a parallel journey and within one's own sangha or community.

The Buddha discerns differences between kinds of friends, particularly those who are at a 'lower,' 'equal,' or 'higher spiritual level' than oneself and prescribes behaviors accordingly. I employ quotes here to sound a note of caution against spiritual arrogance. We should never assume the so-called 'spiritual level' of a care-seeker and maintain unconditional positive regard in our spiritual care relationships.

Let us fist consider those on a lower spiritual level. In general, the Buddha advised us to avoid bad friends. In most cases, the qualities of bad friends are the exact inverse of the qualities of good friends. Just as good friends lead to an increase in wholesome qualities and positive outcomes, bad friends lead to decline in wholesome qualities and increase in unwholesome qualities and negative outcomes. In fact, the Buddha emphatically advised that we should avoid those who are immoral, of bad character, impure, secretive, suspect, corrupt, depraved and rotten; others will assume we are like them and this will damage our reputation. Likewise, we should avoid those who are easily angered, exasperated, irritated, hostile, stubborn, and full of hatred and bitterness; they are the most likely to harm us. We should look on these angry persons with equanimity (AN3.27). We can include them in our circle of unconditional positive regard, even while maintain healthy physical and emotional boundaries. However, it is appropriate to associate with persons "inferior to oneself in virtuous behavior, concentration, and wisdom" out of sympathy and compassion (AN3.26), provided they will not harm you or your reputation. This is how those who are further on the path aid those who are just starting out. We should be an uplifting friend to others.

The Buddha advises associating with those similar to oneself in virtue, concentration, and wisdom. With these friends we can discuss concerns and teachings with ease. Associating with those similar to ourselves helps us maintain the wholesome qualities we strive for (AN3.23). These friendships are often cultivated among classmates in our degree programs, peers in our sanghas, members of our CPE cohorts, colleagues at work, and personal friends. We should seek to create and maintain our professional networks and friendships even after our CPE is completed to maintain our professional competence and spiritual development.

To improve our wholesome qualities, the Buddha advises us to associate with those superior to ourselves in virtue, concentration, and wisdom (AN3.23). We should 'associate with,' 'resort to,' and even 'attend to' those who are pleasing and agreeable, respected and esteemed, give good advice and deep talks, patiently listen, and do not encourage us to do wrong (AN7.37). Just as we must cultivate professional and spiritual friendships, we must also seek and learn from professional mentors and spiritual teachers throughout our careers. The Buddha even advised there are certain people we should never leave, even if told to go: those who cause unwholesome qualities to decline and wholesome qualities to increase in us and aid us in reaching fulfillment on the spiritual path. Whether life is easy or difficult[28] with them, we should not leave them "even if one is dismissed" (AN9.6). The final instruction may be hard to carry out in the present day (and I would not recommend it, as stalking and trespassing are both illegal), but the intention of the passage is clear. Maintain relationships with those who aid you on the spiritual path, even in the face of difficulties. In the modern world, this often means our spiritual mentors may be hundreds or thousands of miles away and we must make a conscious effort to remain in regular contact. Ultimately, this will benefit us and those we serve.

---

28 This sutta, which is intended for a monastic audience, elaborates the pragmatic meaning of this phrase. An easy life is one in which robes, food, lodging, medicines, and provisions for the sick are easily obtained while dwelling with that teacher, as teachers and their students commonly lived together in ancient India (and many monastic communities still live communally today). The difficult life is the opposite. Even if one should find oneself in a poor sangha, if one's spiritual life is being cultivated, one should not give that up to join a rich sangha where material comforts are plentiful if it means that one's spiritual life is neglected. In other words, money isn't everything.

The second theme explores how good friendship is the whole of the spiritual life because it is a necessary precondition on the path to enlightenment, according to three sections of the *Aṅguttara Nikāya*. First, good friendships are among the four powers (with wisdom, energy, and blamelessness) that enable one to transcend the five fears along the path, namely the fear of loss, fear of disrepute, timidity, fear of death, and fear of a bad destination after death (AN9.4). Good friends encourage us, help us give voice to our fears and overcome them, and encourage the development of the other three powers within us. By associating with good people, we preserve our reputation and support one another through the inevitable loss of loved ones. Second, one must be first surrounded by good friends and those friends must act to continuously support one's spiritual development. Good friendship is the first of the nine proximate causes for the development of aids of enlightenment. One must start out with good friends, only then can one develop virtue, be able to hear the teachings, abandon unwholesome qualities, cultivate wholesome qualities, and develop wisdom. When one has developed these nine proximate causes, one then cultivates loving-kindness and mindfulness, abandons lust and sensual desires, perceives impermanence, and eradicates the conceit of 'I am' to experience nirvana (AN9.1). Without first obtaining good friends, nirvana is impossible. Third, this chain of causation is explained again in the next book of the *Aṅguttara Nikāya* as being as natural as rain flowing downhill to the ocean. Through good friends, one hears the Dharma, then develops faith, and so pays careful attention to develop mindfulness and clear comprehension, then used to restrain the sense faculties, develop three kinds of good conduct (bodily, verbal, and mental), the four establishments of mindfulness (contemplating the body, feelings, mind, and phenomena), and the seven factors of enlightenment (mindfulness, discrimination of phenomena, energy, rapture, tranquility, concentration, and equanimity), leading to true liberation and knowledge. I cannot unpack the full complexity of this chain of causation here, except to say that good friendship is the necessary precursor. Thus, my preferred translation of kalyāṇamitra as 'spiritual friend' rests on its role within a chain of causation leading to spiritual fulfillment.

Finally, when describing the spiritual benefits of good friendship, the Buddha generally addresses "Bhikkhus!" or his fellowship of monks. In the *Tikaṇḍakī Sutta* (AN5.141-150) the Buddha advises his monks not to take as friends Bhikkhus with five qualities: those who instigate work projects, take up disciplinary issues, are disrespectful towards eminent monks, wander ceaselessly without settling, and cannot instruct, encourage, inspire, or gladden anyone with their Dharma talks. In other words, avoid being friends with nit-picky bureaucrats. Even those of us who are not monastics can take instruction from this passage.

For advice specifically for laypeople, then we need look no further than the *Dīgha Nikāya Sigālaka Sutta* or *Advice to Laypeople* (DN31.22) in which the Buddha advises the layman Sigālaka to beware of false friends (and how to spot them) and cultivate 'loyal' or 'good-hearted' friends. There are four types of loyal friends: helpful, steady, guiding, and sympathetic. First, the helper is generous, guards one's best interests, and is "a refuge when you are afraid." The last concept may be particularly poignant for chaplains, as Edward Ng writes for the Buddhist Peace Fellowship that "Refuge welcomes vulnerability and entangles the self with others and the world." As Buddhists we discuss the practice of 'taking refuge' as part of the ritual for 'becoming' Buddhist; it is in many of our daily chants and ceremonies. Ng reminds us that the Buddha instructs us to also make refuge for others through "mutual recognition, respect, care and concern." Second, the steady friend remains true in happy and unhappy times, guards your secrets, shares their secrets, and protects one in times of misfortune. Certainly, chaplains are there through times of deep misfortune and guard the confidentiality of careseekers. While we do not always 'share our secrets' the way we would with a personal friend, in the context of chaplaincy, this can be a call towards a professional form of authenticity and vulnerability – to be fully present with the suffering of another and to deal with them honestly and forthrightly. Third, the guiding friend advises against doing wrong, towards doing what is good, shares information, and "points out the path to heaven." In this sense, the friend is both a moral and spiritual guide. So being a good friend, even among laypeople, has spiritual connotations and responsibilities. Finally, the sympathetic friend rejoices in your good fortune, speaks well and encourages others to speak well of you, never rejoices in your ill fortune, and prevents others from speaking ill of you. In modern idiom, this friend 'has your back.' These kinds of friends, one should "cherish them with care."

As of the 1st Century CE, the characterization of kalyāṇamitra added a new dimension in the Aṣṭasāhasrikā Prajñāpāramitā Sūtra or *The Perfection of Wisdom in Eight Thousand Lines*. Throughout this work, three things are referred to as one's 'good friends:' the Buddhas, Bodhisattvas, and the Perfections (or the Dharma), particularly the perfection of wisdom (prajñāpāramitā). Within the *Nikāyas*, kalyāṇamitra is always a literal human person. Written several hundred years later, the metaphor of the Dharma itself as a good friend appears throughout the *Prajñāpāramitā Sūtra*. According to Läänemets, this could also be a reference to the scripture itself, since the "perfection of wisdom" is also the title of the work (2015, p. 174). Thus, sacred texts, or in the modern day, books, can also be considered friends (which is happy news to a bookworm such as myself).

The first theme we are examining – the characteristics of a good friend – appears early in the *Prajñāpāramitā*. In Chapter 1 of Edward Conze's translation of *The Perfection of Wisdom in Eight Thousand Lines and Its Verse Commentary*, as part of a dialogue with Sariputra and Subhuti, the Buddha explains that newly set out bodhisattvas may tremble when they hear these teachings only if they are in the hands of bad friends, but not if they are among good friends (Conze, 1994, p. 88). Good friends provide courage and reassurance. Specifically, good friends show four kinds of behavior to the new bodhisattva; they instruct, admonish, demonstrate and expound the Dharma. Demonstration of the Dharma by a good friend is described in two primary sets of virtues explored in the *Prajñāpāramitā Sūtra*: the Six Perfections and what Conze translates as the Four Unlimited, but most Buddhists known as the Four Immeasurables or Divine Abodes. The Six Perfections are giving, morality, patience, vigor, concentration, and, most important of all, wisdom (Conze, 1994, p. 320). The Four Unlimited (from apramāṇa), Conze (1994, p. 324) translates as friendliness (from maitrī, also frequently translated as loving-kindness), compassion, sympathetic joy and impartiality (also frequently translated as equanimity). Friendliness, per Conze, "consists in bestowing benefits on others, is based on the ability to see their pleasant side, and results in the stilling of ill will and malice" (1994, p. 316). This is a slightly unorthodox translation of maitrī, which is usually referred to as loving-kindness, kindness, beneficence, or goodwill. Maitrī "is considered one of the factors that motivates the bodhisattva to seek to save all beings from suffering," per the *Princeton Dictionary of Buddhism*. For the authors of *Prajñāpāramitā Sūtra*, the relationship is reciprocal, "For this perfection of wisdom entails an attitude of friendliness and compassion toward all beings." (Conze, 1995, p. 109) Friendliness leads one to pursue wisdom in the company of good friends and wisdom leads one to cultivate an attitude of friendliness and compassion. Likewise, the chaplain acts with friendliness or unconditional positive regard towards all, while also continuously growing in the wisdom to act skillfully for their benefit.

The second action of a good friend is admonishment, which we should also carefully consider for its implications on the caregiving relationship. Good friends will admonish the new bodhisattva and "point out to him the deeds of Mara," (Conze, 1994, p. 88) who is the personification of evil in Buddhism, a deity of sensual pleasures who tries to prevent beings from achieving liberation and 'conquering death.' In the early teachings, Mara is a personified being, though later and in modern instruction, Mara is often a metaphor for one's own aggregates, afflictions (i.e., greed, hatred and delusion), and death itself. We see the beginning of this shift in the *Prajñāpāramitā Sūtra* when the Buddha instructs Subhuti that a good friend says "'this is how the faults and deeds of Mara should be recognized. These are the faults and deeds of Mara. You should get rid of them after you have recognized them.'" We see that the "faults and deeds" are our own character flaws and bad behavior. Were they the faults and deeds of an external being, we would have no control over them, but as we are to recognize and shed them, they must be our very own. Chaplains should maintain relationships with their own circle of peers, mentors, and supervisors throughout their practice so that they always have around themselves someone willing to admonish them when it is needed.

The second theme – friendship as an important factor on the spiritual path – appears throughout. Chapter 22 is titled "The Good Friends" and encourages the aspiring bodhisattva to "tend, love and honour good friends," who are "The Buddhas and Lords, and also the irreversible Bodhisattvas." Moreover, the six perfections (giving, morality, patience, vigor, concentration and wisdom) and "the perfection of wisdom in particular should be regarded as a Bodhisattva's good friend" (1994, p. 236). The *Prajñāpāramitā Sūtra* identifies as a good friend anything that teaches the aspiring bodhisattva and aids her on her path to irreversible enlightenment. Good friends demonstrate and expound wisdom, they instruct and admonish the aspiring bodhisattva, and they are one's teacher, path, light, torch, illumination, shelter, refuge, place of rest, final relief, island, mother and father because "they lead him to cognition, to understanding, to full enlightenment," (Conze, 1994, p. 236). We find this view repeated and expanded upon throughout the sutra and its verse summary. The third theme – the outcomes of good friendship – exists as part of the overall descriptions of the bodhisattva's path culminating in enlightenment and nirvana.

In another Mahayana scripture, the *Gaṇḍavyūha-sūtra* or *Supreme Array Scripture*, Manjushri tells the disciple Sudhana that if he wants to become a bodhisattva, he must first "respect, revere, attend, and tirelessly seek good friends," (Läänemets, 2015, p. 175). The scripture is a series of pilgrimage stories as Sudhana visits over fifty good friends who share their wisdom with him as he advances through various 'gates' of insight to achieve enlightenment as a bodhisattva. Each teacher is recommended by the previous one as Sudhana advances, thus giving kalyāṇamitra the connotation of 'advanced teacher.' Yet at the same time, the author points out that "the concept of a 'good friend' is universalized" through the myriad kinds of people who serve as Sudhana's teachers: monks, peddlers, prostitutes, kings, and children of deities. In each case, Sudhana's devotion and gratitude to his teachers is emphasized (Läänemets, 2015, p. 176).

We see many of the qualities of bodhisattvas echoed by Śāntideva in the *Śikṣā-samuccaya* composed several centuries later, where he quotes the *Precious Lamp Dharani*:

> Through an unlimited number of different Dharma doors,
> They [bodhisattvas] discipline sentient beings in the world, in accordance with their intention.
> They act as friends in times of happiness and suffering;
> They are friends in good times and bad,

> And, having become friends in all activities,
> They discipline sentient beings through friendship.
> They are able to bear the problems caused by pain and disaster
> For the sake of friendship;
> As friends, they can bear torments
> For the welfare and happiness of the whole world.
> (Goodman, 2016, p. 307)

Here we see the attitude of friendliness mixed with the aspirational vows of the bodhisattva to save all sentient beings (though infinite) from suffering. We can see that the role of the bodhisattva as a good spiritual friend remained consistent throughout Mahayana teaching. Likewise the role of good friendship is emphasized on the path to awakening as "Those who are surrounded by religious friends / Gather a huge quantity of what is wholesome" (Goodman, 2016, p. 4). However, unlike the earlier Pāli literature, the *Śikṣā-samuccaya* (quoting the *Precious Lamp Dharani*) does not claim good friendship as the first link in the chain of causation leading towards enlightenment; rather it starts with faith:

> Because of having faith in the Victorious Ones and their teachings,
> And by having faith in the practice of the Buddha's heirs,
> Because of having faith in the highest Awakening,
> The mind of a great person is born.
> Faith, coming first, is the mother,
> (Goodman, 2016, p. 3)

While this passage states that faith comes first, the good friendship of the Buddha and having come to know the Buddha and bodhisattvas (his heirs) logically precedes faith. Without knowledge of the Buddha and his teachings, it would not be possible for faith to arise for there would be nothing to have faith in. Thus, we can read this passage as praise for a principle virtue, rather than a clear explication of causation. Indeed, as the passage continues, it contains many looping chains of causation, which return frequently to a praise of faith and its effects.

Śantideva builds on this in his second text, the *Bodhicaryāvatāra* or *Introduction to the Way of the Bodhisattva*. Friends are those who drive away the darkness of ignorance and inspire one to pursue the bodhisattva path; this includes the buddhas and bodhisattvas working for our endless welfare. While no friend, not even the Buddha, can save us from death, they can show us the path of virtue and liberation from the suffering of samsara, which is our only defense. Śantideva warns us to beware "childish beings" who lead us away from virtue (v8.9) and enumerates their vices. We should treat them with courtesy, but avoid their company, preferring the solitary life. If we do happen to find "your virtuous friend, your teacher" (v5.102) of the bodhisattva discipline, we must show them respect and never forsake them. They will help us master our mind and become a "true and honest friend to all" (v5.71). Śantideva also warns that we have often in the past brought about evils for the sake of our friends, so if our friends and teachers are harmed, we must control our anger and remain equanimeous. We can see that good friends are an aid along the path, but only when we ourselves have also developed skillful qualities. We find in Śantideva a complete intermingling of the three themes, discussing the characteristics of good friends, their role on the path, and the outcomes of good friendship sometimes within a single verse.

Finally, we turn to the last text consulted in this survey, the lojong texts in *Mind Training: The Great Collection* translated by Thupten Jinpa. This text adds a new dimension to the second theme by using the concept of good friendship as part of contemplative exercises intended to cultivate particular dispositions and mental states. Here we find several instructions guiding the practitioner to see all beings as friends. Indeed, one has no enemies, save one's own selfishness, which one must relinquish on the path. One surrenders selfish attachment through a focus on others, by adopting and cherishing them as dear friends. The lojong collection quotes Śāntideva:

> Whatever suffering is in the world
> Arises from wishing for one's own happiness;
> Whatever happiness is in the world
> Arises from the wish for others' happiness. (Jinpa, 2014, p. 100)

By "upholding sentient beings with deep concern" we "cripple this self-grasping" (Jinpa, 2014, p. 101) that prevents our own awakening. Moreover, one can distinguish friend from enemy within oneself, using your Dharma name for the part of yourself that is concerned with others' welfare and using your lay name for the part of yourself that is only concerned with one's own welfare (Jinpa, 2014, p. 102). In order to see others as friends, the lojong texts guide the practitioner to contemplate their great kindness; even those who harm you in this life have done you great kindness in previous lives. They are to be viewed as precious pieces of one's own heart. We should understand with sympathy that they only harm from a deluded mind and we should recall with empathy that we too have been selfish and accrued much negative karma. In this way, we come to see them as friends (Jinpa, 2014, p. 103).

These teachings can be hard for modern Americans to hear, especially coming from a culture that valorized self-esteem among children in the 1980's and 1990's as the cure for many social ills and now valorizes self-care and self-love as antidotes to perfectionist striving and material consumption. We must recall that this is a provisional teaching, a skillful means to progress along the path and cut "the jaundice of self-centeredness" (Jinpa, 2014, p. 129) and the arrogant boastfulness that often result from a sense of spiritual superiority that accompanies rigorous religious practice. We must remember these instructions are primarily given to monks, who are full-time religious seekers. While I would not necessarily suggest these contemplations as a starting point for ordinary laypeople, I believe they can be useful for those who pursue spiritual vocations, in whom (myself included) I have observed the occasional growth of harmful spiritual pride.

In addition to the three themes, we can take five major lessons from these texts. First, we need spiritual friends to inspire and accompany us on our own spiritual journey. These can be our religious teachers, professors and other educators, peers within our sangha, classmates, CPE cohort, chaplain colleagues and multidisciplinary teammates where we work, CPE and chaplaincy supervisors and professional mentors, the Dharma or religious teachings themselves, and the buddhas, bodhisattvas, or other divine/celestial beings in whom we place our faith. Second, we must avoid the company of unwholesome friends and cultivate healthy relationships within our personal lives. We cannot claim our personal lives have no bearing on our work, when the Buddha makes it clear that unwholesome relationships can inhibit our spiritual formation and lead to poor outcomes (e.g., loss of reputation, bad habits, or even physical harm). Those who act unskillfully should be treated with courtesy and compassion, even if they harm us, but we should distance ourselves from such individuals and keep healthy boundaries in our personal and professional lives. Third, we must cultivate virtues within ourselves in order to act as good friends to others, including generosity, wisdom, compassion, and ethical behavior. There are many Buddhist practices to aid in this, including psychological exercises to overcome 'Mara' in ourselves and train our minds to recognize internal and external friends. Fourth, we can act as kalyāṇamitra toward careseekers in our professional capacity through embodying these virtues in our interactions with them, serving as a spiritual and moral role model, guiding, advising, admonishing as appropriate (rarely and with caution), acting as a refuge for them in times of distress, and, perhaps most relevant to our role as chaplains, 'non-abandoning' them in times of trouble. It is our ability to be with careseekers during moments of profound suffering, to 'bear their torments' alongside them that is perhaps our most profound demonstration of kalyāṇamitra. Finally, this practice has spiritual benefits for both careseekers and chaplains. It supports careseekers through difficult times, accompanies them along their spiritual path, and can even facilitate their spiritual growth. For chaplains, it is also a practice for spiritual growth, aiding us to eradicate the selfish conceit of 'I am' and achieve realization. It helps both careseeker and chaplain to develop confidence (or faith), hope, virtue and wisdom. In short, we need kalyāṇamitra to become kalyāṇamitra in an eternal interconnected process of reciprocal friendship leading to mutual spiritual growth and, for Buddhists, enlightenment.

Modern Authors and Kalyāṇamitra

Rather than look to purely scholarly literature (as academic studies often examine the root texts themselves, as I have done above) for the meaning of kalyāṇamitra in modern times, I briefly review some popular Buddhist literature to show how the term is commonly understood. Namely, I have searched for the use of the term in *Tricycle* and *Lion's Roar* (formerly *Shambhala Sun*) magazines. Kalyāṇamitra is employed in various ways. All authors recognize religious teachers as spiritual friends, but the definition of spiritual friend and the kind of people who are considered spiritual friends are often much broader. This work shows kalyāṇamitra understood two ways: 1) as one role among many inhabited by a teacher according to the needs of their student and 2) as a universal paradigm accessible to many people in many circumstances, including non-Buddhists. This section presents several examples of each type from Theravada, Mahayana, and Vajrayana teachers of the present age.

Trish Deitch Rohrer likens the kalyāṇamitra to a 'special friend' and sees that friend embodied in the Buddhist teacher Sharon Salzberg of the Insight Meditation lineage. In a 2003 article for *Lion's Roar* magazine, Rohrer calls her "a mirror that shows you – if you care to take a look on a dark Saturday night – your mind" through her ability to sit in quiet awareness. Again we see an example of an advanced teacher being likened to a kalyāṇamitra, though this time not due solely to her position within the lineage, but due to the quality of presence she brings to her relationships with others. Andrew Cooper, writing about the Zen teacher Lewis Richmond in 2010 deliberately contrasted spiritual friendship against that of an 'authority figure.' As with Salzberg, Richmond simply seemed to embody kalyāṇamitra when he "guided the discussion gently – posing questions, sharing from his own experience, supporting what others had to say, contributing a timely quote, and so forth – and in that way, he helped the participants bring forth what is best in themselves." This ability related directly to the quality of his attention, which Cooper described as "genuinely fascinated by the experience of other people," in an article for *Tricycle*. Likewise, I encountered this description in interviews I conducted leading to the development of kalyāṇamitra as the culmination of the four-stage framework. In particular, it is the chaplain's ability to bring a particular type of presence, attention, and gently guided conversation to their interactions with careseekers that typifies this stage. This might sometimes seem at odds with the prevailing view of an authoritative teacher as spiritual friend, but it is not unprecedented.

Zen master Norman Fischer also identifies kalyāṇamitra with a teacher, while, like Cooper, also using the term to contrast it against authoritative ideas of the student-teacher relationship. He writes in a 2017 article for *Lion's Roar* that,

We often think of spiritual teachers as parents or authority figures. Maybe we think of them as coaches or trainers. But in the Mahayana sutras, teachers are referred to as *kalyanamitras* – spiritual friends. They are people who see us as we are, love us anyway, and care absolutely for our ultimate welfare.

A teacher's job is to model spiritual friendship. While at first we may be intimidated by the teacher, imagining him or her to be far more spiritually developed than we are, as time goes on the teacher transforms from a scary boss to a trusted friend.

Over time, we develop relationships with many such spiritual friends within our sangha. Fischer points out how essential such friendships are to the spiritual journey, quoting the Buddha's conversation with Ananda that began this review. It is important to have good friends beside us during difficult times and equally important to be a good friend to others when they are going through hard times; friends enable us to develop compassion and other virtues.

Fischer points out that as good as ordinary friendship is, the Buddha's spiritual friendship is different, deeper, more profound, and "takes place within the context of community," such as the sangha. In such a community, there is less need for the personal connection we associate with friendship. Members simply help each other as a matter of course. Fischer posits that this is because members of a sangha are bonded by the shared purpose of spiritual growth. However, I believe it could also be that the members of a sangha are inhabiting a role. They act as spiritual friends to each other because there is an expectation that they will. Likewise, the chaplain in a hospital inhabits a certain role that allows her to quickly achieve the intimacy and comfort necessary to act as a spiritual friend to those outside her spiritual community. Careseekers expect the chaplain to care, listen, put their wellbeing first, and aid them on their spiritual path. To the extent that the chaplain does this, she is kalyāṇamitra to those for whom she provides spiritual care. Fisher notes that spiritual friendships across religious borders can be particularly fruitful, such as his friendship with Rabbi Alan Lew, which began in 1968.

To Chögyam Trungpa, the spiritual friend is a role inhabited by a teacher at a particular stage of their student's development. As much as we may disagree with certain aspects of Trungpa Rinpoche's teachings and lifestyle, his presence and writing has been enormously influential on American Buddhism, as evidenced by the fact that his words on this subject were published in 2012 by *Lion's Roar*, several decades after his death. In this article, Trungpa likens the teacher to being a parental figure, taking care of their students as if they were 'infants' at the start of their journey and maturing with the student. It is as the student grows up spiritually that the teacher becomes kalyāṇamitra, who Trungpa likens to a "rich uncle" who wants to take care of you but also urges you to make something of your life. In this phase, the teacher has a stronger ability to advise and criticize because we take the criticism of our friends more seriously than that of our parents.

Thai practitioner and Nobel Peace Prize nominee (1993 and 1994) Sulak Sivaraksa would agree on this point, according to Matteo Pistono in his 2013 article in *Tricycle*. Sivaraksa was a 'razor-sharp' critic of Buddhists and non-Buddhists alike and saw this as part of the role of a *kalyanamitta* (Pāli) or spiritual friend. "According to Sulak, critique and debate is one of the most expedient means to progress along the spiritual path, and using such methods to expose flaws and deviations from the path allows for their correction." Sivaraksa was also no hypocrite and welcomed the criticisms of his own friends, even when it was his own ego they were deflating, on his path to spiritual growth. Sivaraksa was less interested in teaching the Dharma than he was in using it to address social issues such as poverty and environmental degradation and is hailed as one of the founders of the Engaged Buddhism movement. As such he may be considered more a Buddhist leader or activist than a teacher.

On the Vajrayana path, according to Trungpa, spiritual friendship is only the middle stage; eventually the teacher becomes a Vajra master to the student who is ready to be initiated into Vajrayana practices. At this stage the teacher can still be caring like a parent and warm like a friend, but also 'ferocious' like a samurai demanding the highest form of discipline from their student. At this point, the student must generate faith in the teacher to allow them to create situations where the student can grow. Of course, as noted, Trungpa was controversial for his relationships with students, some of which were sexual and there have been allegations of abuse.

Another Vajrayana teacher, Lobsang Rapgay, questions if the traditional Vajrayana understanding is still a good idea. In an interview in *Lion's Roar* in 2019, he asks "The question is this: in the twenty-first century, can we see someone as the embodiment of the Buddha, or is it better to regard him as a spiritual friend?" He thinks western students, in particular, have a hard time seeing their very human teacher as a perfect buddha (a problem I share) and it is exacerbated by unscrupulous teachers who use this to their advantage. Pema Khandro Rinpoche, in the same article, points out that the Vajrayana includes many models for student-teacher relationships, including that of the spiritual friend. She hints that problems may arise when practitioners cling to strictly to just one model. Both continue to identify spiritual friend with teacher, though teacher in a particular role different from that of guru or enlightened being.

In a 2017 article in *Tricycle*, Stephen Batchelor points out problems with guru devotion in a modern context. He believes it is based more on feudal (and thus hierarchical) social values and assumptions that do not mesh well with individualized, democratic western culture. At the very least, this caused his own attempts to practice guru devotion to feel hollow and inauthentic. At worst, it creates opportunities for abuse, such as we have witnessed with Buddhist teachers in recent years (Batchelor cites the case of Sogyal Rinpoche, recently accused of sexual abuse of students going on for decades). Pastoral care literature is aware of the dangers of abuse of spiritual authority. Some chaplains in this study expressed hesitation with the idea of assuming spiritual authority in caregiving situations, even when encouraged to do so by their non-Buddhist colleagues and supervisors.

Stephen Batchelor sees the kalyāṇamitra model as a corrective to the guru model, at least within Buddhist communities. He writes, "While the concept of the guru was present in the Upanishads that predated the advent of Buddhism, Gotama rejected it in favor of finding a good friend (*kalyanamitta*), whose role was to help you enter the eightfold path and thereby become independent of others in your practice of the dharma." He believes this model lost ground in favor of the guru model of the later Mahayana and Vajrayana lineages due to the influence of feudal social norms. Whether or not we believe that the role of the spiritual friend is to encourage one toward "independence" (a curiously American value I'm not sure was that prevalent in fifth-century BCE northern India), Batchelor does provide an alternative reading that may suggest a way to move forward.

The strong identification of kalyāṇamitra with teachers permeates all forms of Buddhism in the west (though it seems particularly strong in Vajrayana Buddhism). If we are to adopt Buddhist models of spiritual care, the hierarchical model of the teacher-student relationship will inevitably influence our thinking. (This relationship is not inherently abusive. Indeed, most student-teacher relationships deeply benefit both parties. However, it does tend to create a power-over relationship and opens up the potential for abuse.) I believe Buddhist chaplains should *not* regard themselves as teachers in relation to their careseekers, most of whom are not Buddhist and have not consented to enter into the kind of teacher-student relationship common in Buddhist lineages (even healthy ones). If this is our only or overriding understanding of the role of kalyāṇamitra, then this may not be a helpful paradigm. Or, at the least, we must carefully reflect on whether we can adopt an alternative understanding of kalyāṇamitra – and I argue there are many to choose from, as the ancient literature makes clear – to integrate with our work as chaplains.

Stage Four: Kalyāṇamitra

This section returns us to my research with practicing Buddhist chaplains. It is a continuation of the four stages of the Three Prajñās Framework for Spiritual Care begun in Chapter 3. In reading what the chaplains I interviewed had to say about kalyāṇamitra and their practice of spiritual care, you can compare their descriptions to the literature reviewed above and evaluate similarities, differences, and the suitability of kalyāṇamitra as a model for Buddhist chaplaincy. Recall what we have already reviewed in stage one: self, stage two: student, and stage three: chaplain. At each stage, the chaplain-to-be progresses through developing wisdom based on the three Prajñās of listening, contemplating, and practicing. Each of these can be further broken down based on intention, tasks and outcomes. Stage four: kalyāṇamitra is no different. We shall start with a general overview and then a description of the wisdom developed from listening, contemplating and practicing. We begin with the intention, tasks and outcome of listening.

The intention of listening to develop wisdom in stage four is more altruistic than in stage three. The chaplain listens to the other for the sake of the other and, in doing so, enables the careseeker to 'listen' to the sources of their own spiritual, religious, existential, and philosophical wisdom. The tasks involved in listening in stage four are very similar to those involved in stage three, including listening to both the careseeker and oneself, but the balance has shifted to the careseeker. Awareness of one's responses remains, but one's sense of self fades into the background or, in some instances, disappears altogether into a selfless awareness. Chaplains often found the simple term 'listening' inadequate, even when adjectives like 'deep' or 'supportive' were added. Some described this task as "holding their suffering," a "human connection…that stems beyond words…that breaks down all the labels," "being with patients who are critically ill and dying and not flinching," and "safe and compassionate accompaniment." The outcome of wisdom developed from listening at this stage is twofold. First and most importantly, the careseeker feels truly heard and witnessed in a profound way. They gain access to their own wisdom that empowers and strengthens them. Through being listened to, careseekers experience catharsis, clarity and a sense of value or worth that is affirmed by the chaplain's unconditional positive regard. Second, the chaplain experiences a sense of the sacred through the act of witnessing. One participant "learn[ed] how to be comfortable with other forms of the sacred moving through [me]" than those described in Buddhism.

The intention of contemplating as the basis for wisdom in stage four is likewise other-directed. While the chaplain will also contemplate, they primarily intend to facilitate contemplation for the careseeker. The intention is to make time and space for that contemplation to take place (but not necessarily be the one doing it), especially amid the hustle and bustle of a medical situation or daily life. The tasks associated with helping careseekers contemplate their situations are largely conversational. In addition to being present and listening, they include an ability to tactfully inquire and learn more, empathize with and understand the careseeker's situation, gently challenge and question a careseeker's perspective or understanding, help them interpret or reinterpret their own religious or spiritual tradition, suggest alternatives, support the careseeker's needs and goals, pray with careseekers, and, sometimes, help diffuse conflict between family members or family and medical staff in order to clarify issues or decisions. Vignette 2 with Chaplain B presents a clear example of several of the tasks involved in accompanying a careseeker as kalyāṇamitra while respecting the careseeker's religious tradition and aiding in spiritual growth. The fruition of wisdom developed through contemplating also relates to both the chaplain and careseeker. To the chaplain, it improves their understanding of the wide variety of human situations and responses to suffering. More importantly, however, it offers the careseeker the ability to think through their situation and clarify or change their perspective or behavior. The chaplains I interviewed reported numerous incidents in which careseekers were able to develop a sense of empowerment or determination, recognize a painful truth, accept or let go of a situation they could not change, make an important decision, achieve a sense of clarity or calm, find a new meaning, deepen their relationship to God, repent or seek forgiveness, become aware of and begin to process their emotions, and seek, find or offer family support.

The intention of practicing kalyāṇamitra is inseparable from an intention toward awakening, both for oneself and for others. Three different chaplains spoke directly about the practice of kalyāṇamitra. It is characterized as the whole of the spiritual path because it is the practice whereby one transcends one's preoccupation with self to pursue liberation from suffering for all beings. At this stage, the chaplain treats each person's awakening as equally important, seeing all suffering as equally in need of liberation, whether it is one's own or another's (i.e., seeing no distinction between them). Chaplains reported that the intention of equanimity eliminates the conceptual barriers between self and other, enabling them to be less protective of what they are conditioned to view as the 'self' and therefore more present for others. The tasks associated with practicing kalyāṇamitra include an ability to accurately assess the careseeker's spiritual situation and intervene appropriately to diminish suffering. In this process, the chaplain must often demonstrate 'code-switching' and translation. For example, in assessing a careseeker's needs, the chaplain may see their situation through the lens of the Three Poisons – greed, hatred and delusion – and then offer an appropriate intervention from the careseeker's own tradition, such as addressing an alienating conception of God (aversion combined with delusion) by discussing Jesus's love and forgiveness.

Appropriate interventions were as varied as careseekers and their situations, but were based in common values, documented in the data as positive emotions and values, and common outcomes, the most frequent of which was alleviating suffering, both short- and long-term. The outcomes of wisdom derived from practicing as kalyāṇamitra includes most of the positive values and emotions reported by chaplains, such as acceptance, accompaniment, awe, compassion, devotion, dignity, emotional awareness, empathy, equanimity, generosity, gratitude, happiness, humility, love, mindfulness, peace/calm/ease, and relief from suffering for both the careseeker and chaplain. Through accompanying careseekers as kalyāṇamitra, chaplains both experience a sense of selflessness themselves and also observe the nonself nature of the careseekers they accompany. One chaplain wrote in their reflection:

> [The careseeker's] experience of identity shift and health loss bring up the central Buddhist concepts of impermanence and non-self. This woman was once healthy and out in the world. Now she lies in a hospital bed with a medical bracelet around her wrist. She still has the same job

title, and can even do some of this work from her laptop in the hospital, and yet it feels "weird" and "different to be a patient," "like, this isn't me." She was aware of change happening in her life, which can loosen one's sense of who exactly "me" is.

Nonself and related concepts, including emptiness, impermanence, and interdependence, were referenced by almost all chaplains at some point in their interviews or reflections. The chaplains in this study find deep correlations between their work as spiritual caregivers and these foundational Dharmic principles. Direct, nonconceptual insight beyond words into these principles is the very nature of prajñā and the ultimate outcome on these chaplains' spiritual paths.

Implications, Applications, and Limitations

There are several implications and applications for the Three Prajñās Framework for Spiritual Care and the kalyāṇamitra model based on context and audience. First, I consider the normative paradox that is describing what is can sometimes imply what ought to be. I then proceed to the various uses of this research, including facilitating reflection, guiding education, discerning spiritual formation, suggesting spiritual care praxis, and developing wisdom. These are not the only implications and applications of this work, but they are the major ones. I must also be honest about the limitations of this work. This section is also critical of potential applications. It acknowledges their potential, as well as their pitfalls. More work is necessary and I encourage my readers to contribute their own reflections and research to the field.

First, the normative paradox is that in describing what is, we imply what ought to be. I began my research to describe and interpret what Buddhist chaplains do, why they do it, and how they understand it. I concluded it by recommending a normative Framework and model for how Buddhists ought to go about their work. Have I fallen into the normative paradox? I identified a progression common to the chaplains who participated in this research that may also be common to other Buddhist chaplains. But just because something is common does not mean it ought to be normative.

To resolve the normative question, others need to join the conversation, especially the faculty and CPE supervisors responsible for training Buddhist chaplains and the Buddhist teachers and masters with more experience teaching the Dharma and gauging the spiritual formation of students. This requires broader dialogue with the practice and professional community. Moreover, it may be that what is appropriate for one Buddhist in one context may not be appropriate for another in a different context, let alone appropriate for non-Buddhists. The pragmatic task (what we do) will depend on the outcomes of the normative task (what should be).

Second, the Framework was originally developed to describe how Buddhist chaplains facilitate 'theological' reflection in the context of pastoral care. The interview process revealed its broader applicability. The flow of the Three Prajñās of listening, contemplating, and practicing repeats across the four stages, and gains particular relevance in stages three and four. Moreover, the thesis asserts that chaplains with a strong experience of employing listening-contemplating-practicing to develop wisdom in stages one and two will be better equipped to enter stages three and four. In stage four, the chaplain facilitates reflection for others in the context of spiritual care by listening to them, assisting them in contemplating their situation, and helping them develop insight that can, if appropriate, predicate action, decision-making or personal growth. During this process, the chaplain practices many of the crucial skills for spiritual care, including: active listening; astute observation; skillful responding, reframing and questioning; and careful assessment and intervention. In describing how these Buddhist chaplains behave and what outcomes they achieve, the Framework can serve as a template for how other Buddhist chaplains might achieve similar results. We can learn from example.

Third, Buddhist chaplains working in interreligious settings receive their training through two primary venues: graduate education and clinical pastoral education. Graduate school consists of advanced coursework in religion and pastoral care. Standards are set by the Association of Theological Schools (www.ats.edu), the Association of Professional Chaplains (www.professionalchaplains.org), and other groups. Buddhist chaplains must meet these standards by receiving a seventy-two-unit graduate-level degree, usually a Masters of Divinity (MDiv), or proving equivalency. Clinical pastoral education (CPE) is a separate process governed by the Association of Clinical Pastoral Education (www.acpe.edu) and similar organizations. Chaplains who wish to become board-certified (bcci.professionalchaplains.org) must complete four units of CPE, amounting to 1200 clinical and 400 educational hours of training. Thus far, there has been limited dialogue between Buddhist traditions and these standards, and that dialogue has not yet been grounded in empirical research about the effects of this curriculum and these standards on Buddhist chaplains or those they serve. This research is thus an important addition to this conversation.

The roles of faculty and supervisors in these programs are distinct but overlapping. Both play a part in the education, both academic and practical, and spiritual formation of the chaplain-in-training. The Framework can be applied for both purposes and in both contexts. Academically, the Three Prajñās have often been used as a structure for learning the Dharma. They can be applied on a small scale, such as in a two-hour class on meditation that involves first listening to instructions, then a period of discussion, and culminates in actual meditation practice and the development of direct insight. This progression can also be used on a larger scale, over several weeks, months, or years. In their first semester or year of education, for example, students might be expected to listen and absorb new information. Later, they would reflect on that knowledge and integrate it into their own understanding. Finally, they would be able to practice that knowledge both through academic accomplishments and caregiving skills in CPE and other venues. This process is not necessarily neat and linear, but rather iterative and cumulative.

Fourth, the Framework could also be a useful tool in helping students, faculty, and supervisors gauge spiritual formation. Because the Three Prajñās focus on developing wisdom, not just on the tasks themselves, it also describes the hallmarks of wisdom at each stage. In relation to spiritual formation, for example, one can discern if one has developed wisdom based on listening when one is no longer 'hooked' by the careseeker's distress, avoiding what Doehring describes as "empathic contagion" (2015, p. 65). This would be a hallmark of stage three of the Framework. Naturally, the stages are not meant to be a neat and tidy progression, like ever-higher levels of a video game. However, when a student displays this attitude/behavior consistently, one can discern their skill-level and help them progress further.

The Framework also serves a further purpose for non-Buddhist faculty and CPE supervisors: placing the Buddhist chaplain's spiritual formation in a Buddhist paradigm. This is especially helpful when judging the fruits of prajñā, such as emptiness, nonself, and nonattachment, which may not be classically associated with advanced spiritual formation in other religious and psychological paradigms. The sometimes esoteric and frequently 'foreign' nature of these ideas to non-Buddhist faculty, supervisors, and peers sometimes hinders the spiritual formation of Buddhist chaplains. When a Buddhist chaplain is talking about the exchange of self with other in reference to egolessness, it would be easy for a non-Buddhist to become concerned about boundary issues and the risk of burnout, without realizing that a genuine experience of nonself obviates these concerns. Assessing whether or not such an experience is genuine may be difficult but can generally be demonstrated by the level of distress present in the chaplain. Nonself is characterized by the sense of 'nothing to protect,' which leads to setting down one's normal burden of egoic preoccupation, a sense of spaciousness or relief, and gentle confidence beyond one's ability to justify with words. My description is imperfect. This is an area in which further research with qualified Buddhist teachers is needed.

Fully assessing the spiritual formation of a Buddhist chaplain in their progress toward awakening is and should remain the purview of trained and recognized Buddhist teachers, masters, and institutions. Nevertheless, non-Buddhist faculty and supervisors could benefit from this Framework as a useful heuristic for making an 'educated guess' and either referring chaplains-in-training to their own spiritual resources or consulting with other professionals (including Buddhist professionals) should something seem amiss (if, for example, a student is spiritually bypassing signs of unhealthy attachment and burnout by claiming egolessness as the basis for their behavior). Faculty and supervisors will continue to be able to assess their performance *as chaplains* according to this and other frameworks.

Fifth, the Framework provides new chaplains with a flexible structure to follow in their interactions with careseekers. It is both a tool for discernment – to discover where a careseeker is and what they might need – and a guide for appropriate interaction. It describes intentions to cultivate before entering this work; tasks that one may use, as appropriate; and the outcomes of those tasks, by which to judge the efficacy of one's actions, particularly in relation to one's own spiritual formation as a chaplain. Judging the efficacy of these actions for careseekers with more certainty will require research involving the careseekers themselves.

Listening, contemplating, and practicing is a simple process, but it is also infinitely deep. It can be broken down in many ways and adapted to many contexts. The spiritual care literature, both Buddhist and non-Buddhist, provides many helpful guidelines for individual pieces, such as active listening or reframing techniques. This Framework helps place those techniques in relation with one another in a way that improves comprehension and retention. Thus, the Framework serves as a useful heuristic and mnemonic during spiritual care. The chaplains I interviewed reflected on how even a simple structure can help them be less anxious and more intentional when entering caregiving situations. One chaplain developed a four-part process as a result of their own reflection on practice:

> And the one I came up with was going through four phases, where it was arrive, allow, invite, and bless. Where I would arrive, and that's kind of the muscle memory, the real slow and present way of embodying myself in the room. Allow was allowing them to lead the conversation, like letting them be where they're at, and not trying to force anything. And then invite was inviting, whether there is something they want to lift up that is of concern or celebration, if it hasn't been done already, or more if they've started to. And bless is, could be just, "I wish you well," or, "would you like a prayer or meditation?" So, um, I think before, going through reflection, processing, and feedback, I was not so clear on my approach.

The Framework can serve as a guide in this way and help chaplains reflect on their practice and devise their own theories and guides. In the latter instance, I sincerely hope that fellow chaplains take the time to devise, share, and discuss their own practices to enrich the profession.

Sixth, the Framework is, through its reliance on the Three Prajñās, a method for developing wisdom. We have already discussed the nature of the wisdom developed by those who listen, contemplate and practice in relation to each of the four stages, characterizing it as the outcome or 'fruition' of each task at each stage. The progression of wisdom begins with the development of Right Intention and a cursory understanding of Right View or, at least, language to articulate it, if not directly experience it. Slowly, this language is internalized, integrated, and used to understand and interpret one's own experiences, providing insight into causation, followed by further insight into the pervasive nature of suffering. This is the internalization of the Four Noble Truths.

Through being accompanied by spiritual friends, one begins the process of developing confidence in the Dharma, diligence in one's practice, and a sense of support from a community of practitioners that fuels one's practice to go deeper. As one works with others, one's ability to articulate the wisdom they experience grows, and they also gain access to deeper observations about themselves and their work, perspectives hidden by their own biases and assumptions, which are now brought to light. They begin not only to see the web of causation, but also to understand their place within it and within their own community and context. They can see and apply many of the subtler parts of the Dharma, including the Two Truths and wisdom that serves as the foundation for moral behavior. Their practice of the virtues is enriched, which in turn fortifies their wisdom.

As they come to know themselves (and their nonselves) better, they become more open and receptive to other people, developing a genuine and nonprotective form of listening to others. They develop nonattachment, first to their own assumptions, then to their agendas for others. When one no longer worries over and protects the self, one develops a sense of authentic confidence, mindfulness, and openheartedness. Chaplains report becoming more "authentic," while simultaneously becoming less invested in fixed notions of their identity. They feel sufficient in their Buddhist identity, while they are also able to put that identity aside as needed by careseekers. This allows them to genuinely connect with careseekers and others and respond spontaneously and skillfully (with upāya) in various situations.

Finally, they can facilitate the journey for others. Careseekers experience many benefits as a result, and the chaplain's wisdom continues to grow as they experience a sense of the sacred through this act of placing the other first. By walking with careseekers, they gain far more experience in the specificity and complexity of human suffering than they could derive from their own singular experience, thus driving home the content of the Four Noble Truths. Finally, chaplains experience a sense of selflessness and transcend their own ego. Other is self and self is other; they are not separate or different. This results in liberation from suffering and ultimate wellbeing. Thus, the path of the chaplain as kalyāṇamitra is also the path of the arhant, the path of the bodhisattva, and the path of the buddhas.

Before concluding this section, I must acknowledge some limitations related to language. Even if we, as Buddhists, carefully define the role of the kalyāṇamitra in spiritual care, it will continue to carry the connotations of 'friendship' in the English language. This will cause immediate questions among our non-Buddhist professional colleagues, who will quickly (and rightly) point out that careseekers are not 'friends.' A chaplain can very quickly get into dangerous waters by crossing professional boundaries into the personal relationship that friendship implies. While we may push back against these questions by relying instead on the Sanskrit term (or Pāli, or Tibetan, or Japanese) as I have done in this work, using it in a technical sense, we still run the risk of blurring meanings and boundaries. Our inevitable need to translate the term (even only within our own minds) may lead us to color it with the connotations of the English word. This danger is greater in those chaplains who have are still developing their sense of selflessness, nonattachment and reflexivity. It could be easy to justify behaviors based in attachment and clinging to careseekers as appropriate for a spiritual 'friend,' when they may not be appropriate for a chaplain.

We must remain clear that kalyāṇamitra does not mean the same thing as 'friend' (spiritual or otherwise) in English. Its definition in *The Princeton Dictionary of Buddhism* (Buswell and Lopez, 2013, p. 410) identifies three types of spiritual friends: "An instructor; a fellow practitioner; and a lay supporter." The word 'friend' in English implies a level of personal intimacy that is not necessarily shared in descriptions of kalyāṇamitra. In the cases where they are a teacher, a certain level of distance (and hierarchy) is necessary to make the pedagogical relationship function. In the cases where they are a fellow practitioner, this could connote a true friend, but it could also mean a fellow classmate or a member of the same order who supports one's spiritual goals, but is not personally close. Likewise, in the case of a lay supporter who provides gifts to ensure the survival of an aesthetic or monastic, a certain amount of distance is expected, which would preclude 'friendship' in our modern understanding of the term. In general, one could say that a kalyāṇamitra may be, but need not necessarily be, a 'friend' in the modern sense. Rather, what makes one a kalyāṇamitra is the intention of goodwill and actions that benefit one's progress on the path to awakening. Intimacy at the level of friendship is not a criterion.

In the context of chaplaincy, where does the chaplain stand in relation to the careseeker? This question forces the evaluation of the kalyāṇamitra model. As mentioned above, this paradigm has implications for the relationship between the chaplain and the careseeker, some positive and some negative. These implications change based on how one understands what a kalyāṇamitra is and does. We have seen these types throughout the literature reviewed above. Let us now consider each type of spiritual friend in turn, starting with "instructor" or teacher.

The chaplains I interviewed perceived careseekers more as fellow practitioners or fellow seekers than as students. This perspective is closer to that of 'friend' in the colloquial sense, but continues to carry Buddhist overtones. Steve Collins characterizes the kalyāṇamitra according to three overlapping connotations: 1) in the most common meaning of friend as one "in which trustworthiness, reciprocity and perhaps a consequent mutual regard" are present; 2) as one who behaves within a Buddhist framework for morality; and 3) in "a specifically Buddhist sense [as] someone who helps another on the Buddhist path." However, he points out, "Anthropology suggests that this universal phenomenon need not necessarily involve our modern sense of friendship as two or more persons' mutual liking and enjoyment of each other's company," (1987, p. 52-53) though it can. It may also indicate a more reciprocal, professional, or even contractual relationship. We cannot assume that a 'friend' in other times and cultures is the same as a 'friend' in 21st Century North America. Nevertheless, we cannot escape our modern connotation and the potential for boundary violations it evokes. We would expect a level of mutuality from a friend that we would never expect from a careseeker.

Feminist clinical professors of psychiatry and psychology (respectively), Jean Baker Miller and Irene Peirce Stiver point out that some mutuality within the caregiving relationship is beneficial. They write, "Out of the experience of authentic, mutually empathic interactions, we acquire the 'feeling-thinking' understanding of ourselves and others that gives us a sense of a 'knowledgeable' basis for action" (1997, p. 36). In other words, mutual empathy in which we feel/think what the careseeker feels/thinks and the careseeker recognizes and acknowledges that mutuality (thus confirming our empathy is correct) serves as the basis for informed interventions. Lacking that mutuality, we are just guessing, or worse, projecting. Mutuality of this nature is built on a process of reciprocally sharing thoughts and feelings – not *equal* sharing, but reciprocal sharing. We need not reveal our most intimate thoughts and feelings to careseekers, but it can be useful to share our basic reactions to what they share with us and to confirm that we have an accurate understanding of their feelings and thoughts.

Miller and Stiver describe an example involving Ann, Emily, and Beth. Ann shares her thoughts and emotions around Emily's illness, and Beth responds not just to Ann's thoughts/feelings, but with her own thoughts/feelings. Miller and Stiver write:

> [Beth] puts the sadness they both feel into words and also expresses some fear in her own face and voice. What is especially growth-promoting is that as they talk, Beth shares both her own feelings and thoughts about Emily *and* those that arise in response to Ann's. (For example, she talks about the fear that *she* feels.) Because she does *both* of these things, she adds something to what Ann has expressed, and the two of them can move on to a fuller recognition of their thoughts and feelings, one that may not have been possible a moment before. (1997, p. 27)

In this scenario, Beth is not necessarily disclosing the kind of personal information about herself one might share with a friend. Nor is Beth expecting Ann to respond to her own fear the way Ann might respond to her personal friends. Rather, she is demonstrating to Ann that she empathetically shares Ann's feelings in a way that Ann recognizes. This recognition makes the empathy mutual, and thus the relationship becomes mutually empowering.

Many of these same qualities are described by the Pāli Canon as pertaining to a spiritual friend, including empathy:

> The friend who is a helpmate,
> the friend in happiness and woe,
> the friend who gives good counsel,
> the friend who sympathizes too
> (DN31)

Likewise, could not a chaplain be described as a helpmate through joy and sorrow, who gives good counsel and sympathizes? Yet we must heed warnings about boundaries (which are healthy even among personal friends) or risk what pastoral theologian Carrie Doehring describes as "fusion and empathic contagion, when caregivers feel what care seekers feel without awareness that their emotions have come from the care seeker" ((2015, p. 41). Indeed, one participant described becoming aware that the anxiety they felt during the spiritual care encounter was actually that of the family in the hospital room. The chaplain was able to avoid "empathic contagion" by relying on the awareness and reflexivity they built through their meditative practice. This episode demonstrates that Buddhists are likewise susceptible to this danger and have tools for dealing with it, though we must remain vigilant to apply those tools correctly.

Most careseekers are not Buddhist, which brings us to the second and third of Collins's overlapping connotations. The second connotation invokes Buddhist moral frameworks. In this case, a 'spiritual' friend is a moral/ethical friend. They treat one well and encourage one to also uphold moral standards. The Pāli scriptures include a list of disreputable folks who would not be considered spiritual friends, such as gamblers, drunks, and liars. Meanwhile, righteous folk, however personally close or distant, would be considered spiritual friends. In this case, the role of the chaplain in moral and ethical matters would qualify them as a spiritual friend to all, provided their own behavior is upright. In bringing ethical concerns and challenges to light, even when this provokes conflict, they are also acting as a spiritual friend, though others may not always thank them for it. Several chaplains I interviewed spoke of this part of their role, especially in relation to extraordinary efforts in end-of-life care. Buddhist chaplains are certainly influenced by modern professional and medical ethics (as well as social justice, e.g., feminism, critical race theory, etc.); however, the connotation of kalyāṇamitra in this case still exists within a framework of Buddhist morality.

Regardless of how we understand it, kalyāṇamitra is a Buddhist concept. While there may be analogous Christian (or other non-Buddhist religious) concepts, in both respects, the Buddhist understanding of spiritual friendship is inflected toward the goal of awakening, while the Christian concepts are inflected toward the goal of salvation through Jesus Christ. Behaviors that may seem similar on the surface have drastically different intentions. According to Collins, the third connotation of the spiritual friend is one who aids another on the path to awakening. These goals will nuance chaplain's interventions and may result in a mismatch between the intentions of the chaplain and spiritual goals of the careseeker. This mismatch was, to some extent, evident in our interviews where some chaplains report hesitancy in facilitating spiritual reflection for non-Buddhist careseekers or describe encouraging non-Buddhist careseekers toward particularly Buddhist goals, such as "awakening to the true nature of self." We should be cautious of such intentions. What if their true nature of self is an eternal God-given soul and guiding them through conversations or meditations that evoke experiences of nonself would create a harmful spiritual crisis? While models for care native to Buddhism can be tremendously enriching, we must also carefully consider their implications in interreligious settings, including how we translate and explain them to colleagues.

Conclusion and Reflection

The journey described above is, of course, not that of any one chaplain. It is a composite. Different insights will strike different chaplains at different stages. However, in general, the chaplains I interviewed tend to demonstrate this pattern. Stages one and two function much like the 'preparatory' stage of the *Sarvāstivāda Abhidharma*. Chaplains who have sufficiently traversed these stages and experienced their fruits are then better able to provide spiritual care and facilitate theological reflection for others. This is the primary thesis of this work. Inversely, chaplains who struggle in spiritual care and find it difficult to facilitate reflection for others will need the guidance of strong role models who can accompany them through reflection and build their skills. I have chosen to characterize this as the behavior of a spiritual friend, or kalyāṇamitra. It may also be the behavior of a bodhisattva, a buddha, or, simply, a chaplain.

There are many questions that remain unanswered. My conversations with chaplains suggested many alternative avenues of research that I was not able to pursue. I would like to conclude by listing some of them, in no particular order.

First, the Buddhist chaplains I interviewed provided many enlightening answers to why they chose to pursue the profession. Many saw it as an extension of their Buddhist practice. I wondered about how the social context influenced their choice of profession. In centuries past, a Buddhist who might have wanted to advance their spiritual practice might have become a monk or nun and joined a temple or monastery. In today's context, several chaplains decided that graduate school and a religious vocation was the obvious choice. Did they consider becoming monastics or clergy? Only one layperson mentioned considering this option, and two were monastics before becoming chaplains. Among those who became ordained after their studies began, did they do so out of a desire to become clergy or because ordination is expected of chaplains in a Christian normative paradigm?

In addition to motivations, it was fascinating to hear how chaplains connected their

Buddhist practice with their spiritual care profession. Within these responses were several nascent theories of Buddhist care that could be further researched and developed. Some of them see chaplaincy as an extension of practice, as mentioned above; some rely on classic Buddhist paradigms, particularly the bodhisattva; and at least one saw an inverse relationship, developing their Buddhist practice in order to become a chaplain. Some saw their chaplaincy as a mindfulness-based practice, while others saw it as a compassion-based practice. Yet others were drawn by the need to provide spiritual care to those who suffer, perceiving chaplaincy as a social duty. One described spiritual care as an 'art' and objected to scientific methods to quantify and measure it. What are the implications of the metaphor of spiritual care as an art? Motivations and the relationship between chaplaincy and Buddhist practice is a rich area for research.

Throughout this work, I have tried to outline where more research is needed and described particular audiences to be queried, including careseekers who benefit from the work of Buddhist chaplains, faculty, CPE supervisors, multidisciplinary teammates, and Buddhist teachers, institutions, and authorities. I hope that in completing this work and sending it out into the world, these parties will offer their feedback and correct any errors I have made. I will also continue to proactively reach out and work with these groups to continue advancing the field.

I encourage readers to compose a concluding reflection. Consider using the blank table at the end of Chapter 3 and filling in the boxes for the stage of kalyāṇamitra based on your own experiences. Or use the following prompts:

1. Can you identify anyone in your life who has acted as a spiritual friend to you? If so, in what way? What words or deeds of theirs leads you to consider them a spiritual friend? What has been the outcome of that relationship for you and for them?
2. Can you identify a time when you acted as a spiritual friend towards another person? If so, in what way? Consider the behaviors and paradigms of spiritual friendship outlined in the literature review. Which of these did you exhibit in your relationship with another person? What was the outcome for them and for you?
3. If the kalyāṇamitra model does not resonate with you, what model does? Choose a figure from Buddhism of any other religious tradition, describe their characteristics and behaviors. Why does this model resonate with you? How do you carry this into your work as a chaplain, if at all?
4. What could be the possible limits, dangers, or pitfalls of relying on the kalyāṇamitra model with careseekers? What could be the possible benefits and uses of the kalyāṇamitra model? Does it matter if the careseeker is Buddhist or not and, if so, in what way?
5. In reading this book, what questions have you developed about the work of Buddhist chaplains? What have you scribbled in margins or notebooks? Choose one and describe how you might go about answering that question either through scholarly research (e.g., scriptures and teachings) or qualitative research (e.g., interviews and surveys). What would this contribute to our praxis of Buddhist spiritual care?

~

Thank you for reading. May the merit of this effort release all beings from suffering and the causes of suffering. May all obtain profound, perfect awakening. Sadhu, sadhu, sadhu.

Appendices

Appendix A
Research Methods

If we, as scholar-practitioners, are to continue building the literature in the field we must do so, at least in part, through first-hand research. There are many methods we could use. It is important to be transparent about methods to ensure the best possible critique by fellow scholars and readers, and to encourage new scholars who are employing similar methods to add to the field. However, not all chaplains will be inclined toward research or interested in methods. Therefore, I have limited the summary of my methods to this brief section in the appendices for those who are interested. This section is a summary of material presented in chapter 2 of my dissertation and my earlier qualifying exam paper on the *Bodhicaryāvatāra*. Both are available at monicasanford.academia.edu for those who wish to know more.

Constructivist Grounded Theory Methods

The interviews and written reflections that form the foundation of the Three Prajñās Framework and kalyāṇamitra model were part of a qualitative study using a constructivist grounded theory approach to collecting and analyzing data and building theory. As a result, the lines between data collection, analysis, and theory-building are permeable, as these processes tend to overlap and/or switch back and forth. Grounded theory has precedent as an accepted research practice in relation to both Buddhism and practical theology. An iterative interview process using constructive interviewing practices and constant comparative analysis of the data revealed a substantive theory accounting for the practice/process of Dharma reflection among Buddhist chaplains. In accordance with grounded theory, the data drove the collection and analysis processes through strategic sampling to generate categories, codes, and theories that emerged as the Three Prajñās Framework.

I relied on a constructivist grounded theory model as developed by Kathy Charmaz and presented in her book *Constructing Grounded Theory, 2nd Edition* (2014). Constructivist grounded theory acknowledges the relative and subjective, or "constructed," nature of theories, which are "inseparable from social existence." In other words, rather than assuming the researcher (myself) is an unbiased and objective observer (an impossibility), constructivist grounded theory engages the researcher in the reflexive consideration of interpretive understanding emerging from specific contexts, interactions, and shared (or divergent) viewpoints between researcher and participants. This is distinct from earlier forms of grounded theory, which stressed objective empiricism. Reflexivity is also an important feature of the descriptive/empirical task in practical theology, per Osmer, and a constructivist approach supports this.

I have described my own subjective position to the research as per Charmaz, a position I continued to interrogate throughout the process. I documented and maintained researcher reflexivity through the process of memoing following each interview and at each stage of analysis. Memoing records the researcher's ideas, thoughts, and questions on the way toward developing a theory that accounts for the data.

Semi-structured interviews elicited long-form meaning-making narratives and details of the processes that affect this narrative using "What was it like…?" and "How was it when…?" questions and "Tell me about…"

prompts. Per Charmaz, this form of interviewing "emphasizes going into emergent phenomena and defining their properties." In this case, spiritual care praxis is an emergent phenomena predicated on the situations and contexts in which Buddhist chaplains are trained and work, as well as their personal backgrounds. "What" and "how" questions were used to "shape a subsequent theoretical analysis," per Charmaz, based on the chaplains' narratives. Interviews elicited the reflection process, that is, the methods – formal or informal – used to understand or make meaning. In this instance, the process is more important than the conclusion. As Chenitz and Swanson describe, "The researcher needs to understand behavior as the participants understand it, learn about their world, learn their interpretation of self in the interaction, and share their definitions." In developing the interview script and method, I relied on the work of Svend Brinkmann and Steinar Kvale in *InterViews: Learning the Craft of Qualitative Research Interviewing* (2014).

The chaplains I interviewed were given time and space to reveal or even "muddle through" their narratives, as reflection is not always a conscious, linear process. During interviews, I followed a short set of scripted questions and prompts, but also deviated from the script to elicit additional meaning from the narrative at critical points, particularly in respect to specific language, which is a concern of constructivist grounded theory interviews. For example, I was keen to know how Buddhist chaplains understood the word, "theological," especially in reference to reflection, but other language also emerged as significant, including the term "reflection" itself, and words such as "connection," "mature," and "experience." I followed constructivist interviewing techniques to gently inquire about the meanings of these words from the chaplains.

In addition to interviewing chaplains, I also collected written reflections on careseeker encounters from them. Gathering written reflections has multiple purposes. First, writing is itself a process of thinking and reflecting and, as such, can often lead to more nuanced and/or structured conclusions than a verbal interview. Second, the process of producing written reflections on spiritual care is part of the CPE program and a skill that all Buddhist chaplains and chaplain interns who have been through CPE are familiar with. Third, the written reflection prompts build on a familiar pattern, the last section of the 'theological' verbatim format commonly used in CPE, but with an added emphasis on the particularity of Buddhist experience.

Interviews and written reflections were analytically coded. In grounded theory, interviewing and coding is an iterative process, with frequent pauses in the collection of data to allow for analysis, followed by making adjustments to the interview process in order to focus on important ideas, concepts, processes, and meanings. This process is called "theoretical sampling," in which analysis drives further data collection to focus on particular categories until the data is "saturated," or no new information is being collected. Initial coding was conducted in an open manner advocated by Charmaz, through a combination of "in vivo" coding and thematic coding. I relied on *The Coding Manual* by Johnny Saldaña (2016) as the basis of my methods. Two intermediate coding passes clarified areas for further data collection and theory development. The analysis culminated in theoretical coding to fully explicate the theory emerging from the data. Theoretical codes "[account] for all other codes and categories formulated thus far" and condense the "products of analysis" into their most succinct form.

Literature review in grounded theory is also a continuous process. Some grounded theorists prefer not to conduct a literature review prior to collecting data in order to not bias the outcome. In this case, I conducted a cursory review of the literature related to theological reflection from non-Buddhist sources and a thorough literature review of work on the topics of Buddhist chaplaincy and spiritual care. I conducted a second literature review on the Three

Prajñās following the emergence of the Framework and a more detailed literature review of kalyāṇamitra for this publication. The ultimate goal of this study's methods is to develop an interpretive theory that accounts for the ways in which practicing Buddhist chaplains and chaplain interns currently engage in reflection in relation to spiritual care. My dissertation and this book are the ultimate result.

The Data

Fourteen participants were recruited for this study and completed the demographic questionnaire. Thirteen were interviewed (one was not, due to scheduling difficulties), eleven submitted written reflections, and five provided follow-up interviews. Below is a breakdown of the demographic data of the thirteen interview participants.

Gender	Count	Percentage
Male	9	69%
Female	4	31%
Race/Ethnicity*	**Count**	**Percentage**
White or Caucasian	7	54%
Latino/a, Chicano/a, or Hispanic	1	8%
Asian or Asian American	6	46%
(*participants could choose more than one category)		
National Origin	**Count**	**Percentage**
United States of America	7	54%
Latin American Country	1	8%
Japan	2	15%
Vietnam	2	15%
Sri Lanka	1	8%
Age	**Count**	**Percentage**
25-29	1	8%
30-34	3	23%
35-39	4	31%
45-49	2	15%
55-59	2	15%
65-69	1	8%

Buddhist Branches Practiced*	Count	Percentage
Theravada	5	38%
Mahayana	7	54%
Vajrayana	3	23%
Did not specify	1	8%
(*participants could choose more than one category)		
Multiple Religious Affiliations Identified	**Count**	**Percentage**
None	9	69%
Judaism (cultural or religious)	2	15%
Shinto	1	8%
Integral Yoga	1	8%
Years of Buddhist Practice	**Count**	**Percentage**
6-10 years	2	15%
11-15 years	4	31%
16-20 years	2	15%
21-25 years	1	8%
More than 30 years	1	8%
My entire life	3	23%
Religious Affiliation of Family of Origin (i.e., parents)*		
Same tradition of Buddhism as myself	2	15%
Different tradition of Buddhism from myself	4	31%
Ancestor worship or veneration	1	8%
Shinto	1	8%
Protestant Christianity	3	23%
Catholic Christianity	3	23%
Quakerism	1	8%
Judaism, cultural, but non-observant	2	15%
Indigenous beliefs, shamanism, and animism	1	8%
Atheism	1	8%
(*participants could choose more than one category)		
Ordination Status	**Count**	**Percentage**
Monastic	2	15%
Priest, Minister, or Dharma Teacher	6	47%
Not Ordained	5	38%

Highest Degree Obtained (or pursuing)	Count	Percentage
Other Master's Degree	2	15%
Master of Divinity	11	85%
Graduate School	**Count**	**Percentage**
Claremont School of Theology	1	8%
Harvard Divinity School	3	23%
Institute of Buddhist Studies	1	8%
Naropa University	2	15%
University of Toronto, Emmanuel College	1	8%
University of the West	5	38%
Units of Clinical Pastoral Education	**Count**	**Percentage**
Currently enrolled in first unit	1	8%
One	4	31%
Two	1	8%
Four	4	31%
More than four	3	23%
Other Buddhists in CPE Cohorts	**Count**	**Percentage**
No, I was the only Buddhist	11	85%
Yes, there was one other Buddhist chaplain intern	1	8%
Yes, there were a few other Buddhist chaplain interns	1	8%
Religious Affiliations of CPE Supervisors*	**Count**	**Percentage**
Catholic Christian	3	23%
Protestant Christian	10	77%
Muslim	1	8%
Jewish	1	8%
Unitarian Universalist	1	8%
Hindu	1	8%

(*participants could choose more than one category)

Care was taken to ensure diversity among the study participants in terms of gender, ethnicity, national origin, branch of Buddhism, alma mater, and ordination status. In this study, I have made no attempt to tease apart the perceptions and behaviors of different types of participants based on demographic groups, e.g., male and female, Theravada and Mahayana, etc. That may be an interesting challenge for further research. My goal was merely to ensure the sample itself was as internally diverse (though perhaps not in the same proportions) as the population of Buddhist chaplains working in the U.S. today.

These Buddhists all tended to be fairly isolated from one another during the CPE process in a way that is certainly not true of the theistic religions, particularly Christianity, despite these traditions' internal diversity. This subject was a repeated topic of conversation in the interviews. It was rare for these chaplains to experience extended interaction with another Buddhist chaplain in a clinical setting (such as CPE), where they were far more likely to be surrounded by Christian and theocentric peers. Access to Buddhist peers during graduate school varies by institution, but was far more common than finding Buddhist colleagues during CPE or subsequent professional employment.

I conducted thirteen initial interviews and five follow-up interviews using the constructivist methods described above. All interviews were conducted online using the video conferencing software Zoom, which has a built-in recording function. Chaplains were informed of this and provided verbal permission to record at the start of each interview. Only one participant expressed some concern over being recorded, but ultimately decided to remain in the study after their right to withdraw and the confidentiality and anonymity procedures were explained.

Initial interviews were conducted from June 1st to August 15th, 2017, and lasted from sixty to ninety minutes each. Follow-up interviews were conducted in the same manner from October 5th to 12th, 2017, and lasted from sixty to ninety minutes each. Initial interviews resulted in 194 pages of single-spaced text, or 113,663 words. Follow-up interviews resulted in 81 pages of single-spaced text, or 40,436 words. Interviews were transcribed in Microsoft Word by paid transcriptionists who signed nondisclosure agreements. Audio files were kept until the conclusion of the research and destroyed in December 2018. Transcripts were kept through December 2020 per the Informed Consent and have been used for alternative theoretical subjects; results were presented at the American Academy of Religion in 2018 and 2019. Interview transcripts were analyzed using the software Atlast.ti version 8.

Interviews were performed iteratively, interspersed with memoing and data analysis. Some approaches to grounded theory suggest pausing between each interview (or data collection) to fully code and analyze the data. I find this time-prohibitive and not very fruitful. It is difficult to draw useful theories from a single interview, which may or may not be idiosyncratic. Instead, I produced extensive memos after each interview, usually taking one to two hours to consider the interview, review certain sections of the audio file, and generate new questions. To elicit patterns in the data itself, I performed interviews in two- or three-interview sets.

After collecting and transcribing three interviews, I paused to code the data. The first six interviews were subjected to a single coding pass focusing on thematic and in-vivo codes. After the ninth interview, I began a second coding pass that included the first six, along with interviews seven through thirteen (during this coding pass, I continued to collect data up to interview thirteen), and focused on coding for processes and values. I refined my question set twice, once after the first three interviews and again after the second three interviews. A third question set was then used for the remaining seven interviews, for a total of thirteen interviews. Following the eleventh interview, all interviews were then subjected to a third coding pass, including the final two interviews. Memoing and theory-building occurred concurrently with interviewing and coding. A major pause in data collection at this point allowed for a thorough analysis of all interviews collected to date, as well as the written reflections. At this time, I developed several theoretical hypotheses, which I tested during follow-up interviews.

Follow-up interviews were requested with six participants, and five completed such interviews. By chance, three follow-up interviews were conducted on the same day, as per the scheduling needs of the participants. The question set used in these interviews tested the theoretical hypotheses generated from analysis of the initial interviews. The collection of so much new data in a short amount of time generated an intuitive leap from which the theoretical Framework developed. This Framework was tested during the final two follow-up interviews (and the fourth coding pass), which were conducted the week following the first three follow-up interviews. The same questions were used in these last two interviews, though the order of the interviews was rearranged slightly based on lessons learned from the first three follow-up interviews. In addition, the final two follow-up interview participants were presented with an early draft of the Framework for their feedback and critique. Memoing took place between each follow-up interview, and these were transcribed and included in the final pass of coding and analysis.

In addition to interviewing, I collected written reflections on careseeker encounters from the chaplains. Of the thirteen chaplains who provided initial interviews, eleven also provided written reflections. Reflections varied in length from one-to-three pages, with the shortest being 491 words and the longest being 1,680 words. Some reflections included the reflection questions, below, in the text. A total of twenty-five pages, or 11,116 words of text, from written reflections were analyzed. The following questions were used as reflection prompts related to a spiritual care encounter:

1. What is the key spiritual, religious, or existential issue, content, connection, or assumption that you identified in this encounter?

2. What is your understanding and experience of that issue in relation to the Dharma/Dhamma? (If there is a relation.)
3. Where did you learn about this issue, aside from your own experience? (Please describe sources, such as books, sutras/suttas, teachers or teachings, etc.)
4. Is there a theme or pattern connecting this issue to other spiritual care experiences?

Analysis of essays in *The Arts of Contempltive Care*, as well as the existing structure of the CPE verbatim, contributed to the development of questions that were appropriate and intelligible to the chaplains. Questions were designed to be open-ended enough to allow participants to interpret them as best suited their reflexive process, yet directed enough to elicit data relevant to the research questions.

The Five Hypotheses

The following five hypotheses were developed based on data from the initial interviews and reflections. I also presented an early draft of the Framework to the final two chaplains for their feedback. This section summarizes responses to each of the five hypotheses and references how these responses helped develop the Framework.

Hypothesis One

> Chaplains who have themselves done their fair share of spiritual seeking and experienced a sufficient amount of other-initiated reflection (i.e., been prompted to seek by teachers and supervisors) seem to be better able to facilitate reflection/seeking in careseekers through appropriate questioning, accompanying, drawing out, reframing, and responding (sub-codes).

This hypothesis developed from the memo related to maturity and questions about the relationship between codes for "reflection" and "seeking." It included questions like:
1. "For you, what characterizes mature reflection vs. immature or still-developing reflection?"
2. "If you were helping someone else learn how to reflect, what might you expect to see in a novice?" and
3. "How might you help them mature in their practice of reflection?" Chaplains spontaneously shared or were prompted to provide real examples from spiritual care as well as their own experiences and theories.

Four participants responded to this hypothesis affirmatively and one response was noncommittal (which became typical of this participant throughout the follow-up interview and may be the result of an indirect communication style). Participants further defined what constitutes "mature" and "still-developing" reflection, described how they support others in maturation, and detailed how they were supported when sharing their own reflections with others. Sharing their reflections with others and receiving guidance and feedback was critical to their maturation process, as was effective modeling from more mature spiritual friends. One participant who, in my opinion, seemed highly capable of providing articulate and reflective responses in interviews, described having numerous "spiritual directors" of various faith traditions and groups who helped them "open up for the first time" and learn "how to talk into a group and be held by a group." Through this, they developed a more "mature" ability to reflect on their own.

Responses to this hypothesis informed both "stage two: student" and "stage four: spiritual friend" in the Three Prajñās Framework. Chaplains describing the maturity of their own reflection process in relation to spiritual friends who guided them on their path during stage two helped inform the spiritual friend role, a role the chaplains themselves assumed in stage four. The supportive activities described by the chaplains, the intentions with which they undertake them, and the outcomes they produce inform stage four, particularly in relation to wisdom developed from listening and contemplating. The topic of maturity helped inform the entire developmental arc of the Framework, from stage one to stage four, especially in relation to the outcomes of wisdom developed through contemplation at each stage.

Hypothesis Two

> Chaplains who can form strong connections with careseekers are better able to facilitate 'theological' reflection.

This hypothesis developed from what chaplains said about the importance of connection as an attempt to explore the relationship between connection (and by, extension, being present) and the main topic of this research, 'theological' reflection. As the analysis of significant concepts (above) reveals, participants spoke to different clusters of concepts, one related to reflection – mostly their own reflection – and the other related to spiritual care, but rarely about facilitating reflection for others. It was important to investigate the relationship between these two clusters, and "connection" was the most logical bridging concept. This hypothesis was explored with questions such as:
1. "How would you define a sense of connection with a careseeker?"
2. "What factors contribute to a good or strong connection?"
3. "What factors might make it hard to form a good connection?" and
4. "What do you do or say when you are with a careseeker to initiate or maintain a good connection?"

All participants responded to this hypothesis affirmatively. In fact, most perceived it as a foregone conclusion. Connection is based on rapport, trust, and accompaniment. Not only must chaplains accompany careseekers, but careseekers must also perceive and welcome that accompaniment. When both of those things happen, it is called "connection." Connection serves as the foundation for facilitating 'theological' reflection, even in careseekers who are at first resistant or hesitant.

Responses to this hypothesis helped develop better language for describing the spiritual friend's role in relation to 'theological' reflection, especially the aspect of accompaniment. The spiritual friend is described thus in the Pāli scriptures (DN31):

> [Buddha said:] "These four, young householder, should be understood as warm-hearted friends: he who is a helpmate, he who is the same in happiness and sorrow, he who gives good counsel, he who sympathises... [sic]
>
> The friend who is a helpmate,
> the friend in happiness and woe,
> the friend who gives good counsel,
> the friend who sympathises too – [sic]
> these four as friends the wise behold
> and cherish them devotedly
> as does a mother her own child."

The sutta continues, as the Buddha advises the young son of a lay disciple, defining the actions of the helpmate, the friend in happiness and woe, the good counselor, and the sympathetic. Each of these behaviors were, at some point described by the participants in this study as "spiritual care," many in direct relation to building a connection with careseekers and facilitating 'theological' reflection. Thus, we see a direct parallel between the activities of the spiritual friend and the chaplain: both support and protect others; empathize with the others in joy and sorrow; gently inquire and guide, especially in ethical decision-making; and only have goodwill for the others. Having good friends is the first step in the path to awakening.

Hypothesis Three

> The ability of a chaplain to facilitate 'theological' reflection that enables the careseeker to connect with something beyond oneself is predicated on or influenced by that chaplain's experience of a similar connection to: 1) something sacred; 2) God or the divine; 3) a sense of oneness, wholeness, or interconnectedness; 4) a sense of meaning or purpose for their own life; or 5) other people to whom they look for guidance during reflection.

This hypothesis developed from some statements by chaplains that showed discomfort with the idea of working with careseekers on spiritual concepts with which the chaplain was not familiar or comfortable. This hypothesis is about the chaplain's ability to relate to careseekers' experiences, as was the question my rabbi asked me at the outset of my own CPE ("How will you relate to careseekers who have a strong experience of God?"). The key term in this question is "similar." Does spiritual care only benefit one if the chaplain has a similar experience? Moreover, is similarity of experience predicated on the characteristics of connection or on that which one is connected to (or both)?

Five different types of connections that appeared in the data were used in exploring this hypothesis. Participants were asked questions including:
1. "What is the difference between reflecting for oneself or on one's own experience and "facilitating" reflection for another person? How do you help someone else reflect on their experience?" and
2. "When a careseeker brings up a spiritual or religious topic that is not commonly addressed in the Dharma or that they are clearly thinking of in relation to a theist worldview, such as forgiveness or God's will, how do you understand that topic?" Chaplains often gave specific examples of how they gained insight into such topics; how such conversations went, if any occurred; how they assessed the function of the careseeker's understanding in the situation; and how they facilitated opportunities for the careseeker to reflect and/or mature, including concrete things the chaplain might say or do in such situations.

Responses to this hypothesis were more mixed, with three affirmative and two noncommittal. The three affirmative responses contained different nuances. Therefore, in this section, it may be easiest to describe each response in turn. The first interviewee provided the strongest favorable response, stating, "I think spiritual experience is the same." This chaplain referenced a sense of connection to deeper levels of self/nonself and emphasized practice as a major component, which was corroborated by other chaplains elsewhere in the data. This chaplain remarked, "It's hard to go to the depth of, and really be there in suffering, if you haven't gone through that for yourself."

This was also corroborated by others, who described the necessity of working through one's own issues, past traumas, grief, biases, and emotional processes to come to a deeper sense of awareness of oneself and one's relation to all things. They described connecting both inwardly and outwardly at the same time. This follows a classic formula from the Dharma in which the Buddha demonstrates the nature of nonself by looking in detail at the self. One looks inward to begin to understand the nature of all phenomena, including both oneself and others, and develop wisdom. In the more immediate sense, this provides the chaplain with an up-close and personal view of human psychology. "Your ability to kind of go to the difficult places with patients is kind of predicated on some degree on how much you've done the work. Which I think relates to your experience of God or oneness or you know, gone through the spiritual journey." This participant described an ability to connect based on experiencing a similar process, rather than a similar outcome.

The second follow-up interview also provided an affirmative response, but with a caveat. This participant echoed the necessity of looking at one's own mind as a common aspect of the spiritual journey. However, they also held out the possibility that the interaction between the caregiver and careseeker could also be a space in which sacred connection could spontaneously occur, without being predicated on any previous connection experienced by either party. In that instance, neither party need have any familiarity with the strong sense of connection that could, nevertheless, develop in and through the caring encounter itself. While this possibility always exists, for this participant, certain skills and attitudes in the chaplain (e.g., curiosity, gentle questioning, etc.) and certain predispositions in the careseeker (i.e., some kind of spiritual view, as opposed to complete nihilism) did make those instances of spontaneous connection more likely. This is akin to the Buddhist dialogue on sudden versus gradual enlightenment. Some lineages hold that enlightenment is the culmination of lifetimes of effort and cultivation, while others maintain that it just happens in a sudden moment of awareness of the wisdom that was always present. Their practices look remarkably similar, leading one to conclude that the conditions for sudden enlightenment can be cultivated, though the final moment of enlightenment arrives like lightning.

The third interviewee was more noncommittal on this topic, which was characteristic of this chaplain's responses to four of the five hypotheses, possibly due to their communication style. While the chaplain themselves described a strong sense of interconnection with all things, they were hesitant to ascribe any significance to this in relation to their work with careseekers, particularly Christians. As a result, they "hesitate to talk about my faith to a lot of you, those people who are from different faith traditions. But sometimes they allow me to go talk about my worldview of my faith. Then in that case I talk to them and I wish you feel you are connect or you are supported by others including the God." They wished for careseekers to experience a similarly enriching sense of connection, but were not prepared to speak on behalf of careseekers to characterize that connection, or to assert that such a similar sense of connection was helpful.

While on the one hand stating, "I try not to kind of guide the person to some direction and I am not skillful in this kind of situation," that is, facilitating 'theological' reflection, they also describe behaviors remarkably similar to other chaplains who believe they are doing just that, including asking open-ended questions, showing curiosity, allowing the careseeker to lead, not making assumptions, listening, and holding an intention of compassion and goodwill. This may be due to a misunderstanding regarding the nature of 'theological' reflection and the behaviors necessary to facilitate it for others.

The fourth interviewee affirmed the hypothesis and suggested splitting it into separate concepts. On the one hand, the experience of interconnection:

> …falls more in the category of embodied transmission and the ability to model/lead through/accompany falls more in the category of a learned, albeit often only lately learned skillset. And those, to me, rightly or wrongly, I think of in two different camps. I can see strong arguments being made that they are one in the same thing, but I put one in the skillful means basket and the other in the wisdom basket.

Embodied transmission refers to the experience of having received the Dharma (i.e., it being transmitted by a teacher) and then living in accordance with the Dharma (i.e., embodying it). This is analogous to wisdom, as wisdom is embodied by its nature. On the other hand, skillful means, or upāya, refers more to a particular strategy or method. Methods can, to an imperfect extent, be transmitted independent of wisdom. For example, the Five Precepts (i.e., no killing, stealing, lying, sexual misconduct, or intoxicants) can be followed and will result in spiritual progress even before one possesses the embodied wisdom that fully demonstrates why they should be followed and how they lead to spiritual progress. However, as this chaplain and others affirmed, the ongoing successful use of upāya is dependent upon developing wisdom. Chaplains must practice and develop wisdom of their own in order to correctly employ the right methods with careseekers at the right time to help them develop through 'theological' reflection.

The fourth interviewee, like the former chaplain, stated, "I've never tried to do that particular role [of facilitating theological reflection]," and then they explained what they *have* done with careseekers, which would qualify as just that, including listening, waiting for an opening, gentle questioning, and then assessing "the impact of how they're relating to their belief structure and then their hearing and understanding making meaning." This again, could be due to lack of familiarity with just what it means to facilitate 'theological' reflection in the context of pastoral care.

The final interviewee also provided a qualified response. When asked if "the ability of the chaplain to facilitate theological reflection that enables the careseeker to make those connections is influenced by the chaplain's own history of making those connections," the chaplain responded, "I think the only way that works is if the chaplain is willing to share said connection and I know that a lot of chaplains now, especially, are becoming more and more hesitant with themselves. We can be open. But you have to be very careful with it."

Other chaplains had discussed appropriate self-disclosure during the course of this study, but not in relation to facilitating theological reflection for others. Further probing and clarification revealed that this chaplain also seemed to have a limited understanding of what constituted facilitating 'theological' reflection. They later affirmed, "I think if you frame it in terms of the search rather than the connection, I think that would be a lot better." They felt that sharing a similar faith background could help build a strong connection, but that it wasn't always necessary. The chaplain then described working with a couple experiencing relationship difficulties and facilitating reflection between the husband and wife, though they did not use self-disclosure in this process. Unfortunately, problems with the internet connection precluded further questioning as to whether or not a sense of connection with these two careseekers enabled deeper reflection or not. The interview ended inconclusively.

Those chaplains who do not characterize their own behavior as facilitating 'theological' reflection, yet describe working with careseekers on spiritual and religious topics with strikingly similar language to that of the Christian literature on this kind of facilitation seem to share similar misconceptions. They perceive 'theological' reflection as primarily concerned with correct belief. That is, to facilitate 'theological' reflection, one needs to know what constitutes orthodoxy in a particular tradition, evaluate the careseeker's statements according to that standard, and guide them toward correct belief. Therefore, chaplains claim they don't facilitate 'theological' reflection because they hold concerns such as the fear of not knowing enough about Christianity, "my main concern…is not what they believe in, whether or not it's right," or "I'm not here to preach" and impose my beliefs on the careseeker. I expanded on this theme for a topic present to the American Academy of Religion entitled "Theological Reflection without Theo" and described this phenomenon with the phrase "semantic impasse." This presentation can be found at monicasanford.academia.edu.

The responses from this hypothesis were rich in implications and verified the significance of this research. Buddhist chaplains may find it difficult to relate their work to standards of chaplaincy that are so deeply embedded in Christian language with which they may have little fluency and about which they may have many misconceptions. Developing materials on Buddhist chaplaincy from Buddhist viewpoints, using frameworks, theories, and language native to the Buddhist traditions could have tremendous benefit in helping Buddhists better understand their work as spiritual caregivers.

Hypothesis Four

> Buddhist chaplains infrequently report a sense of personal connection to God or the divine and frequently report a sense of connection or a feeling of oneness, wholeness, interconnectedness, or emptiness; a sense of meaning or purpose for their own life; a very strong connection to other people; and, occasionally, a connection to a something sacred. Buddhist chaplains also tend to locate "authority" in these experiences, rather than in revelation of divine purpose, and use sacred texts as important guides to experience rather than as authoritative in-and-of themselves.

This hypothesis developed from the way participants spoke about the importance of experience, both in relation to reflection and practice, in initial interviews. Some chaplains responded to questions about sources for ideas on reflection by stating they didn't really use them, instead preferring to rely on their own experience. Participants were asked if they experience connection to something sacred and how they would characterize it, as well as where they locate "authority" and how they understand that term. A subset of this question included exploring the difference between analysis and "being present" and the different roles of each in spiritual care.

All participants responded to this hypothesis affirmatively and one, though affirmative, also presented a potential caveat based on a hypothetical situation, though their direct experience also affirmed the hypothesis. Regarding the hypothesis, one chaplain responded, "I think that does make a lot of sense because the experience, the action, you know, the practice, those are the authorities really. The results of the practice show the merit of doing them."

Although this hypothesis was affirmed as a difference between Buddhist chaplains and their theistic peers, the participants were also clear in articulating strong commonalities with peers and careseekers of other religions in relation to religious experience. Responses to this hypothesis helped develop aspects of the thesis related to the importance of spiritual friendship across religious lines. Having spiritual friends of other religions was tremendously enriching for the chaplains in this study. Sometimes that spiritual friendship happened prior to CPE and sometimes during. Many of the more negative aspects of participants' CPE experiences correlated to a lack of spiritual friendship and to behavior that could not be characterized according to the criteria of spiritual friendship. Moreover, Buddhist chaplains who had spiritual friends of other religious traditions seemed better able to accompany careseekers of other religious traditions as spiritual friends themselves. This sample size is, of course, too small to generalize, but this aspect of the thesis holds true at least for the chaplains in this study.

Hypothesis Five

This hypothesis was presented as an either/or scenario from which chaplains were asked to pick which one better represented their experience:

EITHER
Hypothesis 5a

Buddhist chaplains are hindered in their ability to facilitate 'theological' reflection that helps careseekers connect with God or the divine due to a lack of personal experience with this connection.

OR
Hypothesis 5b

Buddhist chaplains are not hindered in their ability to facilitate 'theological' reflection that helps careseekers connect with God or the divine due to their ability to connect with something beyond themselves even though they do not conceptualize it as God or the divine.

This hypothesis developed from a need to clarify the basis for connection and the relationship between the experiences of seeking and connecting with others. This hypothesis often touched on themes explored in the earlier hypotheses, with questions such as:
1. "In what ways, if any, do you find that your experience of also seeking meaning, purpose, and goodness in your life, however understood, helps you connect with careseekers who also seek these things?"
2. "In what ways, if any, do you find that your experiences are so different from those of careseekers that sometimes it is hard to relate to what they're going through or connect with them?"
3. "What hinders or aids your ability to make connections across religious or spiritual difference?" and
4. "What hinders or aids your ability to facilitate theological reflection for careseekers?" As a part of this line of questioning, I also inquired as to whether the follow-up interview participants had experienced situations in which they felt a strong connection with a careseeker that they were then unable to adequately explain to their CPE cohort, as a few participants reported in initial interviews.

Four participants responded in favor of hypothesis 5b, while one participant provided a noncommittal response. The noncommittal response was simply off-topic, and time precluded further investigation. The four who affirmed the second hypothesis were unequivocal. One participant pointed out that spiritual care is "not just about compassionate connection," but about what that connection makes possible, including reflection, healing, and growth.

As a side note, one chaplain also reported a unique experience with her CPE supervisor relating to the fruits of Buddhist practice, especially the development of compassion. It is worth quoting here in its entirety:

> **Participant**: I was so lucky to be in direct contact with my spiritual community. My Buddhist community was very close to where I was staying for the summer [during CPE], and I'm incredibly grateful for that, Monica, because I would have this experience out on the [hospital] floor of just compassion, radiating out of my body like heat, I mean that's powerful. And I could tell other people picked up on it. You know, you can tell by people's responses and that kind of thing and especially the careseekers. And it didn't happen every day. It happened a lot, it happened the most on heaviest clinical days. So, you know the pretty hour on call shift, it was like ka-bam. And even though I wrote about it in my reflections and I made casual, I didn't talk about so much with my peers, because it seemed it might lead to some comparison or not great ideas, but it

did come up on different occasions. All this compassion was coming up and my supervisor just did not get it. She didn't, it bounced off of her and she kept telling me towards the end of our unit that I needed to bring my heart forward more and that my way of dealing with people was, that I use certain language from the Theravada tradition about like, you know, "I felt a flash of frustration arise" or I would say "frustration arises momentarily and goes away" like that's my lived experience of emotion at this point after practicing mindfulness meditation for close to 15 years. And she was like "there's not enough 'I' in there. You need to talk about yourself more," she wanted me to do something that is not in my religious tradition. [laughter] Like, it was the really mind-blowing part about this is, Monica, she was Unitarian Universalist, she wasn't a Christian. She just wasn't getting it. So, it definitely happened and I'm a pretty articulate person verbally, but I felt like there is this whole piece of if you don't have a deist orientation, if you're not super emotional and, I am pretty emotional, but like in the way that CPE wants you to be, somehow you're not making a heart connection and that's a load of crap.
Researcher: I am empathizing with you so strongly.
Participant: It was tough. And I just, it was in me and it was a good thing for me in my practice because it relieved me of the need to be seen by person in charge. I was just like, "you know what, I'm having this experience, this is not about her." It is about, you know, this vessel [myself] and these other care seekers and yep...

Regardless of what this excerpt reveals about assumptions (either founded or unfounded) regarding Christian and Unitarian Universalist supervisors, it also reveals some of the challenges chaplains in this study faced in attempting to justify the fruits of their practice – literal experiences of non-self – against supervisors' expectations regarding the appropriate language with which one ought to describe one's experiences. Were an awakened Buddhist practitioner, having fully realized the truth of nonself and gained the ability to fully prioritize the suffering of others (seeing no distinction between self and other), to enter CPE and describe their experiences to their supervisor, there is a good chance they might be diagnosed with a pathological disorder. Emphasis on appropriate emotional disclosure and self-care is important, especially in developing chaplains, but it need not invalidate the fruits of Buddhist practice. Chapter five describes these fruits in more detail as they relate to prajñā, nonself, impermanence, interdependence, emptiness, and the experience of and liberation from suffering through their realization. Exploring hypothesis five was helpful in not only characterizing the fruits of Buddhist practice, but also highlighting how those fruits interact with the modern context of chaplaincy.

Coding of the *Bodhicaryāvatāra*

Chapter 2 of this book contains an analysis of sections of the *Way of the Bodhisattva* by Śāntideva. This classic Mahayana text was reviewed in much greater detail as part of my doctoral qualifying exams and sections have been excerpted and used in this book. I will briefly outline the methodology used in my analysis of the *Bodhicaryāvatāra* here.

My study of the *Bodhicaryāvatāra* (simplified here as '*Bodhi*') uses both qualitative methods and 'theological' exegesis. First, the Padmakara Translation Group's (PTG) 1997 translation of the *Bodhi* was been selected for study, as I am not fluent in its extant canonical languages. Then several recent commentaries were identified as both well-grounded in traditional training and accessible to modern audiences; chief among those are commentaries by His Holiness the Dalai Lama (HHDL) Tenzin Gyatso (including *A Flash of Lightning in the Dark of Night*, 1991, *Transcendent Wisdom*, 1994, and *For the Benefit of All Beings*, 2009) covering the *Bodhi* either in whole or in part. The Dalai Lama's commentaries also rely on the PTG translations, thus achieving a good fit between primary and secondary sources. Third, tertiary sources were identified both 'upstream' and 'downstream' of the primary text. Upstream sources include an earlier work by Śāntideva, the *Śikṣā-samuccaya*, or *Training Anthology*, and the translations of and commentaries on this work. The relationship of the *Śikṣā*, as I shall abbreviate it, to the *Bodhi* is like that of a course packet of supplemental readings to a more focused textbook, according the Charles Goodman, translator and author of the first major work on the *Śikṣā* in a century. Work on the *Śikṣā* is relatively scarce compared to the *Bodhi*, with only two full-length translations in the past century. The *Śikṣā* is referenced in the *Bodhi*, verses 105-106, demonstrating that Śāntideva was speaking to an audience familiar with this earlier, larger work. It is also referenced by the Dalai Lama in his commentaries on the *Bodhi* (he refers to it as the *Compendium of All Practices*), and by various teachers in the collection of lojong texts referenced below. (Although Goodman admits there is no proof that the *Śikṣā* was composed first; verses 105-106 could have been added later.) Downstream sources include commentaries on the *Bodhi*, such as those by the PTG and the Dalai Lama, as well as others by such notable Buddhist scholars and teachers as Kelsang Gyatso, Pema Chödrön, Pabitrakumar Roy, Francis Brassard, and Paul Williams. In a few instances, a further sacred source was consulted, selections from *Mind Training: The Great Collection*, also known as lojong texts, translated by Thupten Jinpa. The *Bodhi* and *Śikṣā* by Śāntideva and Nāgārjuna's *Precious Garland*, among other texts, form the "scriptural basis" for lojong texts composed from the tenth century onward by various Tibetan masters, according to Jinpa. These "mind training" texts further develop and comment on the contents of the *Bodhi* and often quote it explicitly or reference it implicitly, on the assumption that students would be familiar with it. The lojong texts demonstrate how the *Bodhi* was 'operationalized' through various contemplative practices, how it was understood by later generations, and testify to its continuing impact on contemporary Buddhism. Together, these collected works represent a traditional understanding of the *Bodhi* and its presentation to both ancient and modern audiences.

In attempting to discern the contributions of the *Bodhi* and other Buddhist sacred literature for the field and practice of spiritual care, we must also define what it is we are looking for. Thankfully, chaplaincy is a professional discipline with published guidelines, including training goals and outcomes, a code of ethics, and standards for professional practice. Spiritual care as a field also has some of its own 'canonical' sources, such as *Basic Types of Pastoral Care and Counseling* by Howard Clinebell, *Images of Pastoral Care* edited by Robert Dykstra, among others. Works specifically on Buddhist spiritual care were also consulted, such as *The Arts of Contemplative Care* edited by Cheryl Giles and Willa Miller and the recently released *A Thousand Hands: A Guidebook to Caring for Your Buddhist Community* edited by Nathan Jishin Michon and Daniel Clarkson Fisher. Buddhist works on spiritual care that undertake detailed exegesis of scriptural sources are rare.

These references on spiritual care were used to define a set of qualitative codes relating to the theory and practice of spiritual care, which were then applied to the 917 verses of the *Bodhi*. Each verse was assigned one or, in most cases, multiple descriptive codes, listed below. The method of 'coding' a text allows one to analytically understand its contents, that is, which codes appear most frequently and their connections (aka co-occurring codes) and alienations (exclusive codes). This helps determine relationships between the content of the text from a structural viewpoint. This analysis of the *Bodhi* used twelve unique codes grouped into six code families. They are:

Code	Count	% of Verses
Care of Others (family)		
Regard	164	18%
Action	92	10%
Care of Self (family)		
Boundaries	26	3%
Emptiness	48	5%
Ethics	46	5%
Formation (family)		
Intention	177	19%
Wisdom	300	33%
Virtue	105	11%
Psychology	209	23%
Theology (family)		
Theodicy	152	17%
Soteriology	145	16%
Metaphysics/Ontology	61	7%

A constructive exegesis followed the qualitative analysis; it relies on understandings gained from the above listed literature as well as the first-hand analysis of the primary text. Exegesis of a text is generally considered a 'theological' undertaking. In this case, the following exegesis shall rely on both modern and specifically Buddhist hermeneutical methods (per Donald Lopez's 1988 *Buddhist Hermeneutics*). The term 'theology' and some basic theological categories (theodicy, soteriology, ontology, etc.) are used very loosely in this analysis. The debate on the appropriateness of these terms in relation to Buddhism is not yet settled, and, ultimately, they may be rejected. Until the time that better terms are adopted by the discipline, however, I choose to use terms that possess an analog within other spiritual care literature with the knowledge that changes in religious context may (i.e., Buddhist theodicy vs. Christian theodicy) may lead to startling changes in understanding. Any reader unfamiliar with the basics of Buddhist doctrine should approach these terms in their most basic mode with as few assumptions as possible.

My full exegesis of the *Bodhi* focused on two primary topics: the formation of the spiritual caregiver as an aspiring bodhisattva and the relationship between emptiness of self (i.e., non-self) and care for the other. As we shall see, the formation of the caregiver follows a path reflected in the structure of the *Bodhi* itself, first emphasizing intention, then virtue, and culminating in wisdom. The second section of the exegesis explores the nature of this wisdom in more depth. It attempts to justify the seeming paradox between the necessity to completely abandon the illusion of "I" and the ability of the aspiring bodhisattva to serve others. Common wisdom among spiritual care literature holds that the practicing chaplain should have a 'strong' and 'stable' sense of self to undertake work with others. Some Buddhist teachers, particularly those with a background in psychological sciences, have echoed this sentiment. From a traditional Buddhist point of view, the chaplain should have a strong understanding that there is no "I" while also maintaining a stable and open awareness of the flux of cause and condition that leads to the relative experience of a "self" in relation with to an "other," while knowing that in ultimate truth, both are empty of such existence. I argue, in keeping with Śāntideva, that this understanding is necessary for spiritual progress along the bodhisattva path and that it benefits the careseeker and the Buddhist chaplain.

To my knowledge, this is the first time a major Buddhist scripture has been coded in this manner and only the second time Buddhist scriptures have been deliberately evaluated for their relation to pastoral care. Dr. Pamela Ayo Yetunde completed *Dharma Care: A Handbook on Buddhist Pastoral Care* (Part I) in 2011 based on the Pāli Cannon. Her work draws out several of the same themes as my analysis, including a focus on formation and how the caregiver regards all beings (reflection). Her work focuses more on classic Buddhist virtues such as loving-kindness and compassion, the practice of meditation, and Buddhist wisdom on illness and death. The first two topics are covered in depth in the *Bodhi*, but were not the focus of my exegesis (though this is fertile ground for later exploration). The *Bodhi* also has a narrower focus than the Pāli Cannon, which is much larger and more varied in both subject matter and type of contents (e.g., verse, prose, disciplinary rules, etc.). In contrast, my analysis focused more on pastoral care themes from the professional discipline of chaplaincy.

Conclusion on Methods

The methods employed have both benefits and drawbacks. On the one hand, they are well developed and tested by previous scholars. On the other hand, they have been combined here in somewhat novel (and untested) ways on a topic about which there is little prior literature against which to validate their use or findings. Methodological confusion is the primary drawback of this approach. This confusion results from applying practical theological methods developed in relation to Christianity and from a western intellectual tradition to a religion (Buddhism) that is, in many ways, very different and arises from an eastern intellectual tradition that does not share many of the foundations upon which practical theologians have traditionally based their work.

My use of constructivist grounded theory is colored by the Buddhist approach to language, the constructed-ness of all conceptual knowledge, teachings on causation and conditionality, emphasis on direct experience as the primary source of authority in developing wisdom (and the final source of awakening), and emphasis on reflexivity in the practitioner in relation to their own perceptions and the nature of mind. All of these concepts uphold and reinforce Charmaz's explanations and methods of grounded theory, which is why I have such a strong affinity for the constructivist model. However, these epistemological commitments are not the same as Charmaz's epistemological commitments. They may come to similar conclusions, but they flow from very different sources. Charmaz notes that grounded theory is adaptable, as we have seen in her evolution of Glaser and Strauss's original model into her constructivist one. It remains useful in the face of whatever adaptations I have naively forced upon it in this study.

Methods are not value-neutral tools. They come complete with commitments to particular worldviews and embedded assumptions. Applying a set of methods developed in one context to an activity that takes place in a different context with a different operative worldview could result in the "corruption" of the ultimate findings. Indeed, this is the entire critique regarding the development of a Buddhist 'theology.' Although we know there is no such thing as a "pure" worldview, or even a "pure" method for that matter, critical theory has identified the dangers of applying theories developed by one population to a different population. Feminists, queer theorists, racial theorists, and others who employ critical theory in their work are mindful of these dangers. I have not employed critical theory in this study, which may be to its detriment. Instead, I have chosen methods that I find well aligned with the Dharma (though there is little scholarly work to support my viewpoint) and hoped that they would allow the data to speak for itself. I have followed the classical Buddhist path of resorting to direct experience to validate (or critique) the Dharma and resorting to the Dharma to help understand direct experience. Wherever possible, I have attempted to maintain reflexivity and note my own biases, assumptions, and commitments, but this task is impossible to do perfectly.

Some confusion seems an inevitable consequence of this kind of methodological construction. I am developing a way to qualitatively study the methods used by Buddhist chaplains that is, I hope, both academically sound and appropriate to the Dharma. This has never been done before, which is one of the reasons why this research is significant. The strengths of this approach include the application of a meticulous and accepted method for data collection and analysis to generate new theories where none have yet been articulated. Some new scholars in this field, such as Bhikkshuni Trinlae advocate for a full-fledged discipline of Buddhist practical theology. While I find many correlations between the methods of practical theology, particularly Osmer's tasks, I am not yet ready to go that far, for the reasons explored by Richard Payne and others. However, lack of clarity about the boundaries and methods of some new discipline for Buddhist thought need not prevent us from moving forward with constructive projects to benefit Buddhist practitioners who are already out there doing the work, which is precisely what I have done. This research is ultimately intended to help them alleviate suffering where ever they find it and train those who will follow after.

Appendix B
Sources for Kalyāṇamitra within the Pāli Canon

Source: Bodhi, Bhikkhu (trans.) *The Numerical Discourses of the Buddha: A Translation of the Anguttara Nikaya*. Boston, MA: Wisdom Publications, 2012.

Good friends/friendship
They cause/Benefits
- Wholesome qualities to arise (AN1.71, p. 101) (AN9.1, p. 1245-1247) (AN9.3, p. 1247-1250) (AN10.61, 1415-1418)
- Unwholesome qualities to decline (AN1.71, p. 101) (AN9.1, p. 1245-1247) (AN9.3, p. 1247-1250)
- Great good (AN1.111, p. 104)
- Non-decline and non-disappearance of good Dharma (AN1.127, p. 105)
- Become more virtuous (AN4.242, p. 240) (AN6.67, p. 968) (AN9.1, p. 1245-1247) (AN9.3, p. 1247-1250)
- Grow in concentration (AN4.242, p. 240) (AN10.61, 1415-1418)
- Improve wisdom (AN4.242, p. 240) (AN9.1, p. 1245-1247) (AN9.3, p. 1247-1250) (AN10.61, 1415-1418)
- Approach liberation (AN4.242, p. 240) (AN10.61, 1415-1418)
- Fulfil the duties of proper conduct (AN6.67, p. 968) (AN10.61, 1415-1418)
- Fulfill the duties of a trainee (AN6.67, p. 968)
- Abandon sensual lust (AN6.67, p. 968) (AN10.61, 1415-1418)
- Abandon lust for form (AN6.67, p. 968)
- Abandon lust for formlessness (AN6.67, p. 968)
- A good layperson life (AN8.54, p. 1194-1195)
- Able to hear the teachings (AN9.1, p. 1245-1247) (AN9.3, p. 1247-1250) (AN10.61, 1415-1418)
- First of nine proximate causes for the development of aids to enlightenment (all included in the list above), together leading to: (AN9.1, p. 1245-1247) (AN9.3, p. 1247-1250)
    - Loving-kindness
    - Mindfulness
    - Abandon lust
    - Perceive impermanence
    - Eradicate "I am"
    - Collectively leading to Nibbana
- One of four powers (with wisdom, energy, & blamelessness) leading to transcending five fears: (AN9.4, p. 1254-1256)
    - Fear of loss
    - Fear of disrepute

- Timidity
- Fear of death
- Fear of a bad destination after death
- Good friends lead to the following chain of causation (like rain flowing downhill to the ocean): (AN10.61, 1415-1418) (AN10.62, p. 1418-1419)
  - good friends →
  - hearing Dhamma →
  - faith →
  - careful attention →
  - mindfulness & clear comprehension →
  - restraint of sense faculties →
  - 3 kinds of good conduct →
    - Bodily, verbal, and mental conduct (AN1.287, p. 114-115; etc.)
    - Acts, speech, thoughts (AN3.2-3, p. 202-203; etc.)
- 4 establishments of mindfulness →
  - Contemplating the body, feelings, mind, and phenomena (AN1.402-405, p. 125; AN3.156, p. 372-373; etc.)
- 7 factors of enlightenment →
  - Mindfulness, discrimination of phenomena, energy, rapture, tranquility, concentration, and equanimity (AN1.424-430, p. 126; etc.)
- true liberation and knowledge

To be associated with (AN3.135, p. 363)
- Similar in virtue, concentration, & wisdom (AN3.23, p. 220-221)
  - Discuss and be at ease
  - Maintains wholesome qualities
- Superior in virtue, concentration, and wisdom (AN3.23, p. 220-221)
  - With honor and respect
  - Improves wholesome qualities
- Virtuous, good character (AN3.27, p. 221-223)
  - People will think you are like them
- Take as a friend a monastic who (AN5.146, p. 762-763)
  - Do not instigate work projects
  - Do not take up disciplinary issues
  - Is respectful towards eminent monastics
  - Not a wanderer
  - Can instruct, gladden, and encourage others
- Associate with & resort to, attend to: (AN7.37, p. 1022)
  - Pleasing and agreeable
  - Respected
  - Esteemed
  - "Is a speaker" (per note 1491 this means gives good advice)
  - Patiently endures being spoke to
  - Gives deep talks
  - Doesn't enjoin you to do wrong

- Do not leave people who cause: (AN9.6, 1256-1259)
  - Unwholesome qualities decline
  - Wholesome qualities increase
  - Life is difficult with them OR Life is easy with them (do not leave even if dismissed)
  - Reach fulfillment

Qualities of (also to be associated with; AN7.36, p. 1021-22)
- Gives what is hard to give (AN3.135, p. 363) (AN7.36, p. 1021-1022)
- Does what is hard to do (AN3.135, p. 363) (AN7.36, p. 1021-1022)
- Patiently endures what is hard to endure (AN3.135, p. 363) (AN7.36, p. 1021-1022)
- Reveals secrets to you (AN7.36, p. 1021-1022)
- Preserves your secrets (AN7.36, p. 1021-1022)
- Does not forsake you in times of trouble (AN7.36, p. 1021-1022)
- Does not despise you (AN7.36, p. 1021-1022)
- Virtuous (AN8.54, p. 1194-1195)
- Faithful (AN8.54, p. 1194-1195)
- Generous (AN8.54, p. 1194-1195)
- Wise (AN8.54, p. 1194-1195)

Do associate (& resort to) with persons who
- Right … all qualities of 8-fold path (AN10.155, p. 1507)
- Right knowledge & liberation (AN10.155, p. 1507)
- Preserve life (AN10.199, p. 1527-1528)
- Do not take what is not given (AN10.199, p. 1527-1528)
- Do not commit sexual misconduct (AN10.199, p. 1527-1528)
- Do not lie, speak divisively, harshly, or with idle chatter (AN10.199, p. 1527-1528)
- Have few desires, good will, and right views (AN10.199, p. 1527-1528)

Those who display the seven qualities that lead to non-decline include: (AN7.35, p. 1021)
- Reverence for a teacher, Dharma, sangha, training, concentration, being easy to correct, and good friendship
  - Reverence for good friendship includes: has good friends and speaks in praise of good friendship; encourages those who do not have good friends to find good friends, and (at the proper time) praises those who have good friends [same list for other six factors]

Bad friends/friendship
Causes/Detriments
- Unwholesome qualities to arise (AN1.70, p. 101)
- Wholesome qualities to decline (AN1.70, p. 101)
- Great harm (AN1.110, p. 104)
- Decline and disappearance of good Dharma (AN1.126, p. 105)
- Cannot fulfil the duties of proper conduct (AN6.67, p. 968)
- Cannot fulfill the duties of a trainee (AN6.67, p. 968)
- Cannot have virtuous behavior (AN6.67, p. 968)
- Cannot abandon sensual lust (AN6.67, p. 968)
- Cannot abandon lust for form (AN6.67, p. 968)

- Cannot abandon lust for formlessness (AN6.67, p. 968)
- Not associating with good persons leads to the following chain of causation (like rain flows downward and fills up the ocean): (AN10.61, p. 1415-1418)
  - Not associating with good persons →
  - Not hearing the Dhamma →
  - Lack of faith →
  - Careless attention →
  - Lack of mindfulness and clear comprehension →
  - Non-restraint of sense faculties →
  - 3 kinds of misconduct →
    - Bodily, verbal, and mental conduct (AN1.287, p. 114-115; etc.)
    - Acts, speech, thoughts (AN3.2-3, p. 202-203; etc.)
  - 5 hindrances →
    - Sensual desire, ill will, dullness and drowsiness, restlessness and remorse, and doubt (AN1.11-15, p. 90-91; etc.)
  - Ignorance →
  - Craving for existence, aka rebirth in the suffering realms of samsara (AN10.62, p. 1418-1419)

To not associate with
- Inferior to oneself in virtue, concentration, and wisdom (AN3.26, p. 220-221)
  - Except out of sympathy and compassion
  - Declines wholesome qualities
- Immoral, bad character, impure, secretive, suspect, false claims, corrupt, depraved, rotten (AN3.27, p. 221-223)
  - People will think you are like them
  - Look upon with disgust
- Angry, exasperated, irritated, hostile, stubborn, full of hatred and bitterness (AN3.27, p. 221-223)
  - They might harm you
  - Look upon with equanimity
- Do not take as a friend a monastic who (AN5.146, p. 762-763)
  - Instigate work projects
  - Take up disciplinary issues
  - Are hostile toward eminent monastics
  - Given to lengthy wandering
  - Cannot instruct, gladden, or encourage others
- Do not follow people who cause: (AN9.6, p. 1256-1259)
  - Increase in unwholesome qualities
  - Decline in wholesome qualities
  - Life is difficult with them OR life is easy with them
  - No sense of fulfillment
- Do not associate with persons who
  - Wrong … all qualities of 8-fold path (AN10.155, p. 1507)
  - Wrong knowledge & liberation (AN10.155, p. 1507)
  - Destroy life (AN10.199, p. 1527-1528)

- Steal (AN10.199, p. 1527-1528)
- Commit sexual misconduct (AN10.199, p. 1527-1528)
- Lie (AN10.199, p. 1527-1528)
- Speak divisively (AN10.199, p. 1527-1528)
- Speak harshly (AN10.199, p. 1527-1528)
- Idle chatter (AN10.199, p. 1527-1528)
- Full of longing (AN10.199, p. 1527-1528)
- Full of ill will (AN10.199, p. 1527-1528)
- Full of wrong views (AN10.199, p. 1527-1528)

On qualities of persons in general
- Four monks ask the Buddha if the person who perfects concentration, wisdom, or faith is best. The Buddha states we cannot tell by these qualities alone who is furthest on the path, each could be non-returners. (AN3.21, p. 215-217)
- Three types of helpful people: ("no one is more helpful")
  - Have gone for refuge
  - Understand the Four Noble Truths
  - Has attained wisdom/direct knowledge (AN3.24, p. 219)
- Speech like: (AN3.28, p. 223)
  - Dung = lies
  - Flowers = truth
  - Honey = truth, gentle, pleasing, lovable, heartfelt, courteous, agreeable, and desired
- Gifts of a good/bad person (AN5.147, p. 763)
  - Gives respectfully/casually
  - With reverence/without reverence
  - With their own hand/not by their own hand
  - Gives what is worthy of keeping/what is not worth keeping
  - With view of the returns of giving/without view of the returns of giving
- Returns of a good person giving gifts (AN 5.148, p. 763-764)
  - Out of faith → wealth and beauty
  - Respectfully → wealth, good family and servants
  - Timely → wealth and timely benefits
  - Unreservedly → wealth and the 5 sensual pleasures
  - Without injuring oneself or others → wealth and protection from manmade and natural disasters
- Good/wholesome qualities (AN8.24, p. 1153-1154)
  - Faith
  - Virtue
  - Moral shame
  - Moral dread
  - Learned
  - Generous
  - Wise
  - Few desires

How to sustain good relationships
- Giving (AN4.23, p. 419-420; AN8.24, p. 1153-1154)
  ○ Dhamma is the best gift (AN9.4, p. 1254-1256)
- Endearing speech (AN4.23, p. 419-420, AN8.27, p. 1153-1154)
  ○ Teaching Dhamma to someone who is interested is best speech (AN9.4, p. 1254-1256)
- Beneficial conduct (AN4.23, p. 419-420, AN8.27, p. 1153-1154)
  ○ Encouraging faith, virtue, generosity, and wisdom in others is most beneficent (AN9.4, p. 1254-1256)
- Impartiality (AN4.23, p. 419-420, AN8.27, p. 1153-1154)
  ○ Seeing people as they are (e.g. an arahant as an arahant) is impartiality (i.e. lack of bias) (AN9.4, p. 1254-1256)

BIBLIOGRAPHY

A

Abbot, W.W. (editor), *The Papers of George Washintgon*, Colonial Series, Vol. 3, 16 April 1756 – 9 November 1756, Charlottesville: University Press of Virginia, 1984. Accessed at *Founders Online*, National Archives, https://founders.archives.gov/documents/Washington/02-03-02-0358

"About the HBC Buddhism & Race Conference," *Harvard Buddhist Community*, April 2016, https://harvardbuddhistcommunity.wordpress.com/

Alexander, Michelle. *The New Jim Crow: Mass Incarceration in the Age of Colorblindness*. New Press, 2020.

The American Heritage Dictionary of the English Language, 5th Edition. Houghton Mifflin Harcourt Publishing Company, 2020, www.ahdictionary.com

Anderson, Lorin W., and David R. Krathwohl. *A Taxonomy for Learning, Teaching, and Assessing: A Revision of Bloom's Taxonomy of Educational Objectives*. New York: Longman, 2001.

Association for Clinical Pastoral Education, Inc. *APCE Standards and Manuals: A Standard for Spiritual Care and Education*, last modified January 1, 2016, http://www.manula.com/manuals/acpe/acpe-manuals/2016/en/topic/cover-page

—. "Information For Prospective Students: Frequently Asked Questions," https://www.acpe.edu/ACPE/_Students/FAQ_S.aspx

Association of Professional Chaplains. "Common Standards for Professional Chaplaincy." http://www.professionalchaplains.org/files/professional_standards/common_standards/common_standards_professional_chaplaincy.pdf

Association of Theological Schools. "Standards and Notations." https://www.ats.edu/accrediting/standards-and-notations

Astin, Alexander W., Helen S. Astin, and Jennifer A. Lindholm. *Cultivating the Spirit: How College Can Enhance Students' Inner Lives*. Wiley, 2010.

B

Baranyi, Gergõ, Megan Cassidy, Seena Fazel, Stefan Priebe, and Adrian P. Mundt. "Prevalence of Posttraumatic Stress Disorder in Prisoners." *Epidemiologic Reviews* vol. 40,1 (2018): 134-145. doi:10.1093/epirev/mxx015

Bastis, Madeline Ko-i. "A Buddhist Response to Larry Dossey." In *Scientific and Pastoral Perspectives on Intercessory Prayer: An Exchange Between Larry Dossey, M.D., and Health Care Chaplains*, edited by Larry Dossey and Larry VandeCreek. New York: Haworth Pastoral Press, 1998: 87-96.

—. *Heart of Forgiveness: A Practical Path to Healing*. York Beach, ME: Red Wheel/Weiser, 2011.

—. *Peaceful Dwelling: Meditations for Healing and Living*. Boston: Tuttle Publishing, 2000.

—. "Thom's Garden." *The Journal of Pastoral Care* 50, no. 2 (Summer 1996): 221-222.

Batchelor, Stephen. "Why I Quit Guru Yoga." *Tricycle*, Winter 2017, https://tricycle.org/magazine/quit-guru-yoga/

Bidwell, Duane. "Collaborating with the Spirit: Brief Spiritual Direction in Congregational Ministry." In *Strategies for Brief Pastoral Counseling*, edited by Howard W. Stone, 122-138. Minneapolis: Fortress, 2001.

Blum, Harrison. "Mindfulness Equity and Western Buddhism: Reaching People of Low Socioeconomic Status and People of Color." *International Journal of Dharma Studies* 2, no. 1 (2014): 1-18.

Board of Chaplaincy Certification, Inc. "BCCI Certification." http://bcci.professionalchaplains.org/content.asp?pl=25&contentid=25

Bodhi, Bhikkhu. *The Suttanipāla: An Ancient Collection of the Buddha's Discourses Together with Its Commentaries*. Boston, MA: Wisdom Publications, 2017.

—. *Dhamma Reflections: Collected Essays of Bhikkhu Bodhi*. Onalaska, WA: Pariyatti Publishing, 2016.

—. *The Numerical Discourses of the Buddha: A Translation of the Aṅguttara Nikāya*. Boston, MA: Wisdom Publications, 2012.

—. *The Connected Discourses of the Buddha: A New Translation of the Saṃyutta Nikāya*, vol. 1 & 2. Boston, MA: Wisdom Publications, 2000.

Brassard, Francis. *The Concept of Bodhicitta in Śāntideva's Bodhicaryāvatāra*. Albany, NY: State University of New York Press, 2000.

Buddhaghosa, and Bhikkhu Ñāṇamoli. *The Path of Purification: Visuddhimagga*. Seattle, WA: BPE Pariyatti Editions, 1999.

Buswell, Robert E., Jr., and Donald S. Lopez, Jr., eds. *The Princeton Dictionary of Buddhism*. Princeton, NJ: Princeton University Press, 2013.

Butler, Katy. "Encountering the Shadow in Buddhist American." *Tricycle: The Buddhist Review*. August, 1, 2018, https://tricycle.org/trikedaily/encounter-shadow-buddhist-america/

C

The Chambers Century Dictionary, 13th Edition, Hodder & Stoughton, 2014, www.chambers.co.uk

Charmaz, Kathy. *Constructing Grounded Theory*, 2nd ed. London: SAGE Publication, 2014.

Chickering, Arthur W., Jon C. Dalton, and Liesa Stamm. *Encouraging Authenticity and Spirituality in Higher Education*. Wiley, 2006.

Chödrön, Pema and Helen Berliner. *No Time to Lose: A Timely Guide to the Way of the Bodhisattva*. Boston, MA: Shambhala Publications, 2007.

Clarke, Stephen. "Kalamitra: A Buddhist Approach to Pastoral Counseling." In *Understanding Pastoral Counseling*, edited by Elizabeth A. Maynard and Jill L. Snodgrass, 2015. New York: Springer, 275-289.

Clebsch, William A., and Charles R. Jaekle. *Pastoral Care in Historical Perspective: An Essay with Exhibits*. Englewood Cliffs, NJ: Prentice-Hall, 1964.

Clinebell, Howard and Bridget Clare McKeever. *Basic Types of Pastoral Care and Counseling*, 3rd Edition. Nashville, TN: Abingdon, 2011.

Colins, Charlotte, "Report on the Sakyadhita USA One-Day Conference," *Sakyadhita USA*, http://sakyadhitausa.org/conference.html

Collins, Steve. "*Kalyāṇamitta* and *Kalyāṇamittatā*." *Journal of the Pali Text Society* XI (1987): 51-72.

"Conference on Buddhism and Race in America," *Harvard College*, https://college.harvard.edu/college-events/conference-buddhism-and-race-america

Conze, Edward (trans.). *The Perfection of Wisdom in Eight Thousand Lines & Its Verse Summary*, fifth printing. San Francisco, CA: Four Seasons Foundation, 1995.

D

Dalai Lama. *A Flash of Lightning in the Dark of Night: A Guide to the Bodhisattva's Way of Life*. Boulder, CO: Shambhala Publications, 1994.

"The Dhammapada: The Buddha's Path of Wisdom", translated from the Pali by Acharya Buddharakkhita, with an introduction by Bhikkhu Bodhi. *Access to Insight (BCBS Edition)*, 30 November 2013, http://www.accesstoinsight.org/tipitaka/kn/dhp/dhp.intro.budd.html

Doehring, Carrie. *The Practice of Pastoral Care: A Postmodern Approach.* Louisville, KY: Westminster John Knox Press, 2015.

Dossey, Larry and Larry VandeCreek (eds.). *Scientific and Pastoral Perspectives on Intercessory Prayer: An Exchange Between Larry Dossey, M.D., and Health Care Chaplains.* New York: Haworth Pastoral Press, 1998.

E

Ellison, Koshin Paley and Matt Weingast. *Awake at the Bedside: Contemplative Teachings on Palliative and End-of-Life Care.* Somerville, MA: Wisdom Publications, 2016.

F

Faure, Bernard. *Double Exposure: Cutting Across Buddhist and Western Discourses.* Translated by Janet Lloyd. Stanford, CA: Stanford University Press, 2004.

—. *Unmasking Buddhism.* Chicester, UK: Wiley-Blackwell, 2009.

Fisher, Danny. *Benefit Beings! The Buddhist Guide to Professional Chaplaincy.* San Bernardino, CA: Off the Cushion Books, 2013.

Fitchett, George and Steven Nolan (eds.). *Spiritual Care in Practice: Case Studies in Healthcare Chaplaincy.* London, UK: Jessica Kingsley Publishers, 2015.

Foley, Edward. *Theological Reflection across Religious Traditions: The Turn to Reflective Believing.* London, UK: Rowman & Littlefield Publishers, 2015.

Forster-Smith, Lucy A. *College & University Chaplaincy in the 21st Century: A Multifaith Look at the Practice of Ministry on Campuses Across America.* SkyLight Paths Publishing, 2013.

Franklin, Cynthia, and Rowena Fong. *The Church Leader's Counseling Resource Book: A Guide to Mental Health and Social Problems.* Oxford: Oxford University Press, 2011.

Friedman, Dayle A. *Jewish Pastoral Care: A Practical Handbook from Traditional and Contemporary Sources.* Woodstock, VT: Jewish Lights Publishing, 2010.

Fronsdale, Gil. "Not-Knowing." *Insight Meditation Center.* February 10, 2004. http://www.insightmeditationcenter.org/books-articles/articles/not-knowing/

G

Giles, Cheryl A. and Willa Miller, eds. *The Arts of Contemplative Care: Pioneering Voices in Buddhist Chaplaincy and Pastoral Work.* Boston: Wisdom Publications, 2012.

Gilliat-Ray, Sophie, Mansur Ali, and Stephen Pattison. *Understanding Muslim Chaplaincy.* Routledge, 2013.

Gilliat-Ray, S. From 'visiting minister' to 'Muslim chaplain': the growth of Muslim chaplaincy in Britain, 1970-2007. In: Barker, E (ed.) *The Centrality of Religion in Social Life: Essays in Honour of James A. Beckford.* Aldershot: Ashgate, (2008): 145–160.

Glassman, Bernie. *Bearing Witness: A Zen Master's Lessons in Making Peace.* Harmony Books, 1998.

Gleig, Ann. "From Buddhist Hippies to Buddhist Geeks: The Emergence of Buddhist Postmodernism?" *The Journal of Global Buddhism* 15 (2014): 15-33.

Gordon, James S., Leslie Blackhall, Madeline Ko-I Bastis, and Robert A. F. Thurman. "Asian Spiritual Traditions and Their Usefulness to Practitioners and Patients Facing Life and Death." *The Journal of Alternative and Complementary Medicine* 8, no. 5 (2002): 603-608.

Gotama Buddha. *Vibhanga: The Book of Analysis.* Translated by U. Thittila. Rangoon, Burma: Pali Text Society, 1969. http://tipitaka.wikia.com/wiki/Vibhanga-Scanned-Chap.16

—. *Vibhanga: The Book of Analysis, Pali.* Rangoon, Burma: Pali Text Society, 1969. http://tipitaka.wikia.com/wiki/Vibhanga,_Pali

Graham, Elaine L., Heather Walton, and Frances Ward. *Theological Reflection: Methods.* London: SCM Press, 2005.

Gyatso, Geshe Kelsang. *Understanding the Mind: Lorig, the Nature and Power of the Mind.* Ulverston, UK: Tharpa Publications, 2007.

H

Hakanson, J. Michael. *The Spiritual Side of Traumatic Stress Normalization: Christian Spirituality and Social Neuroscience Considerations for Clinicians and Military Chaplains.* CreateSpace Independent Publishing Platform, 2008.

Halifax, Joan. *Being with Dying: Cultivating Compassion and Fearlessness in the Presence of Death.* Boston: Shambhala, 2008.

Hanh, Thich Nhat. *The Heart of the Buddha's Teaching: Transforming Suffering into Peace, Joy, and Liberation.* Harmony Books, 1998, 2015.

—. *Be Free Where You Are.* Berkeley, CA: Parallax Press, 2002.

Herman, Judith. *Trauma and Recover: The Aftermath of Violence – from Domestic Abuse to Political Terror.* New York, NY: Basic Books, 2015.

Hickey, Wakoh Shannon. "Two Buddhisms, Three Buddhisms, and Racism." *The Journal of Global Buddhism* 11, no. 1 (2010): 1-25.

Hilsman, Gordon J. *Spiritual Care in Common Terms: How Chaplains Can Effectively Describe the Spiritual Needs of Patients in Medical Records.* London, UK: Jessica Kingsley Publishers, 2016.

Holifield, E. Brooks. *A History of Pastoral Care in America: From Salvation to Self-Realization.* Nashville: Abingdon Press. 1983.

Hsu, Fannie. "Lineage of Resistance: When Asian American Buddhists Confronted White Supremacy." *Buddhist Peace Fellowship*, May 8, 2017. http://www.buddhistpeacefellowship.org/lineage-of-resistance/

—. "We've Been Here All Along." *Lion's Roar*, May 17, 2017. https://www.lionsroar.com/weve-been-here-all-along/

I

Inada, Kenneth K. and Nolan Pliny Jacobson. *Buddhism and American Thinkers.* Albany, NY: State University of New York Press, 1984.

Ireland-Verwoerd, Francisca. "Sharing Faith, by Thomas Groome," [book review] *CPT Today*, Boston University School of Theology, Center for Practical Theology, August, 3, 2015, https://www.bu.edu/cpt/cpt_today_blog/

Iwamura, Jane Naomi. *Virtual Orientalism: Asian Religions and American Popular Culture.* New York: Oxford University Press, 2011.

J

Jacobsen, Douglas and Rhonda Hustedt Jacobsen. *No Longer Invisible: Religion in University Education.* Oxford, UK: Oxford University Press, 2012.

Jinpa, Thupten. *Mind Training: The Great Collection.* Boston, MA: Wisdom Publications, in association with the Institute of Tibetan Classics, 2006.

K

Kelly, Ewan and John Swinton. *Chaplaincy and the Soul of Health and Social Care: Fostering Spiritual Wellbeing in Emerging Paradigms of Care.* London, UK: Jessica Kingsley Publishers, 2019.

Kennedy, Nancy B. (editor). *Miracles and Moments of Grace: Inspiring Stories from Military Chaplains.* Abilene, TX: Leafwood Publishers, 2011.

Kandro Rinpoche, Pema, Lama Rod Owens, Lobsang Rapgay, and Lama Rigzin Drolma, "Is the Guru Model Broken?" *Lion's Roar*, March 15, 2019, https://www.lionsroar.com/guru-model/

Kidd, Robert A. "Foundational Listening and Responding Skills." In *Professional Spiritual & Pastoral Care: A Practical Clergy and Chaplain's Handbook*, edited by Stephen B. Roberts. Woodstock, 92-105. VT: SkyLight Paths Publishing, 2012.

Kilts, Thomas. "A Vajrayana Buddhist Perspective on Ministry Training." *The Journal of Pastoral Care & Counseling* 62, no. 3, (Fall 2008): 273-281.

Kim, Sumi Loundon. *The Buddha's Apprentices: More Voices of Young Buddhists*. Boston, MA: Wisdom Publications, 2005.

—. *Blue Jean Buddha: Voices of Young Buddhists*. Boston, MA: Wisdom Publications, 2001.

Kim, KiDeuk, Miriam Becker-Cohen, and Maria Serakos. "The Processing and Treatment of Mentally Ill Persons in the Criminal Justice System: A Scan of Practice and Background Analysis." The Urban Institute, April 7, 2017, https://www.urban.org/research/publication/processing-and-treatment-mentally-ill-persons-criminal-justice-system/view/full_report

Kirkwood, Neville A. *Pastoral Care in Hospitals*, 2nd Edition. New York, NY: Morehouse Publishing, 2005.

Kujawa-Holbrook, Sheryl and Karen Montagno, eds. *Injustice and the Care of Souls: Taking Oppression Seriously in Pastoral Care*. Minneapolis: Fortress Press, 2009.

L

Läänemets, Märt. "On the Meaning of 'Good Friendship' in Buddhism," in Peeter Espak, Märt Läänemets, Vladimir Sazonov (eds.), *When Gods Spoke: Researches and Reflections on Religious Phenomena and Artefacts*. Studia in Honorem Tarmo Kulmar. (Studia Orientalia Tartuensia. Series Nova, vol. VI), (2015): pp. 161-181, https://www.academia.edu/19745290/On_the_Meaning_of_Good_Friendship_in_Buddhism#:~:text=171%20M%C3%A4rt%20L%C3%A4%C3%A4nemets%20Further%2C%20'good,to%20such%20great%20harms%20as

Larson, Duane and Jeff Zust. *Care for the Sorrowing Soul: Healing Moral Injuries from Military Service and Implications for the Rest of Us*. Eugene, OR: Cascade Books, 2017.

Lartey, Emmanuel Yartekwei. *In Living Color: An Intercultural Approach to Pastoral Care and Counseling*. London: Jessica Kingsley, 2003.

—. "Pastoral Theology." In *The Cambridge Dictionary of Christian Theology*, edited by Ian A. McFarland et. al. (Cambridge: Cambridge University Press, 2011), https://dtl.idm.oclc.org/login?url=http://search.credoreference.com/content/entry/cupdct/pastoral_theology/0?institutionId=8909

Lee, Aaron. *Angry Asian Buddhist*. Blog, 2009-2016. http://www.angryasianbuddhist.com/

Lee, Lewis Jeffrey. *Moral Injury Reconciliation: A Practitioner's Guide for Treating Moral Injury, PTSD, Grief, and Military Sexual Trauma through Spiritual Formation Strategies*. London, UK: Jessica Kingsley Publishers, 2018.

Lester, Andrew D. *The Angry Christian: A Theology for Care and Counseling*. Louisville, KY: Westminster/John Knox Press. 2003.

Liew, Jew Chong. "The *Sarvāstivāda* Doctrine of the Path of Spiritual Progress: A Study Based Primarily on the *Abhidharma-Mahāvibhāṣā-śāstra*, the *Abhidharmakośa-bhāṣya* and Their Chinese and Sanskrit Commentaries." PhD diss., University of Hong Kong, 2009.

Lopez, Donald S., Jr. *Buddhist Hermeneutics*. Honolulu: University of Hawaii Press, 1988.

M

Makransky, John. "Contemporary Academic Buddhist Theology: Its Emergence and Rationale." In *Buddhist Theology: Critical Reflections by Contemporary Buddhist Scholars*, edited by Roger Jackson and John Makransky, 14-24. London: Routledge, 2000.

Masters, Ruth. *Counseling Criminal Justice Offenders*. SAGE Publications, 2004.

Maull, Fleet. *Dharma in Hell: The Prison Writings of Fleet Maull*. Boulder, CO: Prison Dharma Network, 2005.

McMahan, David L. *The Making of Buddhist Modernism*. Oxford: Oxford University Press, 2008.

Michon, Nathan Jishin and Daniel Clarkson Fisher, eds. *A Thousand Hands: A Guidebook to Caring for Your Buddhist Community*. Richmond Hill, ON: Sumeru Press, 2016.

Miller, Jean Baker, and Irene Peirce Stiver. *The Healing Connection: How Women Form Relationships in Therapy and in Life*. Boston: Beacon Press, 1997.

Miller-McLemore, Bonnie. "Practical Theology." In *Encyclopedia of Religion in America, Vol. 3*, edited by Charles Lippy and Peter Williams, 1741-2. Washington, DC: Congressional Quarterly Press, 2010.

Mills, L. O. *The Concise Dictionary of Pastoral Care & Counseling*, s.v. "Pastoral Care (History, Traditions, and Definitions)." Nashville, TN: Abingdon Press

Mitchell, Scott. "'Christianity is for Rubes; Buddhism is for Actors': U.S. Media Representations of Buddhism in the Wake of the Tiger Woods' Scandal." *The Journal of Global Buddhism* 13 (2012): 61-79.

Monnett, Mikel. "Developing a Buddhist Approach to Pastoral Care: A Peacemaker's View." In *Injustice and the Care of Souls: Taking Oppression Seriously in Pastoral Care*, edited by Sheryl A. Kujawa-Holbrook and Karen Brown Montagno, 125-131. Minneapolis: Fortress Press, 2009.

Montross, Christine. *Waiting for an Echo: The Madness of American Incarceration*. Penguin Publishing Group, 2020.

N

Ñānamoli, Bhikkhu and Bhikkhu Bodhi. *The Middle Length Discourses of the Buddha: A Translation of the Majjhima Nikāya*. Bonston, MA: Wisdom Publications, 1995.

The National Center on Addiction and Substance Abuse at Columbia University. "Behind Bars II: Substance Abuse and America's Prison Population." Columbia University, February 2010, https://files.eric.ed.gov/fulltext/ED509000.pdf

O

Oates, Wayne E. *The Christian Pastor*. Louisville, KY: Westminster/John Knox Press. 1982.

Opata, Josiah N. *Spiritual and Religious Diversity in Prisons: Focusing on How Chaplaincy Assists in Prison Management*. Pennsylvania State University, 2011.

Osmer, Richard Robert. *Practical Theology: An Introduction*. Grand Rapids, MI: W.B. Eerdmans, 2011.

P

Parks, Sharon Daloz. *Big Questions, Worthy Dreams: Mentoring Emerging Adults in Their Search for Meaning*. Wiley, 2000.

Patton, John. *Pastoral Care in Context: An Introduction to Pastoral Care*. Louisville, KY: Westminster/John Knox Press. 1993.

Payne, Richard. "Why 'Buddhist Theology' is Not a Good Idea: Keynote Address for the Fifteenth Biennial Conference of the International Association of Shin Buddhist Studies, Kyoto, August 2011." *The Pure Land* 27 (2012-2013): 37-72.

Pew Research Center, "Belief in God," *Religious Landscape Study*, 2017. http://www.pewforum.org/religious-landscape-study/belief-in-god/

—. "Religion in Prisons: A 50-State Survey of Prison Chaplains," *Pew Research Center: Religion & Public Life*, March 22, 2012, https://www.pewforum.org/2012/03/22/prison-chaplains-exec/

138, 144, 148, 150, 152, 154, 157-159

Compassion (karuna) 13, 30, 35, 37, 40, 42, 44, 46, 56, 63, 68-71, 73, 82, 96, 98, 100, 103-104, 107-108, 113-114, 116, 126, 128, 131, 133, 136, 144, 155, 158-159, 162, 168

Confidentiality 24f, 60, 62, 128, 150

    Limits 24f, 144

Connection 68-70, 74, 77, 79, 108-109, 133, 135, 148, 151, 153-159

Contemplation 17, 64, 72, 83-86, 88-93, 95-97, 103, 106, 117-118, 135, 153

Contemplative Care 12, 15, 17, 21-22, 36, 43-44, 46, 48-50, 53, 55-56, 58, 61, 63-65, 67, 160

Correlation 11, 36, 55, 57, 59

Dalai Lama 31, 57, 112-116, 160

Dhammapada 51

Death (end-of-life care) 12, 15, 26, 35, 46, 50, 60-61, 63, 73-74, 76, 89-90, 95-96, 99, 103, 107, 109, 115, 121, 127, 129-130, 133, 162, 166

Doehring, Carrie 17, 20, 138, 142

Dukkha (suffering) 11-13, 15, 18, 30, 35, 42-44, 46, 48, 51, 56-58, 61, 69-70, 73-74, 77, 79, 82-83, 87, 93, 95-96, 99-101, 103-104, 106-107, 113-117, 125, 128-132, 135-136, 140, 144, 154, 159, 163, 168

Eightfold Path, The Noble 13-14, 39, 41, 43, 46, 73, 83, 98-101, 121, 124-125, 134

    Action, Right 83, 121

    Concentration, Right 83, 121

    Effort, Right 83, 121

    Intention, Right 42, 44-45, 77, 83, 99, 101, 107, 111, 121, 140

    Livelihood, Right 15, 31, 83, 121

    Mindfulness, Right 83, 121

    Speech, Right 50, 57-58, 83, 121, 125

    View, Right 13, 21, 77, 83, 99, 101-102, 121, 140

Ellison, Koshin Paley 12, 50, 63

Emotion / emotional intelligence 22-23, 30, 34, 36, 43-44, 54, 56, 63, 68-72, 74, 77-79, 84, 103, 106-108, 115, 119, 126, 136, 142, 154, 159

Ethics 45, 50, 63, 116, 143, 160-161

Feminism 18-19, 45, 141, 143, 162

Fischer, Norman 52, 132-133

Fisher, Daniel (Danny) Clarkson 12, 22, 32, 46, 48-50, 64, 67, 133, 160

Four Noble Truths 11, 14, 43-44, 77, 81, 91-93, 98, 140, 169

    First Noble Truth 11

Second Noble Truth 12-13

    Third Noble Truth 13

    Fourth Noble Truth 13

Gabriel, Victor 34, 49-50

Giles, Cheryl 12, 22, 36, 43-44, 46, 51, 53, 55-57, 61, 64-65, 111, 160

Gaṇḍavyūha-sūtra 129

Halifax, Joan 43, 50, 63

Hanh, Thich Nhat 31, 51-52, 65, 99

Harvard Divinity School 46, 150

Hermeneutics 55, 161

Hirsch, Trudi Jinpu 44

Illness 12, 15, 26, 43-44, 48, 74, 89, 95, 99, 103, 107, 142, 162

Institute of Buddhist Studies 150

Intention (*also see* Intention, Right *under* Eightfold Path) 13, 20, 42, 44-46, 50, 68-71, 74, 77-78, 83-84, 99-108, 116, 118-119, 120-121, 126, 129, 135-136, 139-141, 143, 153, 155, 161

Interreligious / Interfaith Care 12, 14, 18, 32, 47, 49, 50, 58, 62, 68, 107, 118, 123, 125, 138, 143

Jensen, Lin 57-58

Judaism / Jewish 15, 18-20, 22, 32-36, 40, 49, 55, 57, 59, 67, 101, 149, 150

Kalyāṇamitra (Spiritual Friend/Friendship) 13-15, 20, 34-35, 41-42, 44, 51, 70, 81-83, 86, 94, 97-99, 102, 106, 109, 111-112, 118, 121-125, 127-129, 130-137, 140-144, 147,

149, 152-153, 157
As part of the Framework for Spiritual Care (*see* Three Prajñās Framework)
Buddha as 20, 46, 121, 123-124, 143
Compared to bad friendship 124, 126, 128, 167
Dharma as 34, 37, 51, 97, 125, 127-128
Defined 132, 141
   Literature review 123-135
   Qualities of 105, 125-126, 129, 167-169
   Role of (in spiritual formation) 19-20, 23, 33-34, 47, 53, 71, 85, 109, 124-125, 130, 133-135, 140, 142
Karma 45, 90, 93, 99, 131
Kilts, Thomas 54-55
Kinst, Daijaku Judith 20, 46, 51
Laypeople 19, 41f, 45, 52, 124, 127-128, 131
Liberation 13, 45, 55, 57, 73, 82-83, 112-113, 116, 125, 127, 129-130, 136, 140, 159, 165-168
Listening 28, 32, 35, 40, 46, 48, 54, 56-57, 62, 68-69, 78-79, 81-90, 92-95, 97-99, 101-102, 104-106, 108, 112, 114, 116, 118-120, 135, 137-140, 153, 155-156
Limitations (of this research) 94, 137, 140
Lojong (mind training) 56, 122, 124, 130-131, 160
Mahayana 13, 23, 41, 44, 49, 55, 84-85, 87-88, 90f, 112, 116, 122, 124, 129-130, 132-134, 149-150, 159
Maitrī / Mettā (loving-kindness) 26, 37, 39, 41-43, 68, 73, 96, 107-108, 127-128, 162, 165
Meaning (or meaning-making) 12, 16-21, 34, 36, 44, 53, 55, 67, 72, 74-78, 95-97, 99-102, 107, 109, 118, 132, 136, 140-141, 147-148, 154, 156-158
Meditation 17, 22, 26, 28, 36-37, 39, 43, 56, 58f, 64, 68, 71-76, 79, 82-84, 86, 88-89, 91-93, 96-105, 108, 112, 114, 118, 132, 138-139, 143, 159, 162
   Jñāna 92-93, 98
Śamatha 22, 87-88, 91-92, 96, 98, 101, 105

Vipaśyanā 88, 91-92, 96, 98, 105
Michon, Nathan Jishin 12, 22, 32, 48, 49f, 64, 160
Miller, Willa 12, 19, 22, 36, 43-44, 46, 48, 51, 53, 55-57, 61, 64-65, 111, 142, 160
Mindfulness 13, 40-43, 49-50, 54, 63, 68, 72-74, 76, 83, 91-92, 100-101, 121, 127, 136, 140, 144, 159, 165-166, 168
Monastics / monasticism 16, 22, 41, 45, 73, 101, 125, 126f, 127, 141, 143, 149, 166, 168, 63
Monnet, Mikel 49, 50, 53, 58
Muditā (sympathetic joy) 42, 128
Muslim / Islam 15, 17-20, 34-35, 49, 67, 150
Nirvana (Nibbana / liberation) 117, 127, 129, 165
Normative paradox 109, 137
Not-knowing / beginner's mind 58, 70, 72, 78, 107
Pāli Suttas 87, 124
   Aṅguttara Nikāya 17f, 124-125, 127, 165
Dīgha Nikāya 17f, 85-90, 124, 127
   Saṃyutta Nikāya 17f, 121
Pastoral Authority 34
Pastoral Care 15, 17-22, 42, 46, 53, 63-64, 68, 122, 134, 137-138, 156, 160-162
Pāramitās (virtues) 49, 73-74, 108, 116
Pedagogy 32, 94, 117-118, 125
Power, Mark 53
Practice (Buddhist or spiritual) 11, 13, 15-17, 20-23, 26, 29-36, 39-41, 43, 46, 49, 51, 53, 55-60, 62-63, 65, 67-73, 75-85, 87f, 90-98, 100-105, 108-109, 112, 114, 116-119, 122, 124, 127, 129-132, 134-140, 142-144, 147, 149, 152, 154-160, 162
Prajñā (Wisdom) 12, 39, 53, 57, 70, 81, 83, 112, 116
Prajñāpāramitā 49, 102, 122, 124, 128-129
Praxis 39-42, 44, 53, 55-57, 59, 68, 71, 75, 117, 137, 144, 148
Prayer 16, 40, 56-59, 62, 64, 108, 139

Pratītyasamutpāda (dependent co-origination / interdependence) 70, 90, 107, 112, 114, 117, 137, 159

Presence 34, 40, 48, 52, 62-63, 65, 68-70, 101, 105-108, 132-133

Psychology 32, 35, 40, 44, 50, 92, 99, 117, 141, 154, 160

Osmer, Richard 11, 95, 147

Outcomes 32, 40-41, 44-45, 68, 71, 81, 99-101, 104, 108, 116, 118, 125-126, 129-131, 135-139, 153, 160

Race / racism 47-49, 54, 56, 65, 99, 107, 143, 149

Ray, Reginald 85, 87f, 94-97

Rebirth 46, 168

Reflection 11, 14, 16, 30, 32-33, 35-36, 39, 44, 50, 53-59, 68, 70-81, 83-87, 91, 93-98, 100, 106-107, 109, 111-114, 116-118, 124, 136-137, 139, 143-144, 147-149, 151-158, 162

Fabrication / negative aspects 75, 77

Feedback on 16, 33, 61, 70, 75, 78, 102, 104-106, 110-111, 139, 144, 151-152

Progression 77-79, 98, 139, 152

Sharing 16, 33, 36, 47, 70, 74-75, 78, 102, 104, 106, 132, 142, 152

Theological 35-36, 53-55, 57-58, 79, 95, 97, 118, 137, 143, 148, 153-156, 158

Writing 11, 16, 32-33, 35, 72, 104, 106, 114, 124, 136, 147-149, 151

Reflexivity 36, 39, 68, 71-73, 141-142, 147, 162

Relationships 29, 34, 39, 50-52, 63-64, 67, 100, 102, 104, 107, 111, 113, 122, 124, 126, 129, 131-133, 161, 170

Intimate / Romantic 39, 50, 134

Peers / Sangha 34, 52, 104, 111, 129, 133

Teacher-Student 34, 51-52, 104, 134

Ritual 22, 40, 42, 62-64, 82, 127

Samādhi (concentration) 13, 39, 68, 72, 74-75, 82-83, 87-88, 91, 100, 108, 118, 121, 125-129, 165-169

Sangha (community) 11, 12, 17, 22, 29, 31, 33, 41, 47, 48, 49f, 51-56, 66, 80, 82-83, 94, 97-98, 101-102-104, 111, 121, 125, 126f, 131, 133, 137, 140, 158, 160, 167

Śāntideva 41, 44-45, 97, 113, 115, 122, 124, 129-131, 159-161

Sarvāstivāda Abhidharma 85-86, 88, 90, 93-94, 143

Śīla (morality) 18, 39, 42, 45, 83, 100, 104, 108, 128-129, 141, 143

Soteriology 20, 45, 59, 70, 73, 76, 85, 112, 117, 161

Spiritual Care 11, 13-18, 20-23, 30, 32-35, 39-44, 46-47, 49-51, 53, 59, 61-69, 71-73, 75-77, 79-82, 85, 93-94, 97-98, 101, 104, 106, 108-109, 111-112, 114, 116-120, 122-124, 126, 133-135, 137, 139-140, 142-144, 148-149, 151-154, 157-158, 160-161

Spiritual Formation 12-13, 15-16, 30-33, 35, 39, 51, 61, 72, 74, 81, 107, 117-118, 131, 137-139

Spiritual Friend/Friendship – see Kalyāṇamitra

Śūnyatā (emptiness) 70, 90f, 95, 104, 107, 112-117, 137-138, 157, 159, 161

Taṇhā (thirst, clinging, attachment) 12, 13, 42-43, 46, 96, 101, 113, 115-117, 131, 138-141

Teachers 34, 41, 44, 50-53, 55, 70, 82-83, 85-86, 88-89, 94-98, 102, 121, 126, 129-135, 137, 139, 144, 152, 160-161

Theravada 13, 41, 52, 84, 88, 94, 112, 124, 132, 149-150, 159

Theism 50, 58-59, 62, 76, 149, 150, 154, 157

Atheism 50, 62, 149

Nontheocentrism 62

Theology 11, 15, 17-19, 22-23, 34, 36, 48-49, 53-55, 57-59, 71, 147, 150, 161-163

Practical 11, 15, 22, 48, 55, 147, 163

Pastoral 15, 17, 19, 22-23, 36, 53, 55

Three Prajñās 12-13, 15, 32-33, 35, 41, 54, 59, 78-79, 81, 83-86, 88-94, 96-98, 101, 104, 108, 111-113, 117-119, 122, 135, 137-138, 140, 147, 152

Contemplating 32, 54, 72, 78-79, 81-90, 92-

108, 110, 112, 116, 118, 120, 122, 127, 135-137, 139, 153, 166
Defined 32
Framework for Spiritual Care 13-16, 33, 35, 59, 69, 73, 78, 81, 83-85, 94, 97-99, 101, 104-105, 108-114, 116-119, 122, 132, 135, 137-141, 143, 147, 149, 151-153
  Stage One: Self 99-101
  Stage Two: Student 101-105
  Stage Three: Chaplain 105-109
  Stage Four: Kalyāṇamitra (*see* kalyāṇamitra)
Listening 28, 32, 35, 40, 46, 48, 54, 56-57, 62, 68-69, 78-79, 81-90, 92-95, 97-99, 101-102, 104-106, 108, 112, 114, 116, 118-120, 135, 137-140, 153, 155-156
Practicing 11, 32-33, 40, 54, 58, 71, 73, 78, 81-85, 87-94, 96-105, 107-108, 111-112, 114, 116-118, 120, 122, 135-137, 139, 149, 159, 161
Three Refuges / Jewels 51-52, 98, 125
Trungpa, Chögyam 133-134
Two Truths 13, 104, 107, 112, 114, 116-117, 140
  Mundane / Conventional 50, 78, 91-93, 113, 115, 117
  Ultimate / Nonconceptual 50, 78, 88, 93, 96, 105, 112-117, 137, 161
University of the West 32-33, 47, 49, 52, 150
Upāya (skillful means) 45, 50, 74, 76, 108-109, 114, 117, 122, 131, 140, 155-156
Upekṣā / Upekkhā (equanimity) 42, 60, 68, 73, 103-104, 107-108, 114, 116, 126-128, 136, 166, 168
Vajrayana 13, 41, 44, 84-85, 88, 112, 122, 124, 132, 134, 149
Validation (of data) 109-111, 118, 162
Verisimilitude 23, 109, 114
Vibhaṅga 85, 87f, 89
Vinaya 45, 73
Visuddhimagga 85, 88-89
Vows 31, 45, 59, 73, 83, 103-104, 108, 130
Womanist 18-19, 49
Yetunde, Pamela Ayo 41-43, 49-50, 161
Zen 20, 27, 29, 31, 46, 49-50, 52, 58, 64-66, 73, 75-76, 113, 132

www.ingramcontent.com/pod-product-compliance
Lightning Source LLC
Chambersburg PA
CBHW081216230426
43666CB00015B/2758